THE STORY OF SCRIPTURE

Other Books by Daniel Jeremy Silver

A History of Judaism

Images of Moses

Maimonidean Criticism and the Maimonidean Controversy 1180–1240

Judaism and Ethics (ed.)

THE STORY
OF SCRIPTURE

From Oral Tradition
to the Written Word

Daniel Jeremy Silver

BASIC BOOKS, INC., PUBLISHERS   NEW YORK

Library of Congress Cataloging-in-Publication Data
Silver, Daniel Jeremy.
    The story of scripture : from oral tradition to the writ-
ten word /
  Daniel Jeremy Silver.
      p.   cm.
  Includes bibliographical references.
  ISBN 0–465–08205–X
    1. Bible. O.T.—History. 2. Bible. O.T.—Criticism,
interpretation, etc., Jewish. 3. Rabbinical literature—
History and criticism. I. Title.
  BS1130.S54 1990
220.1—dc20   89–28701
                                              CIP

To Adele

Without whose love and help this work

might never have been finished

⋙⋙⋙⋙ Contents ⋘⋘⋘⋘

CONTENTS

❯❯❯❯❯❯ Acknowledgments ❮❮❮❮❮❮

I want to acknowledge the help of Marie Pluth, my most competent secretary; Claudia Fechter, librarian of The Temple and indefatigable researcher; Jean Lettofsky and Merrily Hart, librarians of the Cleveland College of Jewish Studies; Alice Loranth, Director, and Dr. Motoko Reece, of the John G. White Collection of the Cleveland Public Library; Dr. Moshe Berger, Associate Professor, Cleveland College of Jewish Studies; Dr. Eldon Jay Epp, Harkness Professor of Religion, Case Western Reserve University, Cleveland, Ohio; and Dr. Leonard Kravitz, Professor of Midrash and Homiletics at Hebrew Union College–Jewish Institute of Religion, New York, N.Y. Institutions I have relied on are The Temple, Cleveland, Ohio, and the Postgraduate Centre for Hebrew Studies and the Bodleian Library, Oxford, England.

THE STORY OF SCRIPTURE

⇛⇛⇛ PROLOGUE ⇚⇚⇚

THE WORD OF GOD AS UNCHANGED AND UNCHANGING

I was drawn to the study of scripture by the resurgence of scriptural innocence in our times. Powerful forces are at work in the Jewish, Christian, and Islamic worlds: black-hat orthodoxy, evangelical churches, and the Muslim Brotherhood, each out to coerce its community to organize around rules and practices that each insists its scripture prescribes. The revival of fundamentalist scriptural religion is one of the surprises of the late twentieth century. Those of us who received a liberal education in mid-century believed that fundamentalism was a relic of the past. Not so, as the successful activities of the Ayatollah Khomeini, Rabbi Menachem Schneerson, and the Reverend Jerry Falwell have testified. The literal understanding of scripture is very much alive.

Early in 1989, I watched a televangelist urge his viewers to mount a campaign to require their local schools to teach a literal version of the first chapter of Genesis, including the doctrine of man's special creation. The evangelist dismissed the Big Bang and evolution as unproven theories put forward by disciples of a pseudo religion called humanism. He pounded away at his claim that no one should trust mere theories, since God had revealed in the Bible the truth of these matters: that the literal interpretation of the Creation story and other biblical episodes is, in fact, fact. Yet that preacher did not encourage his flock to celebrate the calendar of holidays and the Sabbath requirements that the Bible specifically mandates. His literalism was selective.

This evangelist would claim that those were Old Testament laws, and that he was following the New Testament. But the New Testament is inconsistent on this point: Paul denies the continuing authority of the Mosaic Law; Jesus does not. In Jesus' eyes, the law will remain binding at least until End Time: "Not an iota or a dot of the law would pass away until all will be accomplished" (Matt. 5:18). One can legitimately prefer Paul to Jesus; but at the least, the preacher should recognize that what he teaches is not the Bible but an arbitrary selection of biblical texts. Despite his claims, he does not take the scripture literally: he takes it selectively. His Bible leaves out any and all ideas that do not conform to an evangelical Christianity and small-town, middle-American morality.

One of the least examined commonplaces of our times is that the Bible is a good book, even *the* Good Book. To believers, their scripture is an unmitigated source of blessing and a statement of redemptive truths. It cannot be doubted that the scriptures of the major faiths have been important sources of encouragement and wisdom for millions of people. Many have found the courage to keep going on the basis of texts that have been quoted or read to them. Yet we are more conscious today than perhaps ever before that a scripture, any scripture, is a mixed bag. While we may approve "Have we not all one Father" (Mal. 2:10) or the example of strong, independent-minded women like Huldah, Deborah, and Ataliah, or the moral urgency of "burn out the evil in your midst" (Deut. 13:6), white supremacists, male chauvinists, and defenders of privilege can also cite texts to validate their convictions: texts about "hewers of wood and drawers of water" (Josh. 9:21), laws that give a father control of his daughter's person (Num. 30:4–6), and Samuel's acquiescence in the sacralization of royal prerogatives (1 Sam. 8:10–22).

Though each scripture represents itself as an inspired text and is acclaimed by many as the word of God, no scripture is noble, or even sensible, in all its parts. Read any enshrined apocalypse. The Hebrew scripture includes not only factually suspect history but teachings that seem unworthy of humans, much less of God. Abraham hardly sets an example of manly responsibility when, at Sarah's insistence, he orders Hagar out of his tent. How can anyone consider as inspired the brutal stories of conquest and battle in the Book of Judges? The Koran's concept of a holy war, *Jihad,* gives any humane spirit pause, as must some of Mohammed's demands that various tribes who opposed him be extirpated. The New Testament's bitter and intemperate condemnation of Jewish leaders as deicides, hypocrites, liars, and whited sepulchers are not only baseless charges but have caused centuries of suffering. Unfortunately, when such a text becomes scripture, it cannot be expunged, however pernicious its consequences.

Endorsing a scripture, a community defines it as the speech of God, holy, true, inerrant. Piety is one thing, the text another. Every scripture contains misstatements, false statements, and contradictions—a notion so commonplace that George Gershwin used it in his 1935 opera *Porgy and Bess:* "The things that you're liable to read in the Bible, it ain't necessarily so." Some people see the text as a series of exuberant stories—Joshua commanding the sun to stand still, Jesus multiplying the fish and the loaves—which can easily be explained as the enthusiastic way the ancients treated legends.

But the problem is not simply exuberance. Scriptures contain contradictions. In Numbers, God consecrates the family of Aaron as priests; in Ezekiel, the family of Zadok. According to one *Sefer Torah* statement, the paschal sacrifice must be roasted (Exod. 12:9); according to another, boiled (Deut. 16:7); and the roasting requirement says specifically, "you shall not eat the paschal sacrifice . . . boiled in water." Many texts fail to make clear whom an author was addressing, what specifically he wanted to accomplish, and even what general purpose he had in mind. Is the biblical tradition that says, "Love your friend as yourself" (Lev. 19:18), encouraging simple respect for others, charity, self-sacrificing concern for another's life and person, or simply counseling unselfishness? Who is that "friend"? An intimate, any passerby, or only one of your own tribe? What does the command "love" require? An occasional helping hand? Sacrificial care? The biblical sentence provides few clues. Interpretation is inevitable.

Scriptures first became integral to religion at a particular time in human history which roughly coincides with the spread of literacy and the rise of urban society. Judaism, Christianity, Islam, Zoroastrianism, Buddhism, Jainism, Hinduism, Confucianism, Taoism, all developed sacred books to which was ascribed a high degree of authority and infallibility. In each case these books became central to the subsequent development of religious practice and teaching. Each of these religions has a Book, but none is contained or fully defined by that book. Despite a scripture's dominance in religious life, it can never fully control the upsurge of the human spirit seeking communion with God, the spirit that gives a faith vitality and confidence. Even after The Book becomes consecrated, mystics and others maintain intense spiritual lives only partially determined by it. Nothing can stifle the desire of the human spirit to commune with the divine or the special capacity of those who commune with God and hear His voice. When the gates of revelation are declared closed and the scripture completed, interpreters inevitably appear who claim an authority to construe the text's meaning in ways derived less from logical analysis of the text than from the Holy Spirit or a *Bat Kol,* a voice originating in the heavens.

The Torah, the New Testament, and the Koran rarely enjoyed unquestioned authority within their respective communities, for official practice often deviated from the clear intent of specific scriptural statements. Rabbinic interpretation effectively canceled Torah laws that stipulated death for adultery and witchcraft, by surrounding such cases with complex legal requirements almost impossible to meet. The Gospels assume the Jewish calendar, but the Church soon introduced its own. While each scriptural religion affirmed its Book as God's Book and treated it with reverence, each interpretation became not only a sacred discipline but a battlefield as

4

believers fought to make scripture say what they wanted and needed it to say.

Although scriptures are unabashedly praised by the faithful as books of unique and inestimable worth, such praise does not tell us with any precision wherein lies their special merit. Is the text holy because it presents the inspired wisdom of a God-intoxicated sage or seer? Does its value lie in the fact that it presents the fundamental teachings of a particular tradition? Is it, in fact, God's words?

Why did Judaism, and later other traditions, make much of the possession of a scripture after having flourished—in Judaism's case, for centuries—without a scripture? There have been as many answers to this question as students who have seriously posed it. Some speak of the importance of scripture in providing to a religious enterprise a necessary centerpiece, defining and giving shape, from which all teachings flow. Others emphasize a scripture's importance in confirming certain values and teachings as God's own and, therefore, beyond debate in a world where any teaching or value can be disputed and any assertion questioned. Others argue that a scripture is no more than an artifact of literate societies, an inevitable consequence of the growing number of those who could and did read and write, who sanctified certain teachings and set them into texts. A scripture's shared purposes and hopes, its narratives, wisdom, and idioms, define a universe of discourse. This sense of bonding became particularly important as close-knit tribal cultures began to break down, and the community could no longer count on daily contact, personal ties, and shared customs to hold it together. With the growth of urban societies and the development of schooling, a scripture provided members of far-flung communities with a focal point, the knowledge that they belonged to a single community.

The shrine libraries of ancient West Asia included works of law, myth, hymn, and wisdom—in style, and sometimes in substance, not unlike much of the material that found its way into the Bible. In Hellenistic times, the Temple in Jerusalem had a sizable library which included, among many other works, scrolls that ultimately would be chosen as part of the Hebrew scripture. Many of these rolls, those that would be chosen and those that would not, were studied and believed in biblical times. Few besides the Five Books of

Moses were treated as sacrosanct. No one was disturbed to find different versions of various classic narratives in circulation, nor to find scribes who copied them adding and emending.

However valued, a classic is not yet a scripture. A question not often put, and less often answered, is: Why, beginning in the late pre-Christian centuries, were first the Jews and then others no longer satisfied to have a library of thoughtful and inspiring religious classics but impelled to turn certain of their scrolls into scripture? That they did feel so impelled cannot be denied. If we define religion as the emotional and intellectual response to the anxiety-laden fact of being alive but never fully at peace in a world not fully understood, it follows that a religious belief grows out of a personal search for a sanctified purpose and a believable hope. Beyond the troubles of each day, there must be some sense of the possibility of peace and security, if not in this world then in some other. In religious terms, the affirmation of life's possibilities is described as a response to the holy, with "holy" a synonym for a dimension of ultimate mystery, God's presence in our lives. A scripture captures and presents that sense of purpose and hope. Scriptures are gospels, "good tidings," as well as Torah, "God's Instructions." Human life, fragile and pressured, holds as one of its fondest hopes the impossible dream of total security. Projecting this need onto written documents that deal with themes of purpose and permanence, the religious response personifies the sense of holiness in the concept of scripture: unchanging, the immutable heart of the faith, God's certain teaching and promise. In this sense, a scripture is the quintessential religious object.

But you cannot build a complete understanding of any religion on the basis of its scripture. Even if you have a thorough knowledge of another religion's scripture, you would have, observing its adherents' ways and listening to their views, a difficult time relating what you saw and heard of the living community to what you had read in their Holy Book. The Hebrew scripture does not mention the synagogue, the rabbi, the separation of men and women at worship, or even the requirement of reading publicly from the scripture. On the other hand, the Five Books of Moses go on at great length about the sacrificial cult and a dynastic priesthood, and stipulate that a witch must be burned and an adulteress stoned, all completely irrelevant to today's practice. The New Testament makes no mention of popes, the divinity of Mary, Christmas, or tithing.

Once a tradition enshrines a scripture, it discovers that it needs a second scripture. The original scripture may be imaginative, even powerful, but it is an expression of private experience rather than systematic. Its ideas are expressive of the soul reaching out for new understanding of God and the purpose of life. Much is omitted. The second scripture is conceived for a more practical purpose: specifically to provide the faith with an inclusive and functional text in which doctrine and duty are defined. These second scriptures, though not given a major place in the worship hall, are essential in study hall and council chamber. The Talmud is a child of the classroom, primarily a manual of discrete statements about Torah law and practice broadly arranged by topic. The Church tradition is a collection of individual council decisions which became canon law. The Shariyah was drawn together by Islamic jurists whose approaches to the law were in general agreement but who differed on specifics.

Whereas the original scripture tends to be effective, dramatic, and compelling as literature, the second scripture—the Talmud, canon law, and the Shariyah—tends to be prosaic, not at all the kind of book you would pick up to calm distress or anxiety or to find encouragement in sorrow. These second scriptures are academic and scholastic documents, written in dry, legal style. Scholastics and theologians turn to their second scripture for definitive answers on issues of obligation and structure. The general community acknowledges the importance of its second scripture but tends to leave its study to experts. The importance of the Talmud in advanced Jewish education is probably due to a recognition of the limitations of the *Sefer Torah* as a basis for teaching the whole range of Jewish obligations.

The relation of a religious community to its two scriptures is not unlike the marriage relationships in polygamous societies where several wives live together in amity for a while under the same tent—until, inevitably, someone or something comes along to disturb the relations among them. In Judaism and Christianity, groups like the Karaites and the Protestants came along and argued that the second "marriage" was not sanctified, that only the original testament was inspired. The second scripture is functional rather than symbolic; yet since its authority must be acknowledged as central to the community's well-being, the second scripture is dressed up with some of the symbols of scriptural authority and presents itself as inspired interpretation rather than as direct or inspired revelation.

While scripture may be venerated and symbolically affirmed as the centerpiece of a religious enterprise, in matters of practice it often does not have the last word. Scriptures are texts assumed to be central; but a scripture's effective meaning is determined by the evolving life of its society: that is, the needs and interests of synagogue, church, or mosque. Most people accept a scripture not for what it is but for what it has become in the hands of their leaders. The Roman Catholic Bible is scripture as interpreted by the teaching of the official church. The Church affirms that its scripture is the ultimate authority on faith and morals; but, clearly, on such issues as birth control and abortion, the Church has made its scripture yield strong positions that the scripture really does not deal with. The Bible as read by liberal American Protestantism is a historically conditioned document espousing Christology and the social gospel; the same Bible in the hands of evangelical American Protestantism is a messianic document espousing the transforming power of faith in a person's life.

So long as each religious tradition endowed its scripture with sanctity and believed it was the word of God, and so long as its belief was reinforced by parochial schooling and communal conditioning, its scripture was the basis of religious life. When in modern times the challenges to beliefs once confidently held became more numerous and more persuasive, the once indisputable consensus began to unravel. As the multidisciplined university curriculum took over from the homogeneous curricula of religious academies—the cathedral school, the *Madrasa,* and the *yeshivah*—the disciplines of history, archeology, literary criticism, etymology, sociology, and a variety of other studies began to raise questions about the reliability of what was in The Book. The world was not created in six days. During the Conquest the sun did not stand still for the Israelites to complete their destruction of an Amorite army (Josh. 10:12). The story of a virgin birth and an immaculate conception were not historical facts but re-creations of pre-Christian myths.

In the nineteenth and twentieth centuries, people began to notice the seams that hold the parts together, and to question the accuracy of scriptural statements. As knowledge grew of the oral prehistory of a scripture, and as recognition grew that scriptures had incorporated materials from other cultures, people began to ask whether a scripture can be accepted either as a full statement of the faith at the time of its composition or even as a unique composition. Questions began to be asked: about the relationship between scripture and current teachings; about varying, even contradictory, historical interpretations; about the text's divinity. If the devil can quote scripture to his benefit, so can the minister. If various layers of human concern can be shown to exist within and behind the received text, and if the interpretation of scripture differs from age to age, what about it is divine? If the scripture is inspired, why did interpretations sometimes have to turn it on its ear? How to account for discrepancies? Divergent attitudes toward monarchy appear in the book of Samuel; in one chapter, God orders a judge to anoint a king over Israel (1 Sam. 12); in another, God complains to Samuel because the tribes are demanding that a king be appointed (8). Christian apologetes have spent many lifetimes trying to harmonize the various Gospel accounts of Jesus' career. The Koran affirms free will ("The truth is from you, Lord, so let whosoever will, believe; and let whosoever will disbelieve" [18:28]) and denies it ("God leads astray whom He wills and guides whom He wills" [16:95]).

It was a shock to most believers when research made it clear that the Five Books of Moses, the New Testament, and the Koran were composite and edited works rather than a single record written under the inspiration of God. It was even more traumatic when people realized that the "original words" could not be recaptured, and that some of the text never had been spoken at Sinai. Deuteronomy presents a different view of the Exodus-Sinai trek and different formulas for certain laws than Exodus-Numbers. There are four distinct Gospel versions of Jesus' life, and a single account can be shaped only if the reader arbitrarily decides which version of a particular incident or speech is "original."

Contrary to conventional thinking, there is no single scriptural point of view. Saint and devil, orthodox and heretic, prophet and profit seekers can find texts that seem to justify their approach to scripture. Each will argue that those who quote scripture to contrary purpose wrench the texts out of context. Some seem to do so; others do not. The rabbis frequently admitted that the sages could espouse divergent, but equally defensible, views with the ultimate rationalization: both this and this (one sage's view and a divergent one) are the words of the living God. In fact, there is no methodology that can assimilate, evaluate, and draw every sentence of a scripture into a single coherent and consistent teaching.

Once the community of believers included many who accepted the talmudic teaching that every word of the *Sefer Torah* came down from heaven (b. San.99b); or the Protestant thesis (Calvin's) that the New Testament was "breathed out" by God, and that its teachings are inerrant. Many believers no longer do. Today there is no longer a consensus about scripture among believers. Today many affirm that if there is to be a messianic age, humans—not God—will bring it about. That is the essence of the social gospel. Yet in our era of technical triumphs, we have seen the re-emergence of evangelical groups who, despairing of the human capacity to build a bright future, turn back to texts that speak of a Second Coming and a supernatural intervention.

In modern times, nonfundamentalist communicants prefer to talk of inspiration rather than revelation and to define inspiration in relatively modest terms—as the special insight of someone of high imagination and intellectual capacity who, in thinking about ultimate questions, has touched on the truths that animate the universe. They see the great spiritual truths that underlie their faith. They look on their Bible as a product of a partnership between man and God, a human response to the divine. Their scripture's truth lies in the spirit that animates the whole rather than in the accuracy of particular facts and details. They like to talk of the great themes that presumedly inform the text. They have no trouble admitting that the world was not created in six days, or that the miracle stories told about Jesus are in fact just that—stories. Such is human nature and the need for reassurance that many who no longer believe their

Bible remain easy nonetheless within their faith, easily participate in liturgies that eulogize the Bible, and expect those who preach to them to draw ideas, illustrations, and inspiration from the Holy Book. The Anglican bishop John Robinson gained some notoriety a quarter-century ago by writing about the death of God (1963), yet found nothing unusual not only in speaking on God's disappearance from history but in doing so from a pulpit that prominently displayed a Bible proclaiming God's presence. Scriptures have a power that transcends their contents, and humans have spiritual needs that transcend the need for accuracy in a scripture.

While both fundamentalist and modern believers assert on faith that their scripture presents a coherent teaching (however differently it may be described), a close reading of any scriptural text makes it clear that the work reflects a particular period and a particular culture. This is the paradox that creates commentary—that massive body of interpretation designed to remove anachronisms, rationalize outdated ideas, and read new ideas into the text.

Elaborate and elegant systems of commentary and interpretation were developed by scripture-based traditionalists to save their scripture from any imputation that it was inconsistent, mistaken, or untrue in any of its parts. These interpreters consciously and unconsciously subsumed, or sought to subsume, the entire scriptural corpus into a unitary, coherent, and consistent world view. They were so successful that to this day most believers think of the Bible as a book that presents a consistent theology and ethic. Even those who know that the Bible is an anthology assume that all the parts ultimately reflect a single theme. They argue that the Song of Songs is not a collection of early and earthy love and wedding poems which have no particular reason to be in a scripture, but a sustained poetic allegory in which the lover and his beloved presumedly represent God's love for Israel and Israel's for God. The idea that everything in scripture is scriptural dies hard.

In Judaism this reconciliation was achieved by a process called Midrash. Midrash accepts as self-evident the proposition that the *Sefer Torah* is a unique literature, God's, but is not content to take a biblical text at face value. The literal meaning, its ideas clearly and fully expressed, is only one of many God placed within a particular paragraph or sentence. Each word, each letter of the text, is part of God's revelation; and therefore every sentence, phrase, word, and letter was placed there for a purpose. The Bible's full meaning depends, in part, on understanding these noncontextual matters. To make this understanding possible, God enlightened certain masters and enabled them to interpret the text so that all could understand its real meaning.

The human mind being extraordinarily imaginative, commentators have always been able to manipulate texts to give them acceptable meanings. But what of the obvious contextual meaning that is patently illogical or unacceptable? The Bible speaks of a six-day creation. The New Testament describes Jesus as the son of God. The Koran indicates that Mohammed actually entered Heaven. In earlier times, rationalist interpreters explained these texts as allegories or metaphors. They accepted the idea that there are several levels of meaning in a scriptural text—sermonic, metaphorical, allegoric, esoteric—but also insisted that the straightforward reading must not be dismissed. It was early Protestant doctrine—if one can for these purposes put Luther and Calvin together—that the plain sense of scripture must always be considered. The biblical rabbis said the same of *peshat,* their system of straightforward contextual interpretation (b. Shab. 63b). Yet if the plain sense of scripture is considered and taken as authoritative, then on an issue such as evolution the fundamentalists cannot be denied: the plain sense of Genesis is that Adam was created separately and specially. Similarly, those Christians who argue against an easy acceptance of ecumenism and religious pluralism rely on texts that insist that a true Christian must separate from all who do not accept official doctrine (2 John 9–10). If you do not assume that a scripture is fully revealed by God, these issues can be easily reconciled; but if God is the author, then every part of scripture must be without error.

As today scripture has again become of crucial importance in many parts of our world and among many groups—not only as symbol, but as a first and full statement of the will of God—groups of intense believers insist that they base their ways of life on their Holy Book. In their eyes, it is all-knowing, infallible, the source of all truth. In this country, many fundamentalist believers take a particu-

12

lar side of some of the most contentious issues of the time—birth control, abortion, what to teach about creation and evolution, the place of prayer in public life, the death penalty, and civil rights—not on the merits of the issue but because they believe their scripture has foreclosed all but one choice. Some believe that this kind of piety exists only in the middle American states called the Bible Belt, but that's not quite true. I have a friend who found civil rights and nuclear disarmament in his Bible, where millions of others find an intense and rather narrow piety.

Scriptures have played and continue to play important roles in the everyday lives of the faithful and some of the not so faithful and, therefore, need to be understood. Understanding requires that we search out their symbolic and actual role in faith. The relationship between scripture and faith, even for those who unreservedly proclaim their scripture inerrant and sufficient, is complex. However strong the claims and pressures certain books can exert on us, life cannot be lived from a book.

To understand the complex relationship of faith and text, we shall follow the history of one scripture, the oldest, the Hebrew scripture, seeking to define at each stage the complex relation of a living faith and its texts. We will see that the relation of a faith community to its scripture is never, as piety claims, a submissive and unquestioning acceptance of what the scripture affirms; that while the scripture becomes a sturdy symbol of continuity, in actual practice the community turns from a simple reading of scripture to interpretation and interpretive process. One might say that people turn to their scripture for inspiration and to the second scripture—to the Talmud or to canon law or to Shariyah—for discipline.

In retelling the story of scripture, we discover that a truly creative era occurred in each of the three major Western religions before they developed a written scripture: the time of a faith's beginnings, when the founders developed their ideas, is a period of high energy and creativity. We recognize that, as the religion matures and the insights of the early years need to be conceptualized and defined, the history of scripture tends to revolve around the question of who controlled the apparatus of interpretation and what readings they authorized. No scripture is internally consistent but is made so by believers who ascribe truth to the text, usually out of fear that they cannot manage their lives on convictions that are less than absolute about goals, values, and duties.

The emergence of scripture allowed each tradition to define its faith's teaching with greater precision and to guarantee a relatively uniform set of dogmas and practices. At the same time, the fixed text restricted the faith's development by insisting it conform to the written word. The story of the struggle between definition and restriction, and of a second scripture developed later in each tradition to justify positions not self-evident from the scriptural text, is the story of the Western faiths in their medieval development.

In the oldest of these three Western faiths, the rise of scripture tended to parallel the spread of literacy. Judaism existed a thousand years or so without an authorized scripture and, during that era, enjoyed perhaps its most creative period. Its religious leaders—such as Moses and the other early prophets, all of them probably illiterate—emphasized a living tradition rather than a text.

The story we chronicle here is of a long-lived oral tradition transformed over many centuries into a written scripture which was then embraced and enveloped by oral interpretation that swiftly took to itself the value and validity of scripture. One aspect of the story is inevitably chronological, for it follows the Jews over time as they move, willingly or unwillingly, from place to place, or are governed, even in their own homeland, by a succession of alien rulers and cultures. But the heart of the story is the human—not uniquely Jewish—capacity to adapt to new places, times, languages, rulers, circumstances, needs, ideas. Before the Babylonian Exile, spoken words enshrined in the people's collective memory carried the burden of their religious development. It was the Exile and the attendant loss of land, home, and national shrine that made urgent the transformation of memory into manuscript. Priest-scribes struggled to keep alive the people's history by writing it down. Those Jews who returned from Exile, equally with those who lived in the Diaspora—literally, scattered outside the homeland—shaped from liturgy, prophecy, and history a scroll tradition that served as the basis for an educational system that has lasted until the present day and still serves as the basic religious tradition for all Jews. The story ends with a question—as is, perhaps, the Jewish way: What is the role of scripture in the modern world? It is my hope that a fuller understanding of scripture's changing role over many centuries past helps to answer the modern question.

Today the traditional understanding of scripture as the word of God has tended to be vitiated by the impact of secular thought. Traditional scriptures, though recognized as important as classic texts, no longer have this power for all believers. What happens to a faith when large segments of its community no longer trust or believe its scripture? Can a religious tradition exist without the confidence that it is teaching the word of God? Yes and no. In a strictly logical sense, the answer has to be no. Once scripture is reduced to a great books course, it is no longer scripture. But that is not its only fate. The power of these scriptural works tends to transcend their claim to divine authority. Another answer is yes, it can exist as it exists today, if men and women make individual intellectual adjustments to the problem. Each of the faiths existed before there was a scripture, and can, I believe, exist today without one.

But scripture is there and needs to be assimilated into a community's thought. Even if scriptures are not, in fact, the comforting and rock-solid presences that conventional wisdom insisted they were and should be, they act in precisely that way. Once authorized, they become and remain the most significant symbol of a faith's unique and consistent teachings and authority. In every faith, people are encouraged to turn to their scripture for advice, encouragement, and comfort—advice that, it is claimed, has proven its worth over time. Sermons are preached to show how the text, declared to be the unchanged and unchanging truth, offers answers to the problems of the day.

In an overly complex age such as ours where change is the only constant, there is an urgent and understandable desire for certainty. Modern learning is overwhelming and so full of qualifications that it provides more questions than answers to those, the already confused, who must decide whether to be faithful to a marriage, committed to a particular set of social or political values, strict or permissive with their children, or able to let an aged parent die with some dignity. What American evangelists and Iranian mullahs, and those in the Jewish community who claim to be Torah-true, offer is precisely that sense of certainty, a comforting sense of ancient authority and eternal verities presented as God's will. They insist that the symbol is, in fact, a statement of reality, that their scripture is the truth, the whole truth and nothing but truth. Many seek just such reassurance, and many accept that it cannot be found.

1

FROM WORD TO BOOK: DEFINING SCRIPTURE

Behold My word is like fire—declares the Lord—and like
a hammer that shatters rock.

—Jeremiah 23:29

It was through trial and error people learned that a specific herb is a
proven cure for stomach pains, or that baiting a trap a certain way
catches a rabbit, or that planting crops after the early spring rains is
the best hope of a good harvest. No one felt compelled to investigate
why and how. Each accomplishment stood alone. There were cures
but no field of medicine. When people began to write down their
observations, they began to reflect on them in ways they had not
done before. They now could abstract theory from a maze of discrete statements and, by going back and rereading half-remembered
parts, develop broad concepts.

Since the dawn of what we call history, humans have been conscious of the limits of communication in a purely oral culture and have wanted to equip knowledge with permanence and greater reach. Early attempts to give staying power and transferability were simple: a tribesman might tie knots of various sizes into ropes to represent different weights and measures; a bedouin might draw on a rock the outline of a circle with a line above it as a sign to whoever might come by that he had dug for water at this place and found it. By our standards, this was simple stuff; but by using objects to represent ideas, the tangible to suggest the intangible, society had taken the first step toward a written language. The goal was somehow to reify speech, to convert a fugitive event into an object that could be handled, carried from place to place, and consulted at will.

Mastery of the skills that make literacy possible was a critical step in the development of civilization. To be sure, there were cultures before humans learned to read and write. Pre-literate societies were governed by laws, pleased their gods by formal rituals, healed their sick with herbs and amulets, and accumulated practical knowledge about hunting, food gathering, and child rearing. Few of us would, however, argue against the proposition that literacy allowed civilization to develop at a brisker pace.

In an exclusively oral culture, knowledge reaches no farther than the human voice can carry it, and remains available only as long as it can be recovered from someone's memory. The spoken word is evanescent. As soon as it is spoken, it disappears. If a father did not teach his son his trade, or a shaman reveal to a disciple the magical powers of roots and plants, that knowledge died with him. Literacy provided men and women with a recoverable past and sped the expansion of knowledge by making it possible for information to be stored and retrieved over distance and time. Though no one alive remembered a set of facts or a piece of poetry, these facts and that poetry once captured in written form could be recaptured at will.

THE FIRST WORDS

Elaborate pictographic, ideographic, and hieroglyphic writing systems were slowly and painstakingly developed by Chinese, Sumerian, and Egyptian scribes; but such symbol systems were so complex that literacy remained a technical accomplishment that could be mastered only by professionals who spent years equipping themselves with the necessary skills. These early scripts had many limitations, not the least of which was complexity. Each object and action had its own symbol. Scribes had to memorize thousands of signs. Someone took the trouble to count the number of Chinese characters in the K'anghsi dictionary of 1716 and came up with 40,545. The Egyptian hieroglyphs are of the same order of quantity. Pictograms could suggest simple actions but not tense or relationship. While with pictograms you can make lists that tell the number of barrels of wine or bushels of wheat in a storehouse, you cannot describe the special qualities of a single barrel, say, of a light red wine from the Galilee with its special bouquet or aroma.

During the third millennium B.C.E., the Sumerians, among other peoples, discovered ways to relate their signs to sound rather than to objects. Scribes began to develop syllabaries of language symbols based on sound. This was a major breakthrough, since there is an infinite number of objects but a finite number of sounds. At first these syllabaries were fairly complex, but ultimately a usable consonantal alphabet was developed: in effect, a phonetic system in which a limited number of symbols stood for all the sounds used in a language. Various places and cultures have been awarded the laurel for that critical development—Cyprus, Crete, various tribes of the Sinai Peninsula; but because its final development, a system of twenty-two consonants, is Semitic in origin—the name *alphabet* comes ultimately from the first two Hebrew letters, *aleph* and *beth*—it seems likely that much credit is due the royal scribes of the Canaanite city-states. During the middle of the second millennium, Canaanites developed the consonantal alphabet which later passed from Phoenicia to Greece where, improved by the addition of a vowel system, it became the building block out of which developed the communication systems of most Western cultures.

The alphabet, like the computer in our day, revolutionized information transmission and retrieval. Language signs could for the first time convey ideas, feelings, and shades of meaning as well as designate objects and simple actions. Acceptance of the written word as reliable came slowly, because so much guesswork was necessary in reading the unstandardized texts and early language systems of pictograms or primitive phonetics. As syntax, grammar, and spelling were slowly standardized, much of the guesswork involved in reading disappeared. Societies then began to look on documents as a reliable means for recording a treaty, a business contract, or the testimony of a witness. The new technology was constantly improved, and human beings had at their disposal a new and powerful tool.

The mystery associated with the new, little understood alphabet symbols, which had the wondrous power of conveying sound, gave the early writings a magical presence in the popular mind. We who drown in words and paper, and look at words without any sense that a script is unusual, can hardly accept that literacy was originally seen as magical. We will not rightly appreciate the early scriptures if we do not credit them with a power that transcended their context. At the time only a few men could read. Most could not comprehend how a few black squiggles could communicate meaning; for them, the written word was both indecipherable and magical. Thus, men flocked to scribes for amulets whose images and texts would keep evil spirits from their homes and protect their wives during childbirth. The written words had power—the power to confiscate their lands or conscript their sons; and many people did not understand how this was so.

For us, words lie inert on a page. For the ancient, words were inextricably related to sound. No one read, as we do, silently. All who read read aloud. Words had that miraculous power of becoming another category of being. Stories were heard as well as seen and so summoned as well as described. The name of a god inscribed on an amulet was not simply a name but a spoken appeal and a summons. The god heard the writing. The Bible speaks of priests who "placed" God's special name, YHWH, on the people when they blessed them (Num. 6:27). Egyptians of the Middle Kingdom period wrote on the inside of coffins formulas that mentioned various gods, names that the deceased could use to call these gods to his aid as he passed into the realm of the blessed dead and so assure himself of admission. In India, I have watched illiterates rub their foreheads with palm leaves inscribed with words from the Vedas; and in

Nepal, Tibetan pilgrims circle the great Swayambunath Stupa in Katmandu, twirling prayer wheels whose inscription they cannot read, although the words are alive to them and potent.

Writing was first cultivated for its practical value. The written word allowed kings and governors to keep records of taxes due, treaties entered into, land registries, and inventories of palace possessions. At first, scribes were no more than craftsmen who plied a useful trade; but it was not long before talented practitioners recognized that their skills had other applications. Tablets and scrolls recording magical formulas, venerable myths, and prudential advice appeared, and humanity embarked on the long love affair with the written word as literature which has characterized—indeed, obsessed—Western civilization until our day.

Although writing was first sponsored by tyrants as a way of increasing their revenues and control, people soon recognized its value in the transmission of ideas. By the middle of the first millennium B.C.E., perhaps three thousand years after Sumerian scribes had developed the first system that can be called a proper system of writing, the Greeks, among others, began to insist on a set of radically new ideas: that books contain what is valuable, noble, and worthy of being preserved; that "real" knowledge requires book learning; and that schools are places where young men should learn what is in books. Literacy had become the key to civilization.

The spread of literacy ultimately affected all areas of human culture. The early religions emerged without benefit of the written word and were, as we shall see, never entirely comfortable with it. Judaism emerged in an environment where writing was little known and worship consisted of sacrifices and sacred formulas chanted by priests. The religious spirit, conservative by nature, took a surprisingly long time to recognize the potential of a "scripture." Inevitably, as writing became common, religion began to use the written word to state and disseminate its teachings. However inevitable that every religious culture would have a literature, it was not so that the religions—most notably Judaism, since it was the first to do so—should turn some of that literature into a scripture. The five scrolls of Moses and those of the prophets, which were edited in their present form after the sixth century B.C.E., are, in fact, the first set of religious writings ever consecrated by a community. I make this historical note not to claim that "we did it first," but to show how long it took—there is a gap of at least eight hundred years between Moses and the appearance of the *Sefer Torah,* the writing we call the Five Books of Moses—for the community to set down its religious records, and longer yet to consider such documents as fundamental and divinely inspired elements in their tradition, as scripture.

HOLY WORDS, HOLY BOOK

The word *scripture* comes from the Latin *scriptura,* "writing." As the name suggests, it originally defined a manuscript, any manuscript. For reasons no longer recoverable, early in the development of the English language the word *scripture* began to be used specifically for sacred writings, particularly those sacred to Christians. A catechism of the early fourteenth century already uses the term in this context: "For hi es godd, al sais scripture" (Cursor M. 327).

The *Oxford English Dictionary* narrowly defines *scripture* as books held to be sacred and inspired, and cites the Hebrew Bible and the New Testament. Putting aside the parochialism of this definition— the Koran and the Vedas are also unquestionably scriptures—we can accept a more spacious definition of scripture as a volume or collection of writings held by a particular community to be divinely inspired and, therefore, authoritative.

Each of the major religious communities treasures a scripture, a sacred text, which records and presents its special message, truths that define doctrine and duty and offer salvation. Each believes its scripture was inspired by God. When texts are quoted in the name of Moses, an evangelist, Mohammed, or another authority, it is assumed that these men spoke and wrote under the inspiration of the Holy Spirit; that these texts are free of personal bias; and that, being divine in origin, the texts transcend the limitations of human intelligence.

Scriptures are books that are meant to be heard rather than read. Muslim worship begins with the recitation of the first *sura* (chapter) of the Koran. On certain occasions, the recitation of the whole Koran is required. In church and synagogue, formal cycles of scripture were developed to be read aloud during worship. The spoken word conveys an immediacy denied the written word. When I hear portions of the Torah aloud, I sense its sacredness; when I scan the same text in my study, I search carefully for its meaning. I read to learn. I listen to respond. Scriptures have been carefully studied, declared both pious and meritorious; but their ultimate power comes in hearing God's words spoken, intoned, or chanted. A text read aloud regains some of its original power as God's words. Hearing the scripture read aloud allows the worshiper, even if one does not fully understand the words, to participate in the original revelation and, therefore, in a truly redemptive experience which brings one close to God and can change one's life.

If I hear a prophet speak, I may be moved by his voice, manner, or commanding presence as well as his words. If I am in a room that contains a manuscript of his words but do not open it, it may as well not be there. It is one thing to be, say, part of Amos' audience at Bethel, quite another to read what survives of his speech in the quiet of a study. God did not write to Moses: God spoke to him. God did not send Jeremiah a letter detailing his mission: Jeremiah felt the word of God as a burning fire within him. Paul had a transforming vision on the road to Damascus. Islam accepted the Koran as Mohammed's repetition of the Word of God mediated through the angel Gabriel. The power of the religious moment depends upon immediacy. Congregational worship acknowledges the power ascribed to the scriptural word by always including a section in which someone reads aloud or recites a portion of scripture. A minister, beginning to read the scripture lesson, announces: "Hear the word of God."

Like the pulpit-sized Bible on the church lectern, the presence of the *Sefer Torah* in the synagogue gives assurance that what is prayed and said there conforms to God's wishes and is right. Enter a synagogue and your eye will be drawn to its most prominent architectural feature, an ark, fronted by a brightly decorated curtain or sliding door which closes off the cabinet's interior. The ark houses parchment scrolls, bound and mantled, inscribed with the Hebrew text of the Five Books of Moses. Each Sabbath and on festivals, holy days, and market days, this scroll, the *Sefer Torah,* is ceremoniously removed and carried to the reader's desk where it is unrolled so that a designated portion can be chanted. Like the synagogue's architecture, the liturgy underscores the centuries-old claim that these texts present God's own words and will: in short, that this is scripture, "This is the Torah which God commanded us through Moses" (Deut. 4:44).

Both Catholic and Protestant Christianity taught that the Bible was written by men inspired by the Holy Spirit. Islam knew the Koran as the uncreated and direct word of Allah, "the best of histories" (12:3), Mohammed's recitation of what he had heard from God. As Galileo and many other dissenters from official truth learned to their sorrow, the fact that scripture is believed to be divinely inspired means that it may hold sway even when directly contradicted by empirical knowledge. This intransigence we must credit to—or blame on—the powerful urge for certainty and confirmation that provides the motive power behind the religious enterprise: we need to know that what we have been assured is truth is, in fact, true and has been accurately reported to us. Since the text is ascribed to God or divine inspiration, a scripture is God's teaching, presented exactly as God presented it to the founding fathers. The text of a scripture exudes certainty. Who can argue with God? It was and is more comforting and easier to accept a scripture as truth than to consider it a classic some of whose ideas are valuable, and some not. Believers stake their lives—and the lives of other people—on what they believe, rather than endure the uncertainty of discriminating among ideas. Thus, the believer adores scripture as the word of God.

Rabbinic Judaism describes the *Sefer Torah,* the Five Books of Moses, as spoken and written down by Moses at God's dictation without change or addition. Maimonides' medieval formulation sums up the rabbinic position:

> The Torah has been revealed from heaven. This implies our belief that the whole of this Torah found in our hands this day is the Torah handed down by Moses, and that it is all of divine origin. By this I mean that the whole of the Torah came with him from before God in a manner that is metaphysically called "speaking"—but the real nature of that communi-

cation is unknown to anybody except to Moses to whom it came. In handing down the Torah, Moses was like a scribe writing down dictation the whole of it—its chronicles, its narratives, and its precepts.

(Commentary on Mishnah, Tractate Sanhedrin, ch. 10)

The existence of a scripture, though not a prerequisite for a faith's effectiveness, is not irrelevant to it.* Words are indispensable in communicating the religious vision—"In the beginning was the word and the word was with God" (John 1:1); but the spoken word swiftly disappears. Evanescent and unfinished, the spoken word from the lips of a single individual can be doubted, corrected, argued with, or applauded, and discussion may even persuade the speaker to change his mind. Knowing that the word has become text and assumed a permanent form is reassuring; and having a scripture that has been handled with great care, as books usually were, offers reassurance that God's words have been transmitted faithfully.

The written word is set. Discussion will not change it. One can refute a manuscript point by point while reading it, but the author is not present to argue with, and the text stubbornly remains unchanged. I have often thought that book burnings are fueled by feelings of frustrated impotence: deeply disturbed by what one has read or been told is in a book and anxious to rebut its every argument, one cannot cancel its teachings except by destroying the offending work, consigning it to the flames.

Scribes wrote down and edited the material that became scripture for the simple reason that they were able to do so. They had parchment and quills and the necessary skills. Those who first wrote out

---

*Conventional religious wisdom so emphatically declared the existence of a scripture a good thing that the claim was often advanced that possession of a scripture was clear indication of a religion's superiority over more primitive, largely oral traditions. During Islam's period of rapid military expansion, when Muslim lawyers had to determine how to treat large non-Muslim captured populations, they developed the category of *ahl-ul-kitab,* a people of the book, as a group who could be tolerated in the lands of Islam, *dar-al-Islam.* Followers of faiths that did not hold a scripture sacred were to be eliminated by conversion, exile, or death.

Since the assumption is still widespread that any religion worthy of its salt has a scripture, all the "new" religions—Mormonism, Christian Science, even the recent modish cults—quickly developed one. Indeed, contemporary political and economic ideologies that play the role of religion for millions in our heavily secular age have followed suit and, despite blatant antireligious doctrine, enshrine a scripture: Marx's *Das Kapital,* Hitler's *Mein Kampf,* and Mao's *Little Red Book.* The followers of such doctrines find spiritual comfort in the knowledge that the ideas central to their lives exist on paper as well as in the mind and have a solid form more substantial than evanescent speech.

this material had no idea that anyone would ever treat their text as sacred. Many texts had ordinary origins, in a well-known story or an ancestor's genealogy or royal annals. Others may have been something the scribe had on his mind when he found himself with an unused portion of a parchment sheet and the time to fill it. Though some believers today find it difficult to admit the lack of any real significance in some scriptural texts, since all are now part of a volume they declare holy, much in every scripture is, in fact, mundane. The crucial point is, of course, that much is not.

Religions tend to attribute their scriptures to divine inspiration, but the prosaic truth is that scriptures exist in the first instance because men learned to read and write. The spread of literacy was the proximate cause of the publication of scripture. Contrary to conventional wisdom, religions do not begin with a scripture; rather, a scripture presents some of the literature of a religious tradition at a particular state in that tradition's development. To use a phrase applicable to the Jewish experience, there was Torah, a body of teachings accepted as sacred, long before there was a *Sefer Torah,* a text containing those teachings. Just as eight centuries passed before the Jews wrote down the stories of the patriarchs and Moses, so for several centuries the early Christian Church had texts but no scripture—the Gospels were composed not as scripture but as a life of an exemplary man-God. Several centuries passed before there was general agreement on the contents of the Christian scripture. Critical study of the Koran is still in its infancy; but certainly the first two generations of Mohammed's disciples knew his teachings only by verbal report, and a considerable time passed before the leaders were satisfied that they had fully sorted out authentic teachings from spurious ones.

In religion the message precedes the manuscript. Founders speak; they rarely write. Moses was a prophet, a speaker, not a scribe: "and the Lord spoke to Moses, say to the tribes of Israel" (Lev. 19:1). Jesus talked to his disciples and preached in the synagogue. He did not ask or require his disciples to write down his sayings. The Koran, as the name implies, is a recitation, a record of Mohammed's speech. Mohammed also was a speaker, not a writer. His speeches, with additions and emendations, were written down more than a generation after his death. He saw himself as the last of a long line of prophet-speakers: Adam, Abraham, Moses, Isaiah, John, Jesus. . . . Muslim folklore often portrays Mohammed as illiterate, confessedly to emphasize that he had recited God's message exactly as he had heard it. The most imaginative and radically new religious perspectives often emerged before there was a scripture. A person would hear God or experience a vision: Amos, Isaiah, Jesus, Mohammed spoke under the direct influence of an overwhelming experience in which holy books and proof texts had no part. The written word is a record of such a religious experience, not the experience itself.

Preliterate societies, organized within a tight web of custom, law, and tradition, accepted such experiences of the gods interacting with humans and enshrined them in the collective memory. No one distinguished between revelation and tradition. Formulas for pleasing the gods and keeping evil spirits at bay, along with more homely knowledge, were widely shared, well known, implicitly trusted, and repeated over the generations with a high degree of reliability and the highest authority. This world is still reflected in the Book of Genesis, which never claims that its text is divinely inspired, yet presents a narrative that was clearly fully trusted. The famous first line of the Bible might, without contradicting its original spirit, be translated as an early storyteller might have spoken: "Once upon a time long ago God created the Heavens and the Earth."

The traditions of an oral society, however primitive, have the advantage of a compelling intimacy and directness which tend to be lost when they are written down. Putting words on parchment or paper places them outside the mind, while the wellsprings of commitment lie inside the human soul. A literate culture can have a rich and imaginative religious literature, but its dependence on the written word inevitably creates distance between the community and its faith. Even the most compelling speech, become text, loses something of its power.

Scriptures record primarily the creativity of the past and are themselves creative only in redefining existing traditions by including some and excluding others and thus establishing an authoritative anthology of tradition. A scripture is a repository of ideas rather than their first statement. Despite the claim that the Hebrew Bible gave the idea of monotheism to the world, the truth is that this idea—like the imaginative reading of God's relations to man and history as a drama of God's dependable power and justice—emerged in the minds of Israel's prophets and thinkers long before being reduced to writing.

Once a scripture emerges and is certified, all this changes. Speakers must then tie their message to what is written in The Book. However valid the reasons, no one today could erase or add a text to scripture. Unlike Moses, Jesus knew what a scripture was—the *Sefer Torah* and the Prophets had become scripture by his time—and he referred to ideas he had heard from these books. Yet he showed no eagerness to have his own teachings written down and certainly did not expect that later generations would consider his every word sacred, scriptural.

Most of the texts that became scripture seem little, if at all, different from those that did not. Genesis talks about God and occasionally quotes a few words from Him but does not introduce its narratives as "the words of God spoken to" anyone. Only a small percentage of any biblical text or of the Koran unabashedly presents itself as revelation. In the Book of Jonah, God's only oracle to the community through Jonah is, "yet forty days and Nineveh shall be destroyed" (3:4). The two long histories—Samuel-Kings and Chronicles—make no claim to a nobler status than that of history books. The Book of Esther never mentions God or claims divine sanction. No one, I am sure, would be more surprised than the author of Ecclesiastes that his rueful ruminations on age and the impermanence of life ended up enshrined in a Bible.

A scripture can be taken from place to place; it can be copied over and over again. This was both asset and liability: the text can reach a wide audience, but how to guarantee consistency among versions? In the days of manuscripts, each copy was the work of an individual scribe who worked long and carefully on a difficult text and often saw himself as a partner in the creation of a book. He could, and often did, add or amend, believing that the text was as much his as the original author's. This sense of creative partnership came to an end when the work was declared scripture. A scripture is God's word. No scribe would tamper with God's words.

A scripture cannot be amended: "You shall not add or subtract from it" (Deut. 4:2). Yet a scripture's authority was not always honored. Think of Jesus speaking of the Torah: "You have heard it said but I say." Only a nonbeliever or one who believes he speaks with God's authority can directly challenge a scripture. Such is the hold of a scripture that it is, even when challenged, rarely completely rejected. The Christian Church bound what it called the Old Testament to its Gospel; and Mohammed spoke of himself as the last and ultimate prophet and in his speeches quoted from the Bible.

A scripture is more than a sacred teaching. Its sentences and words, even its individual letters, are accepted by the faithful as having power of their own. As God's own they participate in His power. Christian exorcists held up a Bible as a shield against the forces of darkness. Jewish believers placed cherished phrases from their scripture in protective amulets to shield their persons from harm. In the First World War, soldiers on both sides carried into battle pocket Bibles inside whose covers were inscribed the family's lineage as a way of protecting the living and the dead.

I believe that the claim that a particular scripture was revealed often reflected a desire to protect the specific language of some treasured text as much as it was a claim to God's authorship. As communities became more literate, they recognized the individual ways scribes might handle the traditions; and, needing to believe that they possessed rock-solid, sacred writings, they protected these writings from change both by claiming that they were from and by God and by surrounding them with taboos that humans might fear to tamper with them.

The transformation of a body of religious literature into scripture places authority and truth squarely in the text. Where preliterate societies grounded faith in and derived definition from prophetic statements or community sentiment, literate societies claim faith based in and defined by a text. Text and tradition are declared to be one. Certainty and stability are gained; but as the written word defines, it restricts, and flexibility and spontaneity are lost. A scriptural faith must always consider its texts, but a text is not always relevant or helpful to the community's needs.

To speak of scripture is to speak of a defined body of writings, and of no other, as inspired. Believers may assume that scriptural texts are self-evident; yet the Talmud reports that the sages were still debating in the second century of this era whether Esther, Ecclesiastes, and the Song of Songs were or were not scripture. Greek Jews had a significantly different text of Jeremiah than the one that found its way into our Bible. The early church fathers debated the canonical status of the Gospel of John and a number of apocryphal works, and Christian gnostics had a fifth gospel. Innumerable sayings of Mohammed circulated before and after the official arrangement that is the Koran emerged. Scriptural material is not immediately recognizable. Few scriptural passages begin "thus says the Lord." When a scripture describes the Exodus from Egypt, the miracle of the fishes and the loaves, or Mohammed's ascent from Jerusalem, it does so as if it were writing history, as an observer rather than as God. The begats of Genesis would be nothing more than archaic lists of Israel's presumed ancestors, worth only a learned article on ancient Mesopotamian names, had they not found their way into scripture. God did not determine what is scripture; the community did.

Many of the writings that became scripture originally circulated without sanctifying labels and were treated as no more than pieces of interesting literature. Here and there, for reasons we can no longer detail, a scribe set down a short collection of customary legal formulas or a version of an ancient victory hymn or a well-known story or saga. Once the clay or papyrus had been inscribed, there was a chance that some later scribe might come across it and incorporate it into a larger piece he was working on. Another scribe in a still later generation might introduce this material into a scroll of ancient traditions that he was working on and that, by good fortune, might find its way into an important archive. In these early stages, the writing out of texts did not necessarily define them as divine speech; the Deuteronomic histories (Samuel-Kings) actually cite earlier annals. Those who claim the whole Bible to be revelation are, therefore, forced to affirm the absurdity that God, like any professional historian, needed to provide footnotes to validate His observations. Luke indicated in his opening chapter that he knew of several inadequate biographies of Jesus and intended his book to be a useful and accurate correction of their failings; in his explanation of his purpose, there is not a word that he had prepared his scroll under the guidance of the Holy Spirit. Many of Paul's letters were clearly written as private letters to a particular church.

Yet each scriptural tradition claims otherwise. Islam insists that the entire Koran is the word of God. During the ceremony that attends the reading of the *Sefer Torah* in liberal synagogues, an encomium from Psalm 19 is recited: "The Torah of the Lord is perfect, restoring the soul, the testimony of the Lord is sure, making wise the simple, the precepts of the Lord are upright, delighting the mind" (19:8–9). Unlike Judaism and Islam, Christianity has tended to prefer the term *inspiration* to *revelation* and to describe its scripture as written under the presence and guidance of the Holy Spirit, but has treated the Testament as a unique and sacred literature which it often unabashedly claimed to be inerrant.

Despite its ubiquity, such a sweeping claim presents problems. Some scriptural material is neither high-minded nor significant. "You shall love your neighbor as yourself" and "You shall not hate your brother in your heart" are found in the same list of divine instructions as "You shall not let your cattle gender with diverse kind" and "You shall not round the corners of your heads nor mar the corners of your beards" (Lev. 19). It is hard to imagine what inspirational benefit comes from the New Testament passage, "Come, and I will show you the judgment on the great whore, enthroned above the ocean. The kings of the earth have committed fornication with her" (Rev. 17:1–2). Some passages are ascribed to God, but others specifically to individuals: the psalms of David, Solomon, Asaph, sons of Korah, Agur; the gospels of Matthew, Mark, Luke; and so on. Some material is inconsistent, even contradictory.

Though none of the Western faiths admitted that their scripture was anything but uniformly divine, in practice they tended to emphasize some parts of it over others. The rabbis distinguished the *Sefer Torah,* the Five Books of Moses, from the rest of the Hebrew scripture. The *Sefer Torah* was accepted as directly revealed by God. No one, not even the prophet Moses who presumably first spoke these words to the community, in any way intruded on God's revelation. The special sacredness of the *Sefer Torah* was emphasized by the fact that the only scroll kept in the synagogue ark and read through systematically and publicly, on an annual schedule, was the scroll in which these books of Moses were inscribed. Readings from other parts of the Hebrew scripture, particularly from the Prophets, were chosen for their relevance to the Torah portion; but no attempt was made to place such readings on a symbolically equal level. The Christian Church, too, made distinctions. Old Testament readings were considered scriptural, but not in all aspects definitive for Christians. Many groups within the Church did not treat apocalyptic readings like the Book of Revelation with the same reverence as the Gospels and Pauline literature.

Physically, a scripture looks like any other book but is treated as a book like unto no other. As a physical object, a scripture is handled with great care, lovingly. Piety inevitably surrounds a scripture with rites and practices that emphasize its sacredness and unique importance. A worshiper in a synagogue crossing in front of the ark containing the scrolls of the *Sefer Torah* will stop and bow before passing on, while Muslim law insists a Koran must not be laid on the ground or allowed to come in contact with anything dirty. Jewish scribes developed formal rules for writing the *Sefer Torah*. The Koran could be written in any of a number of Arabic scripts, but care was always taken with the writing, and systems of ornamentation were developed to indicate the beginning and end of verses and when the reciter should prostrate himself. Until quite recently, Muslim religious leaders resisted the publication of printed editions of the Koran on the grounds that there inhered in a hand-copied manuscript a special sense of the sacred which the mechanical process of printing could never impart. Among the glories of medieval Christianity are the magnificent illuminated Gospel and Bible manuscripts inscribed and painted in the monasteries of the time.

EXPLAINING THE WORD OF GOD:
A SECOND SCRIPTURE

Though scripture seems to fix for all time its community's sacred teaching, a scriptural religion must resort to restatements from time to time to resolve problems that arise caused by changing times, contraditions in the sacred writings, and inconsistencies. These restatements—such as Vatican II in our day—speak the old phrases in a "new" light or develop ingenious commentary that permits it to dismiss most changes as no change at all.

Those who wrote official commentary asserted that they were simply making clear God's original intention, presenting to the community what was in their scripture and had always been there; but more was there than met the eye. Though they did not know the term, and would have emphatically denied its implications if they had, the leaders of the scriptural religions took an *existentialist* attitude toward scripture. It meant what they needed it to mean. Christian commentators found references to Jesus and the Christ in literally hundreds of nooks and crannies of the Hebrew scripture, references that were not apparent to non-Christians.

Let me retell a medieval story that effectively makes the rabbinic point that God had intended His word to be interpreted. A king had two slaves whom he loved. Before he left on a journey, he gave each one a measure of wheat and a bundle of flax. The intelligent one wove the flax into cloth and made flour from the wheat, sifted it, ground it, kneaded it, and baked it. The stupid one did nothing with the gifts the king had given him. When the king returned, he asked them to bring what he had given them. One brought out a table set with bread on the tablecloth; the other brought out the measure of wheat in a basket and the bundle of flax with it. This classic *midrash*—a beguiling elaboration of a simple, homely story—not only justifies but encourages and blesses the act of interpretation. It likens the Torah to wheat and flax, and makes of Torah interpretation—turning wheat into flour, flax into cloth—an act of intelligence and devotion to God.

Christians, too, insisted the Bible was infallible in all its parts, without contradiction among its elements, for a properly defined faith was necessary for salvation. "Faith," wrote Augustine in the late fourth century, "will stagger if the authority of the divine scripture wavers" (*On Christian Doctrine*, Book 1, p. 37). For him and other Christians of the time, God had chosen and equipped the Church to be scripture's infallible interpreter. Since a scripture is, as we have seen, an anthology of diverse thoughts and rules, the learned and thoughtful in Judaism, the early Church, and Islam felt impelled to interpret it in order to draw out the unity they knew was there, despite appearances to the contrary.

But a scripture is an elemental force that can be helpful or harmful, and sometimes both. The warning, "Make no mistake about this: God is not to be fooled; a man reaps what he sows" (Gal. 6:7), has caused many people who have been simply unlucky to suffer guilt and heartache. Paul's "it is better to marry than to burn" (1 Cor. 7:9) has seriously confused society's understanding of the appropriate role of the sexual in human relationships. Mohammed's justification of war as a means of gaining authority over unbelievers and converting them to Islam (Koran 9:5, 4:76, 2:214, 8:39) continues to encourage political violence in the Middle East and elsewhere.

When commentary cannot fix up a scriptural text, the text may impose on a community ideas it no longer accepts and burdens it cannot bear. The Torah rule requiring that all debts be remitted each sabbatical year is an example of an idea that has become anachronistic. Designed to prevent the impoverishment of a population consisting largely of farmers and herdsmen who survived on the edge of economic disaster and regularly fell into debt when crops failed or someone took over the market, this rule gave the herders and farmers a second chance and reflects a concept of morality appropriate to a simple agrarian economy. During Hellenistic times, as commerce began to play a major role in the economy of an increasingly urbanized community, the sabbatical rule became a stumbling block to economic development. No one would lend money during the later years of the sabbatical cycle; and without money, the economy ground to a halt. To get around the text, which is presented in the *Sefer Torah* as one of God's specific commands for all times, the sages devised a complicated legal fiction to circumvent the express intent of scripture (M. Shevi'it 10:3–4).

A scripture, as a written document full of worthy themes seen as ultimate truths, is both definitive and restrictive. Writings accepted as sacrosanct provide the faith an unchanging universe of discourse —idioms, personalities, a calendar, laws—but, as conditions change, may be quoted to quite different purposes. The words and ideas of a scripture are used in every generation, not always to the same purpose. Yet a scripture's unshakable presence often serves to limit the faith's ability to adjust to inevitable changes in the social order. The presence of an unchanging scripture cannot in itself enable a community to avoid change. Issues come up that the scripture never imagined; or, as with the sabbatical law, rules that fit one situation may not fit another. A religious tradition must continuously adjust to a changing environment; if it is to survive, commentary is necessary. Commentary and interpretation provide that possibility, finding fresh and unexpected meanings in a text.

THE QUESTION OF LANGUAGE

When speech becomes text, a problem of language often arises. A later reader may not understand the language of the original version. Even if one read Hebrew, Latin, or Arabic, it would likely be a contemporary dialect like mishnaic Hebrew, church Latin, or medieval Arabic, and not the classic tongue. Idioms that meant one thing when they were spoken may now be read differently and suggest other meanings. The meaning of certain words may no longer be known. The best of today's scholars, armed with the results of centuries of textual and linguistic research, admit that many translations present difficulties. One can no longer honestly affirm belief in every line and word of scripture because no one knows exactly what every line means. Until recently, every line of scripture was translated, but some recent translations admit textual difficulties by noting in appropriate places that the meaning is uncertain or that there are other possible translations.

Few of the faithful are put off by the fact that scholars do not fully understand The Book. They accept that The Book is holy, that its language is holy. Many accept that the scripture was written in God's native tongue. Jews assume God speaks Hebrew; Muslims, that He speaks Arabic. To this day, while synagogue liturgy can be recited in any vernacular, the *Sefer Torah* is to be read in Hebrew. Islam discouraged translations of the Koran. Schoolboys in all parts of the Muslim world, even if they do not speak Arabic, learn the

35

Koran in Arabic. To translate God's speech into another language than His own, Arabic, would not only distort its meaning but deprive the words of much of their innate power. Christians have a somewhat different approach to language since, unlike the Torah and the Koran, their Bible is a translation. Jesus spoke Aramaic, not Greek; but the Greek and Syrian Bibles in the East and the Latin in the West were quickly accepted not as translations but as scriptures, and their texts as sacrosanct.

THE QUESTION OF CHOICE

A scripture provides its communicants a powerful and compelling symbol: "Here is your duty. Here are your hopes. It is all here, you do not have to guess about it." But when you look behind the symbol to the text's substance, it becomes clear that the sense of certainty comes at a price, part of which has already been paid during the selection process. In imposing on the text the unity the learned knew was there, they necessarily emphasized some texts and pushed aside others; inevitably, words and themes of beauty were left out. Archeologists recovered from the caves above Qumran, on the northwest shore of the Dead Sea, at various times from 1947 on, a psalter that contained several beautiful psalms not included in the received text. Someone had chosen from the available collection of psalms and hymns in order, for some scribal reason, to limit the collection to one hundred fifty hymns. In defining the scriptural canon, the rabbis excluded a considerable literature. Some, like Ecclesiasticus and the Wisdom of Solomon, have survived outside the canon, and their value can still be appreciated. It would be hard to explain why the apocryphal additions to Jeremiah and Daniel were not included in their respective rolls. Much of the richness and variety of Christianity and Islam's formative periods were also left behind. There were other gospels and many other teachings attributed to Mohammed. A scripture inevitably denies a community some of its past.

The editors of the New Testament were aware that much that they included had not been written as sacred literature. The author of Luke wrote to a friend that "many writers have undertaken to draw up an account of the events that have happened among us, following the traditions handed down to us by the original eyewitnesses," and spoke of his desire "to write a connected narrative for you so as to give you authentic knowledge about the matters of which you have been informed" (1:1–4). This is the way a historian writes who is setting down a particular report of a series of events.

Certainly, in the early centuries no one involved with what became scripture had a scripture in mind. Many of the stories, proverbs, and laws had circulated orally for a considerable period. What was written down can puzzle us in many ways, particularly as to why it became scripture. It may occur in several versions; it may be unedifying (the story of a frightened Abraham passing off his wife as his sister). A particular story may simply have been well known and well loved or part of the established notes from which storytellers recited the life of a patriarch. Familiarity was often enough. Chance also played a role in what became scripture; a scribe might add a sentence or two to the parchment he had copied, and forever after a psalm had a few extra lines. Because we think of an anthology as a collection of the best writing of a certain type, we assume that scripture includes works of high quality important to the community's life; but there is also much that is not. Other criteria as well as that of quality governed what was included in a scripture's table of contents.

Some scriptural texts acquired more importance as circumstances changed. "Repent ye, for the Kingdom of God is at hand" (Mark 1:15) rang with urgency in the first century when people believed that Jesus was about to return, and then lost much of its force when Christians had to abandon hope in a proximate Second Coming. Even if few had confidence it would happen in their lifetime, the Second Coming theme remained Christian doctrine, cherished for its message of hope but not insisted upon in any literal way.

THE QUESTION OF INTERPRETATION

In the first thousand years of the Common Era, Judaism's religious leaders devised intricate systems of interpretation: according to common sense and context, metaphorically, by various techniques of association, allegorically, esoterically. Some of these methods simply drew out a text's logical inference, while others defied every rule of logic. For example, the rabbis prohibited mixing meat and milk dishes on the basis of an old agricultural law—"not to boil a kid in its mother's milk" (Exod. 23:19)—which seems to have been originally designed to protect a farmer in desperate times from the temptation of killing off his only breeding animal.

Complementing a scripture by a body of tradition is not unusual in religious history. The Bibles of the world are powerful, dramatic, and effective documents, but they are neither systematic nor fully consistent. The Catholic Church insists on the infallibility of its scripture, yet derives its teachings primarily from canon law. *Ulemas,* teachers of the Koran, will cite the Sunna and the Shariyah as well as the Koran; and rabbis will quote from the Talmud as well as the Torah. What is surprising is that each of these nonscriptural anthologies became, for all practical purposes, an operative scripture.

The Torah, the New Testament, and the Koran became the scriptures of their communities. Each was a brilliant and imaginative classic, but none was a sufficient guide in all matters. Each required interpretation, and interpretation could not be limited to a straightforward explanation of the text on which all could agree. The difficulty was that new conditions were constantly arising that the classic text had not contemplated; and, moreover, the complex and varied scriptural text had no self-evident unity. Orthodox theologians tried to define interpretation as a natural and logical process with inevitable conclusions. In fact, there is nothing inevitable about any interpretive process. Words can be given almost any meaning. To avoid challenge, each of the major Western religions gathered the desired "interpretations" into a second scripture.

Each of these second scriptures has its own shape and structure and is different in format from the original. The second scriptures are not simply convenient rearrangements of matters dealt with in the original scripture, though they often claim to be that. Each defines a structure of religious practice and a formulation of duty and doctrine which in some ways build on the scriptural text and in many ways go beyond it.

38

Canon law affirms a rigidly structured church hierarchy, requires priestly celibacy, affirms the bodily assumption of Mary and the sacrament of confession, establishes a calendar of holy days and fast days, defines a hagiography, and gives to the priesthood authority to define doctrine and practice and to the Pope infallibility: themes either missing in the New Testament or only vaguely suggested there. Canon law's claims to obedience depend largely on the New Testament's authority; but the degree to which the Roman Church rests its authority on canon law, on what it tends to call tradition, rather than on the New Testament, is exemplified by the trauma that convulsed Western Christendom when the reformers Zwingli, Luther, and Calvin claimed that canon law was the creation of error-prone churchmen, and that divine authority inhered only in the original scriptures.

Each of the scriptural faiths claims that its scripture is inspired, but only Protestant Christianity, and mainly for only a brief period at its beginning, insisted on the sole sufficiency of scripture, what theologians call the doctrine of *sola scriptura.* The Reformation's battle was with the papal tradition, not with Christianity. Protestant Christianity suspected all tradition except that derived directly from scripture. Everyone was to make of scripture what he or she could. Protestant Christianity soon developed its own traditions, since no faith, scriptural or otherwise, can survive without giving authority to the result of years of creativity and teaching.

The Roman Church, like Islam and rabbinic Judaism, insists that authority lies in scripture and tradition and generally defines tradition as the official teachings of the Church. Rome justified its claim by insisting that the Church was established and inspired by God and given special spiritual powers that allowed it to define the meaning of scripture and to define the duties and doctrines of the faith. Most religions gloss over the many ways in which current practice and doctrine diverge from that presented in scripture; but the Catholic Church, which has a penchant for neat and careful formulation, has said openly that the Church affirms teachings not found in its scripture. At the Council of Trent in 1648, and more recently (18 November 1965) at the Second Vatican Council in a Dogmatic Constitution on Divine Revelation entitled *Dei Verbum,* Rome declared: "Consequently, it is not from sacred Scripture alone that the Church draws her certainty about everything which has been revealed. Therefore both sacred tradition and sacred scripture are to be accepted and venerated with the same sense of devotion and reverence" (p. 117).

The Koran was destined to inspire and vitalize Islam, but was not allowed the final word in defining Islam's institutions, doctrines, and practices. For that purpose, Muslims turn to the Sunna and the Shariyah. The Koran assumes that traditions of Arab justice and local custom (Sunna) play a major role in the community as it goes about the task of consecrating a particular way of law and of life. To authorize these practices, new ideas and institutions were needed, and various statements of the prophet were "recalled" which had not been included in the Koran. Some of these statements may actually have been Mohammed's; others certainly were not, though they were claimed to be. The standard used to determine whether a saying was acceptable or not was *sahib*: "is it sound?" The test of *sahib* was extrinsic: Did the saying have a reliable pedigree? Could it be traced back to Mohammed through a chain of reliable transmitters? Islam and its jurists were able to develop and articulate a way of life and a way of faith, including the five mandatory daily prayers, that went far beyond the actual teachings of the Koran. By the ninth century, anthologies of sound traditions *(al-sahib)* had been collected; the most acceptable of these were drawn together and as law codes became the basis of Islam's second scripture (Shariyah). It is the Sunna, as codified in the Shariyah, to which Muslims turn for doctrinal and judicial guidance.

Judaism has its *Sefer Torah,* its scripture, but it also has the Talmud, a massive body of teaching and law, edited more than fifteen hundred years after Sinai, which rabbinic piety associates with that revelation and on whose authority it declares obligatory many practices and principles. For the rabbis, Torah consists of two parts: the written law and the oral law. The written is contained in the Five Books of Moses, and the oral law is made up of the traditional interpretations handed down, by word of mouth through a reliable chain of transmitters from generation to generation, until it was at last embodied in the talmudic literature. They affirm the links over and over, as in the opening of the Mishnah tractate known as *Pirke Avot*: "Moses received the Torah at Sinai and handed it down to Joshua; Joshua to the elders; the elders to the prophets; and the prophets handed it down to the men of the Great Assembly" (M. Avot 1:1). In many discussions, the sages readily admitted that the traditions take precedence over scripture in defining practice.

We are not accustomed to think of works such as the Talmud or canon law as a second scripture. Every faith teaches—and its faithful accept—that its original scripture contains the first and last word. The conventional wisdom has been that Judaism, Christianity, and Islam are, and have been from the beginning, definable and consistent entities. While at times heretics and enthusiasts tried to reshape the tradition, the scripture was there, acting like a magnet, pulling deviants back to the source. An attractive idea, and inaccurate. Most scriptures lacked the range or detail to give full shape to their evolving traditions. They became important symbols, but the actual task of definition was left to the interpretations in a second scripture.

Commentary introduces into the faith a new kind of priesthood— the authority of those who can read and interpret. With commentary comes the dominance of a new élite, the learned and the trained, who "do" the commentary and determine which interpretations are acceptable. Particularly during those centuries when literacy was a rare accomplishment, a scriptural religion tended to give authority to those who claimed the power to interpret. All who could not read were urged to submit and abide. A scriptural religion tends to be defined from above.

Inevitably, distance opens between the leaders, those who define, and the faithful, those who obey. Inevitably, an official church emerges as a separate entity distinct from the community of believers. When this happens, religious coercion is usually not far behind. The community's ultimate response to coercion will be to rally behind leaders who claim that the present élite have misdefined scripture. More often than not, the rebellious message is: "Read scripture. Do not leave it to others to tell you what God has said." That was the basis of the Protestant Reformation, which urged, in effect, that the substance of the faith was not in the Church but in the Bible. The Protestants, quickly finding that many could read the text and make sense of it, had formed, within a generation or two, sects that accepted the interpretation of one or another leader—Calvin, Luther, Zwingli. A measure of unity was achieved because groups tended to follow their leaders' interpretations as they had once followed Rome's lead, the only difference being that Rome had insisted on submission and the protesting churches continued to emphasize independence of thought, making up one's own mind about scripture.

The coexistence of a scripture and an accepted commentary gives institutional authorities a basis for opposing any claim that a new message has been received from God that seems contrary to official teaching. Continuity is assured but at the price of silencing or driving off those who feel they have known God intimately or heard Him speak. Acknowledging many modes of interpretation, the rabbis often quoted a line from Jeremiah: "Behold My word is like fire—declares the Lord—and like a hammer that shatters rock" (23:29). Interpretations, like sparks, fly off in all directions, and each spark gives off some light.

CONCLUSION

The interplay between interpretation and scripture as the final and unchanging word of God is similar to the role played by the American Constitution in our government. The Constitution's text, and the arguments advanced by those who wrote its paragraphs, have a certain force which the courts take under advisement; but in rendering decisions, the courts also take into consideration, though not always acknowledging that they do, the needs and attitudes of contemporary society. The language of the Constitution exerts an authority that cannot be willfully flaunted and is sometimes inescapable; but when they desire to do so, interpreters can stretch the letter of the law until the spirit of the times overwhelms it. The power of judicial review is the power to change the Constitution. Interpretation and commentary are the ways religious leaders changed their scripture and thereby their faith.

A recitation is flexible. A scripture text is frozen. Times and conditions change. Constitutions require amendment. Calling ideas timeless does not make them so. Scriptures claim to present general truths but, in fact, contain materials written at a particular time and place and in the language of a particular day, using its images and idioms as well as its science and superstition. Judaism is like other religions, a complex human institution which evolved slowly and drew ideas from many sources. The *Sefer Torah,* like the New Testament and the Koran, consists of a largely unplanned selection of texts and traditions which have passed through many hands and minds, scribes and editors, until it achieved the form we know today.

A scripture often appears to be what it is not, the source book and summation of a tradition. A scripture presents a selection of cherished traditions found acceptable by a particular group of religious leaders at a particular moment in their faith's evolution. No scripture contains the first word or the last word. Many of the faith's formative ideas precede the assumed moment of revelation, and much of a faith community's subsequent development represents the community wrestling with the text it has declared holy, whose words, ideas, and insights continue to play an important role in the minds and lives of communicants.

2

SACRED SPEECH: BEFORE THE EXILE

> The Lords said this to me: herewith I put My words into your mouth.
>
> —Jeremiah 1:9

Torah min ha-Shamayim, the revelation of the Torah by God, was and remains for traditional Judaism a central tenet of the faith. The Torah is from God. It presents His version of early history, His instructions, and His promises as He wishes them to be known. The Torah was revealed at a particular place and time, early in Israel's history. Sinai, the place, became the rabbinic shorthand for this revelation. If one accepts the biblical claim that it was given just a few months after the Exodus from Egypt, Judaism began as a self-conscious faith in the twelfth or thirteenth pre-Christian century. This view emphasizes the originality of the Torah's teachings and their origin in God's will. Those who accept this view describe the subsequent history of the Jewish people as a conscious effort by the community to understand and abide by these Instructions. Sinai represents the gift of truth, promise, and identity and presumedly set the shape of the religious life of the Jewish people for all time.

There is nothing inherently illogical in the idea that God revealed His will to Israel at Sinai. God is omniscient. He knows what was and what will be, and makes known to those He chooses what He chooses. But today, after several centuries of literary and historical research, it has become clear that Judaism did not emerge as a full-blown religious tradition at Sinai—any more than did Christianity when Paul had his vision on the road to Damascus, or Islam when Mohammed was moved to oracular speech.

The oldest of the classic religions of the West, Judaism went longest without a written scripture. Despite the occasional late biblical reference to Moses writing down God's instructions in a book, the Hebrew tribes of his day were not yet literate or interested in literacy. In such early semi-nomad societies, neither leadership nor a reputation for wisdom depended on being literate. In the development of Judaism, tradition preceded text by a considerable period, precisely when some of the most creative and revolutionary thinking took place. Long before Israel had a scripture, it had developed the idea of the oneness of God and God's incomparability; the idea of God as creator and a dependable power outside nature who judges men and nations by their actions rather than by the gifts brought to His altar; of man as in some measure responsible for his fate, of man created in God's own image, and of the common origin of the nations—humanity. Scripture would embody these ideas and many others, but they did not begin in scripture: they began in the immediacy of individual religious experience, in the minds of prophets and sages, and worked their way toward the forefront of Israel's consciousness in the living situation of the community. The medium of religious revelation was the spoken rather than the written word.

THE SPOKEN WORD

In the beginning, the tribes of Israel, like all pre-literate groups, carried their traditions in their heads and their hopes in their hearts. There was no scripture. They certainly felt that the gods at times made known their will to shamans, prophets, or sheiks; their traditions certainly included reports of oracles and of divine activity, treasured not on clay or papyrus but in the community's collective memory. The historical fact is that for most of what is commonly described as biblical times, there was as yet no Bible. Each tribe had its own oral traditions. Oral traditions use and reuse incident, image, and idiom. These "texts" were written in the mind, stored in the tribe's memory, and subjected to emendation over the years as the community's interests demanded.

The donkeys carrying the worldly possessions of the Hebrew tribes who began to enter Canaan toward the end of the second millennium B.C.E. were laden with tools and textiles but not with inscribed clay tablets or papyrus texts. The various cultures of these semi-nomadic tribes of Israel consisted of seamless webs of practices and of traditions learned by imitation, hands-on instruction, or from the recitations of storytellers. Fathers taught their sons husbandry, the art of self-defense, and a code of responsibility and virtue. Mothers taught their daughters to sew, work in the fields, cook, and care for their infants. Holy men whispered magic formulas to carefully chosen disciples. Old women taught willing girls the skills of midwifery and herbal medicine. Rhapsodists regaled the community with well-known epics about their ancestors and well-known myths which explained the origins of life and the mysteries of nature, and taught their sons those traditions so that they in turn could regale another generation.

The tribes had no written literature. Theirs was an oral culture, an amalgam of law, saga, cherished genealogies, sacred hymns and formulas, myths, a calendar, customs, and, of course, a many-sided folk wisdom which was both practical—when to plant and when to harvest—and philosophic—how life had begun and how evil had come to be. Since their culture and physical environment changed little from generation to generation, conventional wisdom was confirmed by experience, consecrated by time, and accepted as right, sacred to the god(s). The way of the fathers felt natural to the sons. There was no generation gap.

The tribes that ultimately formed the Israelite confederation moved about West Asia and during their migration must have come across scribes plying their trade, but there is no indication that any of the Hebrews undertook to master the art of writing. They had no need of documents. Cases brought before tribal sheiks like Abraham and Jacob were argued orally and decided on the basis of well-known legal norms. Oral testimony was taken, and judgments were publicly announced. A pile of stones at the corners of a field registered ownership. The early biblical narratives confirm this picture: Abraham's purchase of a burial cave, the Machpelah, is described as a purely oral arrangement (Gen. 23:1–20). When Jacob seeks to be reunited with Esau, he sends presents and a spoken message (Gen. 32:14–22). The drama surrounding Jacob's unwanted marriage to Leah assumes a pre-literate society: had there been a written marriage contract, Laban would not have been able to trick Jacob into marrying Leah rather than Rachel (Gen. 29:16–30).

The elders served the god(s) on various high places, seeking protection for the tribe, their trek, and their flocks. They did so without benefit of Bible or prayer book. Those who conducted the mandated rites learned the proper hymns and practices from their predecessors, and the community knew through these what was expected of them. When there was a need to consult the gods, a sheik or a priest cast lots or consulted the oracles and reported back at a public assembly a god's instructions. God repeatedly reveals His will and then tells Moses: "Speak to the tribes of Israel." In most tribes, a family of specialists, speakers, and trained rhapsodists had mastered and practiced the art of the formal recitation of the tribe's myths and sagas and was prepared to rehearse these traditions at appropriate ceremonies, as Moses is reported to have done on the "other side of the Jordan" (Deut. 1) and Joshua at Schechem (Josh. 24).

Thus, Israel's first literature was inscribed in the minds of those who spoke it and those who heard it. Over time some of this literature, after going through many oral revisions as it was told and retold, was written down; but even after an extended passage of time, such a text often reveals its origin in an oral tradition, what Walter Ong has called its "orally constituted sensibility and tradition" (1982, p. 99). The language is spare, highly compressed, lacking embellishment. Stories are simply told, generally in a poetic style because rhythm and assonance make them easier to remember. Nouns and verbs appear without modifying adverbs and adjectives. Phrases tend to be alliterative and rhythmic. An incident is quickly sketched. No attempt is made to analyze motivation. Images are concrete. Lists rely on repetitive formulas ("When Mahalalel had lived sixty-five years, he begat Jared" [Gen. 5:15]) or employ a series of similar incidents as an aid to memory ("The Israelites set out from Rameses and encamped at Succoth. They set out from Succoth and encamped at Etham." [Num. 33:5–6ff]). The apparent willingness of biblical narrative to let the imagination of the reader fill in the details and provide context has often been commented on as one reason for the book's unceasing appeal. It is a virtue born not of a conscious decision but of necessity: compression was the imperative of an oral culture where literature was created and stored in the finite memory.

Such schooling as there was emphasized rote learning. Indeed, rote learning and the memorization of texts would remain the basis of the educational process of almost all West Asian and Mediterranean cultures long after books and literacy had become familiar elements in the community's life. "Once I was a son to my Father, the tender darling of my mother. He instructed me and he said to me, 'Let your mind hold on to my words'" (Prov. 4:3–8). During the entire pre-exilic period, formal education was the exception rather than the rule for boys and almost entirely unavailable to girls. Boys learned by being apprenticed, by listening, and by aping their elders.

Traditions remained alive through the recitals of well-known sagas, and lessons about custom and law were learned in the course of everyday life. People lived within a silence broken only by the sounds of nature and on occasion by the human voice, the voice of the town crier, the storyteller, the chanter of hymns, and the public orator. Prophets brought oracles vouchsafed to them from on high. There were few distractions. One heard what was said and had the quiet in which to reflect on it and a need to remember—as I, when alone for any long period of time, find myself repeating passages of poetry memorized in childhood, in this way providing myself with the companionship of others.

People not only paid close attention to what they heard, but were able to remember the recitations, one speech or story not being immediately followed by another and yet another to blur the impression of the first. Audiences generally anticipated what came next in a recital and were disappointed rather than pleased by innovation. Frequent hearing of the same tale, told in largely the same phrases, imprinted familiar phrases and incidents on the people's minds.

The art of rhetoric was cultivated. The ability to speak effectively was a prerequisite for leadership. A sheik did not have to be able to read or write, but did have to be able to make himself heard and understood. Moses tried to beg off from God's commission to be the agent of the slaves' liberation by arguing that he was slow of tongue and therefore would not be effective (Exod. 4:10).

Words were not merely means of communication but objects of inherent power. Words spoken by priests and prophets, and almost certainly by poets, were felt to possess an innate power not unlike the power of a magical spell. Once uttered, such words took on a life of their own. A spoken oath was binding. Isaac recognized that he had been tricked into blessing Jacob instead of Esau, but his culture did not provide him the means to cancel the blessing (Gen. 27). Legend had Joshua stop the sun in its course with incantation (Josh. 10:12–13). Blessings, curses, and oracles once spoken were believed to carry weight. Had God not put words of blessing, in place of the intended curse, into the mouth of the prophet Balaam, the tribes would have been effectively cursed (Num. 22–24). Jerusalem's conservative nobility demanded that Jeremiah be imprisoned because he had spoken aloud a prophecy of the city's destruction. Presumedly, had he not spoken aloud the oracle, the threat it contained would have remained dormant. By bringing words of promise, a prophet certified the community's hopes: "The word that issues from My mouth does not come back to Me unfulfilled but performs what I desire" (Isa. 55:11).

All voices counted, but the voice that counted most was God's. God speaks: "Thus says the Lord"; Israel is encouraged to listen: "Hear, O Israel." God's spoken instructions lie at the heart of the biblical record. Indifference to God's admonitions was defined as a form of deafness: "You [the prophet] are to them like the one who sings love songs with a beautiful voice and plays well on an instrument, for they hear what you say, but they will not do it" (Ezek. 33:32). It was the spoken, not the written, word that had standing.

One of the signs of the arrival of messianic times is Isaiah's prophecy that "the deaf shall hear even written words" (Isa. 29:18).

THE WRITTEN WORD

The earliest extant Hebrew writings—a number of inscribed ring seals and the Gezer Calendar, a small limestone tablet which presents a list of months together with the agricultural tasks appropriate to each—are generally dated to the century following the establishment of David's monarchy (*c.*1000 B.C.E.). Unfortunately, little Hebrew writing survives from the next three or four centuries, so the spread of the literacy craft cannot be described. But once settled in Canaan, a few bright young Israelites must have set out to master the writing and reading skills in which they found many Canaanites adept and whose value as a useful and administrative tool became increasingly evident and necessary as the community settled in. They knew the scribe as a craftsman who offered his skills in the same way as the local smith or mason; as a tradesman, the scribe learned his art by the time-honored way of apprenticeship.

EDUCATION AND THE POWER OF MEMORY

There was, however, another level of scribe-administrators who had been since Sumerian times (mid-fourth millennium B.C.E.) the real promoters of writing because of its usefulness in managing affairs of state, collecting taxes and tribute, conscripting forced labor and troops, and maintaining land registration, palace inventories, and the like. Such officials worked in the bureaus of the Canaanite city-states. They learned their skills in the way these arts were universally mastered by men of their class in ancient times—in palace schools. There a teacher sounded the letters or spoke the phrases of the poem or saga being used as a text, and the student repeated the lesson aloud while copying the letters on a wooden tablet. This process was repeated until the teacher was satisfied that the text was stored in the student's memory, and that he could write out and perhaps also read aloud his copy.

50

The teacher made sure the neophyte scribe properly understood the text by having him sound it out. The mentor listened and made the necessary corrections. The Chinese schoolroom—whose babble became a byword to Western visitors who compared it unfavorably with our presumedly quiet and orderly classes—is, in fact, similar to what a visitor would have found in a school for scribes in ancient West Asia. All reading was done aloud. Since everyone was conditioned in this way, everyone in the ancient world who could read, read aloud. As late as the fourth century c.e., Augustine in his memoirs expresses surprise when he notices a scholar off in a corner reading silently.

Education aimed at mastering what was already known rather than at enlarging the boundaries of knowledge. One of the paradoxes that accompanied the spread of literacy is that at first the existence of inscribed tablets and scrolls forced scribes to depend more, rather than less, on their memories. Writing was a primitive art, and the written words were not yet corseted with a definite structure of spelling or grammar. Lines were irregular, and text might run in several directions. Scribes compressed as much text as possible on a single surface, for writing surfaces were expensive. As a result, one had to do some imaginative guesswork or be familiar with a text to make sense of it, particularly when a text was not an inventory, a list, but literature. Reading was an uncertain art. No wonder the Greeks taught that Mnemosyne (memory) was the mother of the Muses, and set their sons to memorize the *Iliad*. Even if you had access to tablets or scrolls, what was not stored in your memory might as well not exist. Your library, such as it was, was in your mind. A neighbor or colleague might know a particular tradition you had forgotten, but the outer limit of collective knowledge was the sum of collective recollection.

"My son, forget not my teachings . . . incise them on the tablet of your mind" (Prov. 3:1–3). Acquiring knowledge was a long, laborious, and tedious process, and one never graduated. Each tablet or scroll had to be learned. Adults repeated what they knew all their lives to make sure they had not forgotten. Not surprisingly, the biblical tradition is full of admonitions encouraging the faithful to review God's instructions, lest they slip into oblivion: "Recite [these

Instructions] when you stay at home and when you are away, when you lie down and when you get up" (Deut. 6:7); "Remember the commandments of the Lord" (Num. 15:39); "Remember to do all my commandments" (Num. 15:40). Sin was traced back to forgetfulness: "My people are ruined for lack of knowledge. You have forgotten your God's Instructions" (Hos. 4:6). Righteousness was associated with a strong memory: "The mercy of the Lord is from everlasting to everlasting . . . to those that remember His precepts to do them" (Ps. 103:17–18). In messianic times, people will be "joined . . . in a covenant which shall not be forgotten" (Jer. 50:5).

While we associate intelligence with literacy and creativity, the ancients associated it with retentivity: "Memory," Aeschylus said in *Prometheus Bound*, "is the mother of all wisdom." Indeed, the spread of literacy often raised fears about the future of civilization: that is, one who had access to a library might no longer review regularly what he knew, and so fail to keep it in mind. The concern of these early Jews was fundamentally moral. A well-stocked and active memory, full of noble thoughts, was held to be the mother of virtue, because what was in a person's mind inevitably showed up in his actions. Memory and virtue were, in their thinking, inextricably linked.

Memory was the trusted means of keeping traditions alive. In recent years, much has been written about the role of professional storytellers and rhapsodists in shaping and preserving oral and folk culture. Generally, these professionals have been described as highly reliable transmitters. So impressed have some students been by what they believe to be the fidelity of the oral transmission of narratives and legal formulas that they have come to overdramatic conclusions about the reliability of the Bible's reports of events occurring centuries before they became a part of Israel's written record. We do find details of much older practices and customs as well as venerable idioms embedded in various later biblical narratives. Oral traditions were handled carefully; but the Hebrews, like all peoples of the time, were not committed to an absolutely faithful transmission.

While pre-literate and semi-literate societies treasured traditions that passed on through the generations with a significant degree of fidelity, changes were nonetheless constantly being made in oral presentations. The general conservatism in respect to the transmission of well-known material has led students to exaggerate the fidelity of oral transmission. Studies of rhapsodists and storytellers in traditional cultures have shown that, though they believe that they are repeating stories without change, they never tell a story quite the same way twice. The teller responds to his audience and they to him —an interchange that causes subtle changes as the teller chooses the words and images that seem to strike a responsive chord in a particular audience. Thus, storytellers constantly modify their narratives to make them more understandable or exciting to an audience. Myths were subtly reshaped with each retelling to fit new social or ethical attitudes.

True, the familiar sagas were repeated with considerable accuracy, and familiar details and images reappear with each telling. Yet when anthropologists have been able to compare a spoken version of a pre-literate tribe's history with an earlier telling, they have found that, though neither speaker nor audience were aware of it, the story had changed, the later version containing details that reflected political events subsequent to the earlier version. For example, researchers recorded an African saga about a tribe's origins; a generation later, other researchers heard the same narrative and found that it had been adjusted to reflect the fact that two clans were no longer members of the tribal group (Goody 1968, p. 33).* At every telling the story must be made understandable to those listening to it. The Homers of the ancient world recited with love and respect the well-known sagas of their tribes, using familiar phrases, idioms, and incidents in ways that allowed them to respond to the cultural preconceptions, political knowledge, and emotional interests of their audience, who thus helped to "write" the history. In this way, a culture not yet encumbered with a scripture retains a subtle but

*Similarly, there exist in the biblical literature several different lists of the twelve tribes that presumedly constituted the Israelite confederation: each is obviously the grouping as it was known at a particular moment in the community's history. Thus, an oral culture can forget or change details as long as the general theme—in this case, the existence of a twelve-tribe confederation—is maintained.

Also, comparing a series of recitations by a Yugoslav bard and finding that no two presentations were absolutely identical, A. B. Lord concluded that the singer adjusted his material to the reactions of the audience, the feel of the meeting, and his own feelings, and was unaware of having made any change (1960).

functional capacity to reshape its fundamental traditions without being conscious of doing so.

Such familiar recitations were not simply good theater but tied listeners to their past, to each other, and to their god(s). Part of the joy and power of such moments lay in their familiarity. The audience could anticipate words and phrases and thus have tangible proof that what they believed to be true and right was, in fact, so. The story's value lay in the recital which brought their past to life and guarded their present with the security of trusted teachings. The narrator did not need to belabor the message. The experience was the message. Its value lay in the emotional security that came from sharing a common heritage and present.

Myths can be traced to earlier prototypes in other cultures, a prime example being the tale of the Flood and Noah (Gen. 6–9). The biblical story is not a stencil of the earlier Sumerian epic of Gilgamesh which it so much resembles. Rather, it is a transformed version of a long-familiar story, changed over time and by unconscious design to reflect meanings and purposes appropriate to the Israelite ethos. Where Utnapishtim, the survivor of the flood in the Gilgamesh epic, is saved by the god Ea because he was the god's protegé, Noah is saved by God because he is a righteous man.

The first scriptures were intended to be read aloud. Chants that suggested the inflection and mood created by storyteller or prophet were formalized. Communities encouraged the reader to memorize and publicly recite the text in the same singsong the rhapsodists used in their recitations. Conscious efforts to transmit orally sacred traditions persisted long after literacy had become a much-used social tool. This is true in many ancient cultures. In India, the Rig Vedas, already well known in the thirteenth century B.C.E., were chanted aloud for centuries and not written down for another thousand years. To this day, Muslim schools emphasize the chanted memorization of the Koran, the actual text being used only to ensure against mistakes. And as far back as we can trace public readings from the *Sefer Torah,* we find that they were not read but chanted—as they often are today by those who come to "read" from the Torah in synagogues around the world.

54

EARLY SCRIBES AND RECORD KEEPING

Shortly before the tribes entered Canaan, Canaanite scribes put the finishing touches on a phonetic system that reduced the cuneiform syllabary to a manageable alphabet of twenty-two or twenty-four consonants, a system whose manifest advantage over all previous systems gained for it quick acceptance in the various governmental bureaus of West Asia. Because picture writing required an infinite number of signs, centuries of work had gone into the effort to replace these complex pictorial or hieratic scripts with a manageable system based on sound rather than on image and one in which all the phonetics, the basic sounds used in a spoken language, could be suggested by a few symbols. With this achievement, only one further change would be needed to produce the alphabet that still serves us well: that is, the specific vowel signs, introduced by the Greeks during the seventh or sixth centuries B.C.E., which made it much easier to transcribe pronunciation and, therefore, meaning.

The Hebrews, adopting the alphabet they found in Canaan, never had to wrestle with all the complexities of a hieratic writing system—a fact that may account for their remarkably consistent literary preference for simplicity over complexity. Language patterns affect thought patterns. Did Israel's late arrival into the world of the written word have something to do with its ability to conceive of one God over many, of one creation over separate natural forces, of one human family over separate and distinct tribal ancestors? And did the consonantal alphabet, which made it possible to communicate ideas through a finite set of symbols linked directly to sound rather than to a visual image, make it easier for the Hebrews, who never had to accustom themselves to pictographic symbols, to conceive of a God who could not be visualized or described?

In Canaan, as in all the city-states of West Asia, the development of writing techniques had been encouraged for their practical value as an administrative tool. Palaces sponsored the schools where scribes were prepared and which fostered experimentation designed to improve scribal techniques. As urban life developed and city-states grew into empires, officials found it increasingly necessary to provide help to the clerks trying to cope with the growing elaboration of political administration: the increasing number and complexity of land registries, tax records, inventories of military and palace supplies, census figures, and the palace's correspondence with provincial officials and foreign courts. Most of the inscribed tablets so far recovered from the ruins of the palaces and temples of West Asia—the number runs into the tens of thousands—deal with these and other such practical administrative matters: lists of taxes to be collected, registers of captured booty, inventories of items on deposit, copies of treaties, conscription documents, and royal and priestly genealogies. Only an occasional tablet records a venerated myth, sacred hymn, or collection of wisdom.

This was a world where illiterate kings sponsored schools for scribes, whom they needed for the efficient and effective organization of their power. Literacy was a practical art, not as yet associated with literature. Writing was developed as an instrument of social and political control. Those who attended palace schools and mastered scribal skills tended to be the sons of the lower nobility or minor priests who could, in the ordinary course of events, not expect to inherit land or feudal authority but had every reason to believe that demonstrating usefulness to those who governed was the way to position, preference, and power. An Egyptian text, *Teaching of Kety, Son of Duauf* (second millennium), imagines a father advising his son on the advantages of investing the long years required to master the scribal arts:

> I have never seen a sculptor on an errand [as an ambassador] nor a goldsmith when he was sent out. [But] I have seen the metalworker at his work at the mouth of his furnace. His fingers were somewhat like crocodiles; he stank more than fish-roe. . . . The small building contractor carries mud. . . . He is dirtier than vines or pigs. . . . His clothes are stiff with clay. . . . The tenant farmer's voice is as raucous as a crow's. . . . His sides ache, as if heaven and earth were in them. . . . Behold, there is no profession free of a boss—except for the scribe: he is the boss. But, if thou knowest writing, then it will go better with thee than in these professions which I have set before thee.
>
> (Pritchard 1950, pp. 432–34)

The themes of the scribe's reprieve from manual labor and protection against unpleasant working conditions appear frequently in ancient literature, as do other themes—such as those of prosperity in this life and immortality after this life ends—which are sounded in *Kety*: "Behold, there is no scribe who lacks food, from the property of the House of the King—life, prosperity, health!" (p. 434); and "A man is perished, his corpse is dust, all his relatives are come to the ground—[but] it is writing that makes him remembered in the mouth of a reciter. More effective is a book than the house of a builder or tombs in the West" (p. 432). A millennium later, an editor of the Book of Proverbs still found it appropriate to include a maxim that made a similar point: "See a scribe skillful at his craft. He will serve kings, he will not serve common men" (22:29).

Ordinary folk knew and feared the clerk as an agent of a distant, feared authority whose tablets or parchments often took away their land or added to their tax burdens. The Hebrew term for a scribe emerges from the root *spr*, "to count," rather than from the root *ktv*, "to write." A scribe was originally a *sofer*, a counter. Scribes compiled conscription lists, tax rolls, forced labor assignments, and records of royal lands—all activities that took from the many for the benefit of the few. In the process, scribes wrote the documents that threatened the immemorial routines of tribal life: denying access to customary pasturage or tying up simple folk in a mesh of complicated, and imperfectly understood, contractual obligations. The mysterious marks and lines the scribes produced often served as the basis of proceedings that appropriated land or conscripted sons into forced-labor battalions. The prophet Isaiah voiced the feelings of many in one of his famous "woe" oracles: "Ha! Those who write out evil writs and compose iniquitous documents, to subvert the cause of the poor, to rob of their rights the needy of My people; that widows may be their spoil, and fatherless children their booty!" (10:1–2). Many popular myths named the god of death as the deity who first taught literacy to human beings.

A history of the development of literacy in ancient Israel remains to be written; but it seems likely that at first it was simply a matter of Israel's kings doing what kings elsewhere had long found to be to their benefit. Having established a permanent court for his mini-empire in Jerusalem, David found that the management of his newly acquired kingdom required the maintenance of record keeping bureaus and set about accomplishing his ends by hiring scribes from other courts.

Illiteracy was not seen as a disabling handicap which precluded the exercise of power or even a reputation for learning. Not a single line in the Book of Judges suggests that Deborah, Gideon, Samson or any other leader of the settlement period could read or write. The Deuteronomic histories routinely describe the kings of Israel and Judah as listening to the speeches of their counselors or being read to by a royal scribe. The few stories in the Deuteronomic histories that describe a royal figure as actually writing are clearly revisions of earlier recitals. One is a report that David inscribed the message that ordered a field commander to dispatch Uriah on a suicide mission (2 Sam. 11:14–15); another, that Ahab's queen Jezebel wrote the letter plotting to charge Naboth with treason (1 Kings 21:8–9). Reading both scenes, I feel certain that a later storyteller had reshaped these exciting but unseemly tales, inserting the use of written letters to emphasize the royal personages' need to handle ugly business with maximum secrecy. It is doubtful that either David or Jezebel could read and/or write Hebrew. David is described as a farm boy turned mercenary, an upbringing that would not have provided him the opportunity or wherewithal to attend a school for scribes had one been available to him. Jezebel was Phoenician and a woman: neither circumstance made it likely that she would have been able to write a letter in Hebrew.

Kings were kings, not scriveners. They needed to win wars, not write or even read books. The neo-Assyrian emperor Ashurbanipal (668–33 B.C.E.), who lived three centuries after David, is one of the few ancient kings to boast that he had mastered the scribal arts; what we know with historical certainty is that he was the first to establish, systematically, a literary library (Richardson 1914, pp. 22, 128). In Ashurbanipal's case, literacy became something of a disabling passion. In middle age, he abandoned statecraft for bibliomania and depleted the royal treasury in order to enrich the library of Nineveh, in its day the largest in West Asia.

A capable sword, a strong will, and common sense were the attributes a king required. He could always hire scribes to keep the necessary accounts, prepare and read correspondence, and record his triumphs, as well as storytellers and poets to entertain the court with recitals of the community's sagas and legends. A quick and retentive mind combined with political and military success—and, in Solomon's case, sufficient interest in culture to patronize poets and musicians—easily established a royal reputation for learning, which later generations translated into legends describing Solomon as an author in his own right, having written Proverbs, Ecclesiastes, and the Song of Songs. A critical review of Solomon's skills makes it doubtful that he could read any of the scrolls his scribes had begun to collect in the palace archives. Solomon's wisdom expressed itself in speech rather than script: "Men of all peoples came to listen to the wisdom of Solomon" (1 Kings 4:34).

Solomon was shrewd enough to be concerned that the kingdom be guaranteed a steady supply of able administrators and clerks. His solution was to establish in the palace a school for scribes, Israel's first, and to appoint scribes to major posts where literacy was useful. The register of senior officials in Solomon's court includes: "Elihoreph and Ahijah, sons of Shisha, scribes" (1 Kings 4:3). We hear of scribe-administrators throughout the period of the kingdoms. King Jehoash assigned a scribe to serve as controller of a project to refurbish the fabric of the Temple (2 Kings 12:10–13). When Jerusalem was captured by the Babylonians three centuries later, "the scribe of the army commander who was in charge of mustering the people of the land" became one of an unfortunate group of officials executed on the orders of Nebuchadnezzar (2 Kings 25:19; 2 Chron. 26:11).

Not all scribes, of course, were senior administrators. Most served as notaries who maintained the tax rolls, palace inventories, and lists of tribute; and as clerks who made copies of the court's correspondence with other governments, army commanders in the field, and provincial officials, and maintained the administrative files. As commercial life developed in the larger towns, merchants began to use clerks to record purchases, sales, and inventory. Clans like "the families of scribes who inhabited Jabez" (1 Chron. 2:55) began to specialize in this craft and trained up their sons for the work much as other families specialized in being smiths or vintners. Jars were stamped with the owner's name or mark. Inscribed seals became common, used even by illiterate commercial types to signify that they had heard a contract read out, and agreed that this document recorded the agreements they had entered into. A few such seals have been found inscribed in Hebrew letters, and some who owned them probably learned to puzzle out the signature a professional had pressed into the clay or cut into the stone; but few Israelites felt a need to spend the years required to master the literate arts. While the scarcity of Hebrew inscriptions earlier than the seventh century B.C.E. may suggest simply the use of perishable writing surfaces or bad archeological luck, it certainly also suggests the numerical insignificance of the literate classes.

It is not surprising that neither scribes nor written records played a significant role in the religious life of the pre-exilic community, since no people of the time ascribed holiness to any written document. No West Asian shrine enshrined a scripture, and no liturgy of the time featured readings or recitations from sacred tablets. Some temples had libraries, but these were little more than archives where the priests kept lists of donations and of valuables left on deposit. To be sure, some texts of myths, magical formulas, and sacred hymns have been found in these archives; but none of these tablets or rolls was intended to be publicly exhibited or to be read out during a public service; and as far as we can tell, none was treated with any special ceremony. As I have said, the ancients had little reason to revere the written word, though they most certainly felt its mysterious presence as they did whenever they came face to face with any art or skill they did not fully understand.

One of the reasons, perhaps the main one, that it took nearly a millennium for the Five Books of Moses and the Prophets to emerge as a written scripture is that at this early date people had little reason to assume that the written word provided a truly dependable record. Later communities would be eager to compile a scripture in order to secure the text of their oral traditions; but in the pre-exilic period, the art of writing had not yet developed to the point where people could be sure that anyone reading a text would get it right. Deciphering a written text, decoding its symbols—in short, reading—was not, as it is with us, a fairly simple skill that, once mastered, allows one to read anything.* Not all scribes had a good hand. Writing surfaces were difficult to prepare and consequently expensive. Since compression was required, words and sentences were run together or abbreviated. Texts were inscribed without punctuation signs or word or paragraph divisions, without a system for capitalizing proper names; there were no accepted rules of punctuation, spelling, or grammar. There were no vowels. Few scrolls or tablets were free of scribal mistakes. A text one had never seen before presented itself as a complicated puzzle. Often there were several equally "logical" readings. Even a well-trained and intelligent scribe could not be sure of an author's meaning. Long after writing was developed, oral transmission remained the more dependable way of transmitting sacred traditions.

People who knew how to write, wrote; but people trusted what they heard from those who knew rather than from what was written down. A short oracle in the Book of Jeremiah, which appears to come from the very end of the pre-exilic period, reflects the sense of undependability associated with written texts: "How can you say, 'why, we are wise for we possess the [written] instructions of God.' Assuredly, for naught has the pen labored, for naught the scribe!" (8:8). While literacy was far more widespread in fifth-century Greece than in pre-exilic Israel (1200–600 B.C.E.), and books were more carefully edited, Socrates still felt compelled to rebuke a man full of pride about the invention of writing:

> This invention of yours will create forgetfulness in the learners' souls, because they will not use their memories; they will trust to the external written characters and not remember of themselves. You have found a specific, not for memory but for reminiscence, and you give your disciples only the pretence of wisdom; they will be hearers of many things and will have learned nothing; they will appear to be omniscient and will generally know nothing; they will be tiresome, having the reputation of knowledge without the reality.
>
> (Plato, *Phaedrus* 274–77)

*So difficult has it been to decipher manuscripts that—despite the reverent attention of generations of editors and, in recent years, of experts in linguistics and lexicography—many textual questions involving the biblical text remain unsolved. For example, to this day we are not sure whether an ancient legend about the prophet Elijah indicates that he was fed by ravens or, while hiding from the king's wrath, by wandering Arabs; the consonants in question allow either reading.

An ambassador sent to another court might be provided with a written copy of his message, but was expected to deliver his master's wishes orally. The letter he carried was little more than a way for the recipient to confirm that the message told to him reflected the message with which the agent had been entrusted.

Uncertainty about the value of written records affected all West Asian legal practice. Oral testimony was preferred to documentary evidence. Generally, elders dispensed justice without recording their proceedings. Witnesses could describe what they had seen and heard. They might lie, but there could be no mistaking what they had said in their testimony. By contrast, a written document was inevitably subject to a variety of readings and meanings because of the compression of text, confusion in spelling and word division, and inevitable scribal error. The use of documents in judicial proceedings was limited almost entirely to issues in which there was no alternative, such as divorce, which involved a woman as an interested party. In Hebrew law, and in the law of most West Asian societies, a woman had no standing before a court. As a consequence, the usual procedure in a divorce case of relying only on oral testimony by the husband would have excluded the wife's evidence and put her at an unfair disadvantage. Thus, the necessity of devising a "bill of divorcement" (*get*) which established her rights and could be given into her hand (see page 100).

THE BEGINNINGS OF SCRIPTURE

In these pre-exilic centuries, there may have been lists of *torot,* divine instructions, perhaps set down on papyrus or wood by a scribe associated with one of Israel's shrines who for one reason or another wrote out a list of rules he had heard recited or been taught; but such lists were not treated as holy. At a time when ordinary folk generally feared the written document as a tool of tyranny, the emergence of a scripture that assumed and commanded positive feelings of loyalty and a sense of holy awe was out of the question. The scroll of *torot* found during a refurbishing of the Temple ordered by Josiah in 621 B.C.E. apparently had never been missed; once found, the scroll itself was treated with no particular veneration. Other kinds of lists—such as chronicles of ruling families or the proverbs and maxims exchanged by scribes throughout West Asia—were written down, and written records were useful in organizing the financial and administrative work of the shrine; none were treated as sacred.

As the kingdoms matured and their administrations became better organized, and as trade's importance in the economy grew, the use of scribes increased. Inevitably, so did the number of written records. Record keeping is addictive. After recording the rota of deposits in the shrine treasury, a scribe might record the calendar of holy days observed in that place or the number and form of sacrifices or the hymns sung during the ceremonies. Other scribes, out of interest or when ordered, wrote portions of familiar epics or perhaps a list of *torot,* divine instructions, which local priests had collected. There were writings of various kinds and content, but during the pre-exilic period none of these documents was treated as sacrosanct. Even the record of a divine oracle was simply a record: God spoke; the power was in the spoken word.

No special care was lavished on the form of this written material. Scribes wrote on whatever writing surface was at hand, mostly clay or papyrus, using the same script and forms they employed for their registers or ordinary correspondence: a cursive alphabet, which strongly suggested its origin in a provincial cuneiform script, later generations would call *Ketav Ivri,* "Hebrew writing," and, in our time, paleo-Hebrew.

THE TONGUES OF THE PROPHETS

The ancient world knew and valued sacred speech. Torah was "heard." Prophets spoke God's message. Singers sang God's praise and that of the king. Those who were skilled in speech were much sought after. Priests consulted oracles like the Urim and Thummim and announced God's will. Those who tended the altar knew by heart the sacred hymns. There is no indication of a ritual involving the reading of sacred literature or the public display of sacred tablets or scrolls. Literacy was not required for those who aspired to the priestly office.* The priestly role was deeply identified with the spoken word: "Proper rulings were in his mouth/Nothing perverse was on his lips. The lips of a priest guard knowledge/Men seek rulings from his mouth/He is a messenger of the Lord on High" (Mal. 2:6–7). Jeremiah equated priestly instruction, the counsel of wise men, and the speech of prophets, and describes all three as forms of spoken authority (18:18).

Israel shared with other peoples of that time and place the belief that the spoken word, uttered by a holy man in a holy place, was a vehicle of power. The prophet was a speaker, not a scribe. The tongue was sacred to prophecy. Isaiah knew that his lips had been touched with a purifying coal. Jeremiah recorded, "The Lord said this to me: herewith I put My words into your mouth. See, I appoint you this day [a prophet] over nations and kingdoms; to uproot and to pull down, to destroy and to overthrow, to build and to plant" (1:9–10). And Isaiah: "God made my mouth a sharp sword" (49:2).

The prophet did not need to be literate, and probably few were. The prophet heard the voice of God in a vision; yet what brought to life the events described was not this private vision but the prophet's decision to make public what he had seen and heard. At times it appears that for the words to have effect the prophet must not only speak but speak to a specific audience. The Balaam story in the Book of Numbers assumes that, for the curse he proposed to utter to have effect, the prophet must travel to the place where the tribes were encamped: Amos had to go to Bethel, and Jonah to Nineveh.

Bible manuals sometimes list Isaiah, Jeremiah, Ezekiel, and the Twelve (minor prophets) as "literary" prophets. The term, a modern invention, indicates no more than that, unlike other prophets named in the Bible of whom we know only incidents told about them, we have from these men texts that purport to present passages from their speeches. With one exception, Jeremiah, none of the "literary" prophets seems to have arranged for his speeches to be written

---

*The stories that report the finding of the scroll of *torot* during Josiah's refurbishment of the Temple suggest that the senior priest, Hilkiah, had to ask a royal scribe, Shaphan, to read him the contents (2 Kings 22:8ff.; 2 Chron. 34:15).

down; yet all apparently were confident that their messages would survive.

The occasional reference to a prophet who takes pen in hand turns out, on examination, to be anachronistic revision. The scroll of Isaiah includes two versions of an oracle in which God orders the prophet to give his son a symbolic name—*Maher shalal hash baz,* "pillage hastens, looting spreads" (8:1–3)—as a warning of impending destruction. In one version, God simply orders Isaiah so to name the boy (8:3); in the other, the prophet is told to prepare a poster "and write on it in common script, *Maher shalal hash baz*" (8:1). Today, when no self-respecting demonstration takes place without attention-getting placards, God's demand seems commonplace; but who among an illiterate Judean crowd would have been able to read the emblazoned motto? It seems likely that someone later retelling this story to a post-exilic audience—among whom there would have been a sizable number of readers—felt that it "told" better this way.

While Jeremiah lived over a century after Isaiah, at a time when the urban expansion of Jerusalem was considerably more advanced and literacy far more common, he, too, seems to have had little interest in writing out his speeches. To be sure, the received text contains two references that suggest that God specifically ordered Jeremiah "to write down in a scroll all the words that I have spoken to you in a book" (30:2, 36:2); but in each case, Jeremiah responded by hiring a professional scribe, Baruch, son of Neriah, who "wrote down in the scroll at Jeremiah's dictation all the words which the Lord had spoken to him" (36:4). When a charge of treason was lodged against Jeremiah, the king, Zedekiah, ordered that a scroll containing the prophet's speeches be prepared and brought to him. Zedekiah ordered the royal scribe to read the scroll to him; and, as the reading proceeded, the king cut from the scroll each leaf after it had been read, and threw it into the fire, apparently hoping in this way to cancel the predicted disaster. Determined that there be a written record of God's judgment, perhaps also to dramatize the fact that the king's actions lacked the power to cancel God's decision, Jeremiah had another scroll prepared; again, he himself did not inscribe it. A true child of the age of memory, he knew the oracles by heart, even those that had been delivered years before, and simply dictated his speeches as they had been originally delivered to Baruch, who wrote out the replacement scroll.*

The care with which prophetic statements were transmitted and eventually recorded derived primarily from the interest of various pious groups in using such oracles to "prove" God's power. Events had happened as the oracle, God, had predicted they would. At first, evidence of this oracular kind seems to have been left entirely to the memory of the faithful: "Bind up the message, seal the instruction with My disciples" (Isa. 8:16). Why? For "you are my witnesses, says the Lord" (43:10). Since at times there was a considerable hiatus between the pronouncement and the occurrence of the predicted event, and the witnesses who had heard the oracle spoken were no longer available, the only way to prove that God had announced the event beforehand was to show a written record: "Now, go write it down upon a tablet and inscribe it in a record that it may be with them for future days, a witness forever" (30:8). Such written witnesses must have been particularly important to the exiled community (sixth century B.C.E.) because their hope of return depended on the certainty of God's promises of return, and the audience who had heard the original oracle might have been killed or scattered. Proof that God's word was powerful and certain assured the nation that the promises explicit in the covenant could be expected to be fulfilled if the community proved repentant and loyal.

THE ROYAL CHRONICLES

Throughout the period of the monarchy (tenth through seventh centuries B.C.E.), the kings of Israel and Judah used scribes with some regularity not only to organize tax collections, maintain correspondence, and administer their various bureaus but to prepare dynastic chronicles. Scribes discovered that the royal ego was pleased when they prepared records of royal triumphs. The earliest royal annals have been lost and are known to us by name only because a later gen-

---

*One other reference connects writing with Jeremiah's career: in the narrative sections added to the scroll considerably after the prophet's active career, there is a report that shortly after the defeat of 597 B.C.E. Jeremiah wrote a letter to those who had been taken to Babylon as captives, urging them to settle in. If such a letter were actually sent, it is likely that Jeremiah dictated it to a professional scribe, as was his way.

eration of chroniclers, who edited the Deuteronomic and Priestly histories, cited them in their histories: Annals of the Acts of Solomon (1 Kings 11:41); Annals of the Kings of Judah (1 Kings 14:29); Annals of Samuel the Seer (1 Chron. 29:29). The earliest chronicles recorded the king's noble pedigree, dramatic events in the lives of his ancestors, and his victories and munificences and may be considered Israel's first written literature. The Psalms contain reflections of the courtly ethos in which these scribes worked:

> My heart has composed a sweet melody. I shall recite my work, O King, my tongue the pen of a skillful scribe, you are the fairest of the children of men [45:2–3]. How many are the ivory palaces? How many shall acclaim you? Daughters of kings shall be stationed in your mansions, the queen at your right hand in the gold of Ophir [45:9–10].

Two other early "books" are cited in the later histories: the Book of the Wars of the Lord (Num. 21:14) and the Book of Jashar (Josh. 10:13). Jashar appears to have been a collection of short poems associated with important incidents in the early history of the Israelite confederation. The two surviving citations of the Jashar poems include a few lines of a hymn ascribed to Joshua praising God for having commanded the sun and the moon to stand still so that the military rout of the Amorites could be completed (Josh. 10:12–14); and David's moving lament for Jonathan and Saul: "Your glory, O Israel, lies slain on your heights: How have the mighty fallen!" (2 Sam. 1:17–27). Of the Wars of the Lord we know only that it included a northern Israel boundary list set out in memorizable form (Num. 21:14). The appearance of such material—which seems to reflect the cultural interests of the palace and to be designed for no nobler purpose than to cater to a royal ego—in a text that will be acclaimed as scripture, underlines the role of chance and circumstance in the development of the biblical canon and reminds us that no one set out to write or edit a Holy Bible. Scriptures represent selections from a community's literature—particularly, but not exclusively, from materials of religious interest. Many elements entered in the editorial decisions: availability, presence in a well-known text, general interest. Books became holy because readers declared them to be so, not because of the author's or the storyteller's original intent. The gentile prophet Balaam could never have anticipated that some of his prophecies spoken about Israel would become holy writ.

THE WISDOM LITERATURE

Early on, literacy became associated with a particular "cosmopolitan" culture which developed among the scribes of many nations. Responsible as they were for all correspondence between their court and the outside world, scribes were the first group in each community to break out of its tight-knit envelope of tribal and cultural insularity and to take a serious interest in other cultures. Humans are by nature curious; and some of these men, who were, after all, an educated élite, became eager to learn about the political concerns and even the cultural interests of the scribes of neighboring groups with whom they corresponded and, when deputized as ambassadors, sometimes visited. They discovered what others thought about the brevity of life, the vagaries of individual destiny, the best way to raise a family, advance a career, tolerate fools, and manage relationships with the powerful. In many cultures the community's "wisdom," its advice for the management of a successful life, was encapsulated in compact, easily remembered proverbs and maxims which were passed on as commonplace advice from father to son, from teacher to student, and from native to foreign scribe.

The sum of these reflections and observations came to be called Wisdom. Although each community had its own Wisdom tradition, proverb and observation tended to pass fairly easily from one West Asian community to another; hence, Wisdom had a cosmopolitan character. In time, collections of cautionary sayings and sound advice and sober speculation about the twin mysteries of life and death were compiled, often with large sections of "borrowed" material.*

Wisdom as we know it is a body of literature of which the Book

*A classic example of such borrowings is the close paraphrase in the Book of Proverbs of some thirty Egyptian sayings known as "The Teachings of *Amen-em-ope*" (about eleventh century B.C.E.).

of Proverbs is a classic example. Its style is that of brief, rhythmic, often picturesque adages obviously shaped by the needs of memorization and everyday speech, often in numerical formulas ("Three things there are which are stately in their stride, four which are striking as they move" [30:29]) or acrostic structures, such as the famous woman of valor poem with which the book closes (31:10–31).

Wisdom still reflects its origin in an essentially oral culture. It is assumed that Wisdom's truths enter the mind through the ear rather than the eye: "Hear, my son, and be wise" (Prov. 23:19); "My son, listen to my words, incline your ear to my sayings" (4:20). In Egypt, teachers of Wisdom believed that "a hearing heart" was essential to good character development. I know of no Wisdom maxim that advises: "To be wise, my son, spend your youth with the scrolls of ancient wisdom"; rather, the prodigal confesses: "I did not listen to the voice of my teachers, my ears were shut to those who tried to instruct me" (5:13). It was generally believed that the ideas that were memorized remained active in the mind and helped to determine behavior; it was generally agreed that unless the gods or fate intervened, you made decisions on the basis of the ideas you had appropriated as your own—that is, those uppermost in your mind. It is not surprising, then, that as formal schooling developed across West Asia, teachers used these prudential and monitory observations as set pieces for students who were being introduced to the scribal arts.

Like the scribes who compiled the royal chronicles, these scribes, busy with their musings and their maxims, had no idea that some day their thoughts would be enshrined as scripture. They valued Wisdom highly. It had among them the status that philosophy enjoyed in the Middle Ages, but they made no claim that these thoughts were revealed, only that they were useful, in conformity with what we would call natural law, and in that sense ultimately true. The words of the Proverbs were those of Solomon, Agur, or Lemuel, not God's. The identification of Hebrew Wisdom with God's words developed over a considerable span of time late in the Second Temple period.

THE ORAL TRADITION OF GOD'S INSTRUCTIONS

There were no taboos against making a written record of any part of the oral tradition, even of power-laden sacred formulas. In 1985, an amulet—datable to the late pre-exilic period—was discovered at a grave site at Ketef Hinnon just outside the walls of pre-exilic Jerusalem. The amulet consists of two small, inscribed, cylindrical silver plates. These two thin metal plaques, each incised with a text in *Ketav Ivri* script, bear the names of individuals, possibly the amulet's owners, and a blessing closely resembling the formula that became the most powerful blessing known to ancient Israel, the Priestly Benediction (Num. 6:24–26). The language of the blessing is specific. The amulet writer has appropriated the biblical explanation: "Thus they shall link My name with the people of Israel and I will bless them" (6:27).

The threefold invocation of YHWH's name was spoken by Temple priests on ceremonial occasions and believed by all to offer real protection to the community; it is a custom taken over and continued to this day in the synagogue. Whether the deceased wore these amulets during his lifetime or they were prepared to be placed in his grave, it is clear that they served a protective purpose. Such amulets offer further evidence of the magical power associated with written formulas invoking God's name.*

Incidentally, the use of phrases similar to a well-known blessing is evidence of a universe of discourse rich in familiar phrases which circulated broadly and were used often, sometimes in slightly changed form. Variants on the Priestly Benediction—"May YHWH bless you and keep you"; "May YHWH make His face shine upon you and show you favor"; "May YHWH lift up His countenance upon you and grant you fulfillment"—appear not only on these amulets but separately in various psalms (67:2, 80:4).

The language of well-known forms was probably a greater force behind the persistence of familiar formulas than any conscious effort in that direction. Such phrases were the ready-at-hand building

---

*The existence of a tiny space between the two plaques, through which a string could be threaded, makes fairly certain the identification of these plaques as amulets. The use of a precious metal, silver, and of God's most powerful Name, the Tetragrammaton, makes it clear that this plaque was highly valued as a protective device or charm.

blocks out of which storytellers, priests, and teachers constructed their presentations. Michael Fishbane, in an analysis of a denunciation of priestly activities by the post-exilic prophet Malachi, has shown how a skillful speaker used the idioms of the Priestly Benediction to heighten the sarcasm of his condemnation: "So, now, beseech the countenance of God that He may show us favour . . . will he be gracious to you?" (1986, p. 332).

While there were no cultural bars to the inscription of the oral tradition, there was, at the same time, no compelling reason for undertaking a concerted effort to set down Israel's religious tradition. Indeed, it is doubtful whether during these pre-exilic centuries anyone could have defined with any precision the boundaries of Israel's sacred traditions. Religion permeated every aspect of life. The traditions were set down piecemeal. A scribe who may also have been a priest may have been ordered to prepare a list of divine instructions sacred to his shrine. Another of a more literary bent busied himself after working hours setting down a local version of the Flood story. Such material was all part of a diffuse tradition—or, rather, traditions, since there were local variations based on tribal traditions.

Over time, bits and pieces of these traditions became text. Texts of various kinds existed, but—and this is the crucial point—they were not as yet treated as sacred writings or featured in shrine worship. No presentation, oral or written, of the sagas, genealogies, dynastic chronicles, lists of *torot,* and Wisdom sayings was accepted at any time during the pre-exilic period as sacrosanct or inviolate, though obviously these materials were trusted and believed. Pre-exilic biblical Israel had religious traditions but no Bible.

These early years were a period of consolidation of various strands of tradition. During and after the period of settlement, the separate traditions of the separate tribes were gradually brought together, sometimes by accident and sometimes by design, and various formulations slowly took shape—a process that continued over some centuries. The confederation was composed of tribes, not all of whom shared a common history. The various tribes knew different versions of the creation myths and patriarchal stories, and each tribe held sacred its own sagas. Not all tribes had been slaves in Egypt. Some tribes cherished traditions about the Exodus but not about the Sinai covenant, while others cherished memories of the Sinai covenant but not of the Exodus. Different lists of the Instructions required by God's covenant were cherished at the various shrines: Bethel, Gilgal, and Schechem. It was during the period of confederation and settlement (from about mid-twelfth into the tenth century B.C.E.) that these separate scenarios and themes began to be brought together into a more or less single narrative.

Over time these multiple traditions and discrete narratives were drawn into the chronological framework with which we are familiar. This framework in time had a certain inevitability. Professional storytellers knew that to keep an audience's attention they had best tell the story in sequence: the patriarchal stories, and the David saga, like the *Iliad,* are told in that fashion. The spoken word disappears as soon as spoken; so, for memory's sake, recitation tends to be linear. Walter Ong has made the useful point "that knowledge and discourse come out of human experience [so] the elemental way to process human experience verbally is to give an account of it more or less as it really comes into being and exists, embedded in the flow of time" (1982, p. 140).

The reciters who first drew traditions together, and later the scribe-editors who set them down, felt little need to edit out all inconsistencies. People heard and later read only parts of the tradition, never the whole. When several strands of tradition were brought together, as much of the familiar as possible was maintained even if this meant inconsistent versions. What did it matter if several variations of the Creation myth were in circulation? That's why the animals march into Noah's Ark in pairs and also in families of seven (Gen. 6:20, 7:2). The important thing about these materials is that they were familiar and trusted. Each had developed in one or another section of the community and had survived a thousand retellings and numerous editings.

Much later, looking back on their origins, Jews tended to assume that the now-venerable sacred books, the scriptures, which were central to their culture had played the same role in the lives of their ancestors. Even though these later generations were wrong in so assuming, they believed they had convincing proof of The Book's central role in their faith. The proof was in The Book. It was all there, black on white: "When Moses had put down in writing the words of the Teaching to the very end" (Deut. 31:24). Once they came to accept the *Sefer Torah* as truth, and to believe that what was had always been, it seemed natural to them that Israel had had this teaching, the Torah, from the beginning of its national history, ever since Sinai. Indeed, not only had Israel always had The Book but the community had always been under an obligation to read and study it. Again, the Jews of later times saw the proof as incontrovertible. Deuteronomy contains a paragraph that has been recited daily during the synagogue service for nearly two thousand years, and they understood it to require that each Jew spend some time each day introducing his sons to the sacred book: "And you shall teach them [these laws] to your children and shall speak of them" (6:6). That such a text required an interpretation associating schooling with books was deemed, by these later generations, self-evident. But, again, they were wrong. At no time during the pre-exilic years could the study of the tradition as text have been actively encouraged. Pre-exilic Israel knew nothing of a written scripture. There was Torah, a body of divine tradition; but as yet no *Sefer Torah,* no scripture.

This Deuteronomy sentence encouraged parents to introduce their children to their traditions. Faith was a family affair. In its original context, the sentence read: "You shall impress them *[v'shinantam]* upon your children and you shall recite them" (6:7). The verb *v'shinantam* designated common speech, oral instruction. Thus, recite the traditions to your children until the sagas and Instructions have become second nature to them, indelibly etched in their memory! Books were not meant here. Rote learning and cultural conditioning were. Indeed, neither reading nor writing is encouraged in the Torah. The cultivation of memory is: "My son, attend to my words; incline your ear to my sayings. Keep them constantly in mind. Cherish them in your heart of hearts for they mean life to him who possesses them and health to his whole body" (Prov. 4:20–22).

Torah comes from the root *yarah,* which originally meant "to throw" and came to denote the casting of lots, specifically casting lots to discover God's will. In the Bible, the noun *Torah* defines the specific terms of God's will and embraces many roles and duties. A

73

torah was a commandment the community accepted as divinely ordained and, therefore, obligatory. Originally, these laws (*torot*) were not attributed to any particular historical personality or event. They represented venerable and venerated practice and long-held concepts of right and virtue and so, inevitably, the will of God.

The various collections of *torot* that survive in the received text evince some concern for a content-based arrangement, but none for comprehensiveness. The habit of stringing together related matters to ease the process of memorization seems to have dictated the arrangement rather than any desire to arrange material topically. Matters relating to a calendar of holy occasions and rules governing the sacrificial cult are generally separated from other rules, but often instructions on a variety of topics simply follow each other without apparent logic; and nowhere in the text is there a fully exhaustive list of rules governing any area of practice.

What was unique in the treatment of the emerging collections of *torot* was an increasingly evident determination to root them in a particular act of divine speech and to identify them as the message brought by a single prophet: "And the Lord spoke to Moses." Beginning in the last centuries of the pre-exilic period (8th–7th centuries B.C.E.), a conscious effort was made to root the various collections of *torot* in the Sinai covenant. Some of the *torot* are much older than Sinai and reflect well-known legal traditions of West Asia from the second millennium. Others, like those that were to govern the sacrificial cult, undoubtedly date from the period of settlement when Israel for the first time built shrines. This editorial effort had not been fully completed when the present text of Exodus-Numbers was finalized, and we read in those scrolls that Moses received Instructions on other occasions and in other places, such as the Tent of Meeting. Deuteronomy, the latest book of the *Sefer Torah,* avoids any mention of divine instructions being given to Moses on any occasion other than Sinai.

To explain this tendency to relate all *torot* to Sinai and Moses, those who see self-interest as the primary human motivation point to the interests of the priesthood and the important role priests and priest-scribes played in the drive to set down the tradition. The authority of the priests was linked intimately and dynastically to the authority of Moses. If all the *torot* had been revealed through Moses, and Moses had ordained his brother Aaron to be the founder-dynast of the priest class, there could be no serious challenge to the claims by the existing priestly class that their service and privileges were divinely mandated. But more than priestly self-interest was involved. There was a need for a unifying myth that would give a sense of coherence to the tradition as it slowly acquired a single form.

As the tribes became a confederation and then a kingdom, a need was felt for a single presentation of God's instructions. Each tribe, each shrine, had its own. There was no way to prove one Torah formulation more worthy than another. Since the authenticity of a particular formulation of *torot* could always be contested, a single and singular event, Sinai, was declared to be the source of all accepted *torot*. The reports of the covenant-enabling ceremonies organized at Schechem by Joshua and at Mizpeh by Samuel were stripped of the register of stipulations that must have been confirmed on those occasions. These lists or parts of them may well have found their way into one or another of the anthologies of *torot* that today coexist in the received text. To protect the unity gradually being established, there began to circulate *torot* that proclaimed it God's will that no one add to or subtract from the teachings given through Moses at Sinai.

The texts with the messages brought by the prophets who followed Moses contain no statutory laws. Perhaps Israel's culture did not look to prophetic oracles for laws—but if that is so, how shall we explain the major prophetic role assigned to Moses? More likely, the later prophetic texts came from a time when the myth of Sinai had already become a cardinal article of the faith and when *torot* were expected from shrine oracles rather than from individual prophets. In any case, the Bible presents the prophets as bound to a mission to summon the community to return to God's ways rather than to accept and practice any new duties.

The coexistence in the received text of clearly distinguishable blocks of *torot*, the separate codices which often contain divergent formulations of a particular rule, leaves no room for doubt that each codex developed in its own way. The *torot* did not come as a unit from Sinai but represent separate traditions, each possibly related to the tradition of one or another tribal shrine. One Instruction allows

Levites to begin their Temple service at twenty-five years of age (Num. 8:24); another stipulated thirty as the proper age (4:23). We hear that an Israelite slave girl is to be freed after six years (Deut. 15:12); but another reference to the treatment of Israelite slave girls makes no mention of such a requirement (Exod. 21:7). The spring harvest has three names in three different lists: the Harvest Feast, or *Katsir* (Exod. 23:16); the Feast of Weeks, or *Shavuot* (Deut. 16:9–10); and the Feast of First Fruits, or *Bikkurim* (Num. 28:26); and there is some confusion among them about precisely when this many-titled holiday is to be celebrated.

Those in the post-exilic period who ultimately edited the written records into what we know as the *Sefer Torah* presented those laws that for one reason or another had achieved a particular holiness and probably had served the various pre-exilic shrines as symbols of the entire covenant tradition—an approach not unlike that taken today by many who still see the Ten Commandments as symbolic of all that is good and right, God's will.

There was no original Torah, only various developing streams of tradition which were more or less shaped into a text that gave the appearance of a single tradition. There was a growing sense of national unity and perhaps a natural preference for order over disorder, although the existence of different traditions and codes was not particularly disturbing since there was as yet no scripture and no concept of one. Some in Israel knew one list of *torot;* some, another. Many were not aware that there were lists. The community accepted the authority and consistency of traditions that were part of the warp and weft of daily life. As each generation heard again the tradition, they became increasingly comfortable with particular readings and interpretations; as their world seemed coherent, no one tried to find inconsistencies in what seemed to be a natural unity.

As indicated earlier, many pious folk dismissed this developmental reconstruction out of hand, offering as evidence the *Sefer Torah*'s own testimony: a text or, rather, one or another of a few texts that indicate that Moses actually wrote out part or all of the received text. These texts exist, but they do not provide the solid proof claimed for them and cannot stand against all we now know of the development of Israelite thought and practice.

MOSES AND THE COVENANT AT SINAI

No one knows what happened at Sinai, or with certainty that there was a Sinai. There are no reliable eyewitness accounts, and our texts all come from much later periods. But it is clear that one of the most consistent themes in the telling, one described at length and in various versions, presents Moses as prophet, not scribe. Moses is the prophet through whom God's message is transmitted. He is God's man, *ish ha-elohim,* who cried out to the community the Instructions of the King of Kings. Again and again throughout Exodus, we find the phrase, "The Lord *said* to Moses: 'Thus shall you *say* to the Israelites.'" The one consistent element in the various pieces making up the *Sefer Torah*'s presentation of Sinai is that there was a revelation at that place, an event where the voice of God dominated. God spoke. Moses spoke. The people heard and acclaimed.

The various scenarios of the covenant-enabling assembly presumedly held at the foot of Mount Sinai describe a ceremony that involved a tribal leader acting as officiatory priest or prophet and crying out sacred words, the assemblage affirming and accepting these obligations as forever binding on their community, and an enabling ritual being celebrated, probably a blood sacrifice, which declared the covenant in force. Moses is pictured throughout as a prophet, God's spokesman. The original story focused entirely on the spoken word. There was no stenographer at Sinai.

How and why, then, did the Sinai episode come to include the famous image of the two inscribed stone tablets? They are there, but they were not always there. They represent a storyteller's inescapable need to dramatize events and to do so in ways his audience would appreciate and understand. The tablets served as a dramatic element to reveal the presence of God at the moment the covenant was fashioned. By their presence they served as a visible witness to the covenant's continuing power.

The Canaanites often erected stones, *masseboth,* in their shrines. These stones were held to represent the presence of the god(s) at the rites conducted in their honor. When Jacob fled Esau, he raised an altar on the spot where God promised him protection, and put beside it a stone, a *massebah,* which, in the accepted symbolism of the day, witnessed to the fact that God had been present there, and by inference that God could in the future be approached there. Most of these stones were unadorned; a few, like the plinth found at the Canaanite altar at Hazor, were inscribed with some of the attributes associated with the god(s) worshiped there. An Israelite audience would have understood and appreciated a narrative that associated God's presence at a religious site with a sacred stone. There were such stones all over Canaan. It is unlikely that these *masseboth* were inscribed, but an Israelite audience would have been aware of the not-uncommon West Asian royal practice of setting in various locations stone stelae inscribed with the imperial law, usually prefaced with paragraphs of extravagant praise of the reigning king's magnificence and power. Would the King of Kings, to establish His authority, have done less than the great emperors of the time? Exodus reports, "God spoke [*va'yedaber*] all these words [*devarim*] saying" (20:1), and its narrative about the tablets comes later; here the operative words are *va'yedaber* and *devarim* from the root *dvr,* "to speak." Speech precedes inscription, I would argue, by centuries rather than by just a few paragraphs.

Storytellers must fit well-known images to the events they are describing. Sinai was a way station on the long march out of Egypt. It would have made little sense to set up a sacred stone, inscribed or not, at a place the tribes might never revisit; so the stones had to be portable. There are two tablets; and the explanation is, again, cultural style. One way the ancients emphasized authority was to double a particular phrase. God was the King of Kings. If kings inscribe their law on a selected stone, God would inscribe His law on the stone of stones.

We cannot recover with any certainty how and why Israel's storytellers wove new details into successive retellings of the Sinai events, but I can suggest how eager audiences unraveled the details. God was there. The Law is not only royal but divine, fixed for all time. God gave the law twice to Israel. The Law is unique, God's own. Just as ambassadors in those days took an oral message but also carried their king's instructions in a letter to assure the recipient that the oral message was correct, so the emphasis here is on the stone tablets, on which God Himself inscribed His words, as the confirming document.

78

In another version of the Sinai story, God instructs Moses, His faithful agent, to do the writing. Moses' complete reliability is emphasized in the eulogy that closes Deuteronomy: "The servant of God," whose "eyes were undimmed and his vision unabated" (34:5–7), becomes the text's authenticator. The tablets provide what an ancient audience would have considered tangible proof that Moses had spoken God's instructions precisely as he had been commissioned to do. There were other narrative benefits. The tablets are of stone. Stone suggests permanence. To inscribe God's Law on stone is to testify to durability and immutability. Words cut into stone cannot be readily changed. This is a law for all times.

One of the many uncertainties emerging from the present form of the Sinai narrative concerns precisely what was said. Were there only the ten statements? Precisely those ten? The image of stone tablets suggests that this was the case, but the received text explicitly introduces many other *torot* into its presentation of the Sinai revelation and at least one other slightly different version of the Ten Commandments.

That the tablets came into being in the course of pious narration becomes even more certain when we consider their subsequent history or, rather, lack of history. According to the text we possess, the first set of tablets was shattered by an enraged Moses when he discovered that the tribes were worshiping the Golden Calf; and the replacement set, once engraved, was placed for safekeeping in the Holy Ark, Israel's portable shrine. Then it simply disappeared from history. We hear no more of the tablets, save one bare reference in 1 Kings (8:9), repeated in 2 Chronicles (5:10). Any tablets believed to have been written by God or by Moses surely would have been among Israel's most precious possessions, objects to be revered. Such tablets would have been the making of any shrine. One can imagine a constant stream of pilgrims arriving to venerate those holy objects and to draw on their power; but there is no indication that this was ever the case. After Sinai we hear much about the Ark but hardly a word about the tablets.

The idea that the revelation was inscribed on tablets seems to have emerged at a fairly late stage in the elaboration of the Sinai events and to have served to emphasize God's presence at Sinai and the importance of the text; but both Moses and God are unlikely scribes. Of God I cannot speak, but what we know about the cultural and social level of the Hebrew tribes in Moses' day makes it extremely doubtful that he could read or write. Even if we assume that the legend of a childhood spent in an Egyptian palace is not the pure invention it seems to be, we cannot take for granted that he would have been schooled there in the scribal arts, certainly not in the languages required of a Hebrew scribe. Egyptian princes were taught the arts of governance and war, not how to read and write. In the unlikely case that Moses was enrolled in such a palace school, he would have become adept in the hieratic script favored in the New Kingdom, not in the *Ketav Ivri,* the quite different script and alphabet in which the Israelites kept their records. If we assume Moses was raised as a Hebrew, the slave encampments could not provide the young with the time and leisure for extended schooling.

Moses is presented primarily as a speaker. Exodus shows a Moses sensitive to the fact that he lacks the qualifications to be God's spokesman. At the Burning Bush he worries that he will not be an effective messenger: "I have not been a man of words" (Exod. 4:10). Upon his commission, Moses brings to Pharaoh a spoken message, not a letter; and another spoken message, again not a letter, to the council of tribal elders. Deuteronomy is a series of valedictory addresses in which Moses, about to relinquish the mantle of responsibility, reviews Israel's history and discourses on God's redemptive acts and the operation of the covenant: "On the other side of the Jordan, in the land of Moab, Moses undertook to expound this Teaching" (1:5). Phrases in which God orders Moses to speak to the Israelites occur with almost thirty times greater frequency in our text than do sentences in which he is ordered to write something down.

The few references to Moses as writer are uniformly anachronistic. Someone has inserted into Exodus 24—clearly a composite of various traditions about the events at Sinai—this sentence: "Moses wrote down all the commands of the Lord" (24:4). After an unrelated paragraph in which an elaborate covenant-making ceremony is described, the theme of a written covenant is again picked up: Moses "took the record of the covenant and read it aloud to the people"

(24:7). The text is at best unclear. Which commandments did Moses record? What happened to this record? If there was a scroll, why were the stone tablets necessary? None of these questions can be answered. These two sentences in Exodus are a late insertion into an earlier version of the history of the Sinai covenant which described the occasion as one purely of sacred speech and sacrifice.

The why and wherefore of the appearance of the theme of a written record can only be guessed at. Some scholars suggest that, as the nation became more aware of the habits of surrounding cultures, storytellers added to the older narrative details their audiences had come to associate with customs now broadly recognized as linked to treaty making. In West Asia, treaty texts were often placed for safekeeping in a shrine, protected by all kinds of taboos as well as high walls; the texts' presence there implied that the gods approved and took responsibility for ensuring that the agreed-on terms were kept.

Similarities have been noted between the Sinai episode and descriptions of covenant- and treaty-making ceremonies among the Hittites and other peoples of the area. It was common practice, when making a treaty, to include a eulogy to the king's power, a proclamation of the vassal's submission, and their mutual acceptance of the treaty terms. The ceremony usually included a sacrifice, calling the god's attention to the treaty and summoning him to punish disobedience. The terms were written down so that the king could organize an annual ceremony of resubmission at which the terms would again be read to his vassals, who would be forced again to recognize publicly the overlord's superior power.

Numbers introduces a detailed list of the forty-two camps occupied by the tribes during their trek, by referring to Moses writing down the itinerary: "Moses recorded the starting points of their marches as directed by the Lord" (33:2). A sentence such as this proves no more than that a priest-scribe who lived some seven centuries after Moses knew, or thought he knew, of an old tradition of the trek which went back to Moses. Perhaps he even had seen a parchment; but as any guide in the Holy Land will tell you, the document in your hand may be, and probably is, a pious forgery. On the basis of style as much as of substance, scholars can confidently assign this text to priestly traditions drawn together in exilic or post-exilic times.

Finally, there are several references to Moses as a scribe in Deuteronomy 31, which are the texts cited repeatedly by the sages to prove their claim that Moses wrote down the entire *Sefer Torah* following God's dictation. Deuteronomy 31 is set during the last days of Moses' life just before he transferred authority to Joshua. After counseling Joshua on his responsibilities, we are told, Moses wrote down "this Teaching," contents unspecified, and presented the text to the levitical priests and the elders of Israel who were instructed to read from this teaching to the entire community each sabbatical year during the Feast of Booths (31:9–13). The formulaic language seems to pick up on one of the conventional requirements that a treaty be renewed every year by the kind of enabling ceremony already described: that is, an annual ceremony which featured a public reading of the treaty's terms and the vassal's resubmission to them. There is no evidence that the practice of a regular sabbatical reading of the Torah text was ever the custom in Israel; and there is certainly no reason to believe, as the rabbinic tradition would claim, that the document referred to as "this Teaching" necessarily contained the entire Pentateuch as we know it.*

Deuteronomy 31:24 is the text most frequently cited by those who insist that Moses wrote the whole *Sefer Torah* on God's specific command. Moses is described as using his last hours to write the words of "this Torah" to the very end. God further commands Moses to have the Levites place "this book of Teaching [presumedly the scroll he has been working on] beside the Ark of the Covenant of the Lord your God and let it remain there as a witness against you" (31:26). What the phrase "this book of Teaching" specifically refers to can no longer be ascertained. Rabbinic Judaism related it confidently but without warrant to the whole *Sefer Torah*. In recent times, some scholars have claimed it to be a reference to Deuteronomy, which is known to have circulated for a considerable period as a sep-

---

*At this late date, it seems hardly necessary to make the argument that one cannot assume the existence of the received Torah at the time this sentence became part of the tradition. Deuteronomy's history is long and complicated, and any reference to this "teaching" must refer not to the entire scroll but only to specific *torot*.

arate scroll; but this identification assumes a much earlier publication of the Deuteronomy scroll than most researchers would accept. A more enlightened opinion has the sentence refer to some portion of Deuteronomy's legal code, a portion that developed independently of other parts of Deuteronomy. If this is the case, then Moses is described here as writing out a selection of *torot* that were not drawn together until centuries after his death.

As far as we know, during the entire pre-exilic period, such a scroll, which would have been precious beyond price since it contained God's teachings in Moses' own hand, was never consulted or made the centerpiece of tribal ceremony. The reference to it is late and singular; no other reference exists to such a scroll. It disappears without a trace. And there is no suggestion that the scroll found in Josiah's day (late seventh century B.C.E.) was related to it. When, two centuries after Josiah, Ezra brought a scroll of *torot* to Jerusalem from Babylon, he did not advance the claim that he had brought back Moses' scroll or even a faithful copy.

JOSHUA

Joshua almost certainly was not a scribe. He is described as Moses' aide-de-camp, a field commander, who succeeded his leader as sheik of the tribe confederation. Like all other governors of semi-nomadic tribes, Joshua required military skill, courage, and good sense but not the ability to read and write. The details offered about Joshua's life raise the question when this man, born into slavery, who spent his adult life on a desert trek, might have found the opportunity to spend the required years of scribal training.

A scribe has bridged the end of Deuteronomy and the opening of the scroll of Joshua with a speech in which God advises Moses' heir that "this book of the law shall not depart from your mouth, but you should meditate therein day and night, that you may observe to do all that is written therein" (Josh. 1:8); and the Joshua scroll closes with the description of a covenant-enabling ceremony in which he again is made to appear as a writer. The tribes are assembled at Schechem. Joshua presents a lengthy oration in which he details the record of God's protection of Israel. He warns the subchiefs that they must not serve alien gods. The assembly shouts, "We will serve the Lord" (24:1–28).

The earliest presentations of this event probably included a list of *torot,* covenant rules, which Joshua, as was the custom, had recited during the ceremony and which the assemblage had acclaimed; but these have been eliminated in line with the overriding priestly concern to locate all *torot* in the prophetic mission of Moses. What we have instead is an editorial postscript:

> On that day at Schechem, Joshua read a covenant for the people and he made a fixed rule for them. Joshua recorded all this in a book of divine instruction. He took a great stone and set it up at the foot of the oak in the sacred precinct of the Lord; and Joshua said to all the people, "See, this very stone shall be a witness against us; for it has heard all the words of the Lord, which He spoke to us; it shall be a witness against you, lest you break faith with your God." Joshua then dismissed the people to their allotted portions [24:25–28].

Other than the list of *torot* enshrined at this ceremony, what was there for him to record? Again, if there was such a scroll, what happened to it? The stone that witnessed to God's presence reiterates a familiar thematic element in a covenant ceremony, but Joshua's role as a notetaker is clearly out of character for a twelfth-century B.C.E. sheik of semi-nomad tribesmen. It suggests, as does the book's preface, a much later and more literate age, probably the early postexilic centuries, when priests took for granted that lists of *torot* and records were to be inscribed and kept. Otherwise, again, we have to account for the surprising disappearance from Israel's history of what would have been an infinitely precious document. The only other references to Joshua as a writer can readily be dismissed.*

*These references to Joshua as a writer appear in the Book of Joshua and in Deuteronomy. The first, a short insertion which clearly breaks the flow of narrative, says he "inscribed on the altar stones a copy of the teaching which Moses had written for the Israelites" (8:32). That insertion in turn refers to an insertion in the narrative in Deuteronomy of Moses ordering Joshua to erect an altar when he enters the Promised Land: "And coat the stones with plaster and inscribe upon them all the words of the Teaching" (27:2–3). What is pertinent here is that at some point a late priestly editor or historian felt it important to indicate that Joshua had faithfully fulfilled his commission from Moses, however irrelevant it was to Israelite practice. No other reference exists to the inscription of texts on plastered walls.

SAMUEL

Samuel, the last of the trio of pre-exilic giants, is described in the Bible as organizer of a covenant ceremony for the tribal confederation. Presumedly he celebrated it at Mizpeh where he cried out various rules respecting the office of the king and recorded God's instruction in a scroll document we are told "he deposited before the Lord" (1 Sam. 10:25). Samuel may have been literate. By the beginning of the eleventh century, the tribes were already fairly well settled and had adopted many Canaanite ways. Samuel is said to have been raised by a shrine priest and to have lived in settled communities, where literacy would not have been uncommon. Still, the image of Samuel as a scribe is unlikely. A "child of prayer," he is said to have been dedicated at birth to the rules of the Nazarites, an ascetic group which promoted the simple life and sought to revive the austere virtues of Israel's nomadic origins. Nazarites had little need for, and no interest in, the administrative arts; and it is unlikely that they would have sent a neophyte, however promising, to a shrine school to master this Canaanite skill. In later years, Samuel is variously described as a circuit-riding charismatic, clairvoyant, judge, and prophet. None of these roles required literacy.

JOSIAH'S SCROLL

There is in the entire pre-exilic literature only one creditable reference, a late one, to a scroll of *torot* that was apparently of some religious significance. The story is that, during a refurbishing project organized by King Josiah in 621 B.C.E., a "scroll of the Teaching" was found in the treasury of the Jerusalem Temple. Two reports of this incident exist (2 Kings 22; 2 Chron. 34): in one, workers discover the scrolls; in the other, the high priest does. In both versions, the find is treated as interesting and unexpected but not momentous. In both versions, the scribe-administrator who reports the find to the king raises with him routine business matters before mentioning the find.

Set against the unexcited reaction of the court officials, the king's reaction seems surprising. Once the scroll had been read to him, Josiah is said to have rent his garments, adopted a formal state of mourning, and ordered his staff to inquire of God what must be done. A prophetess, Huldah, was consulted. She confirmed that the Instructions were authentic, and announced that God intended to punish Jerusalem because of the sin of idolatry, but that the king would be spared because he had humbled himself and devoted his energies to religious reform. This scroll then seems to have become the centerpiece of a covenant-enabling ceremony of the type with which we have become familiar.

This story in its present form could not have been shaped earlier than Josiah's death in 608 B.C.E. and probably must be dated sometime after the Babylonian invasions of 597 B.C.E. and the destruction of the Temple in 586 B.C.E. That traumatic event and the consequent exile preoccupied the religious feelings of the defeated nation. They wanted to know why the disaster had occurred and why God allowed a king who had permitted idolatry in the royal shrine for the first eighteen years of his reign to escape punishment and die peacefully while many who had never accepted the presence of the idols were made to suffer God's punishment. The answer this text offers is that this was God's will. Josiah had repented. In this context, the scroll seems to be an almost incidental agent of God's will. It seems likely that in the sixth century Huldah's prophecy about Jerusalem's fall and Josiah's reprieve would have been the focus of popular interest, rather than the covenant *torot* that might have been contained in the scroll.

Some scholars have suggested that the scroll was a pious forgery executed on Josiah's order to justify a program of religious reform on which he was determined. In the absence of any other evidence, it seems improbable that at this stage of biblical development a scroll, whatever its contents, could have been considered sufficiently significant to warrant invention. Documents, even ones dealing with important religious themes, were simply confirming records. The spoken word and the oral tradition were still primary.

If the whole episode is not pure invention, then we must suppose that a scroll or *torot* was, in fact, discovered during Josiah's reign, and that memory of this event later was merged with memory of

Huldah's prophecy about one of Judah's best-known and most powerful kings. If so, this is another scroll that is never again mentioned. After the king's first excitement over the find, there is no mention of further exhibition or consultation of the scroll. We are not even told that the text was placed in the Holy of Holies or in some other sacred location. Neither this scroll nor any other is listed among the sacred objects taken as booty from the Temple by the Babylonians. Any such scroll was either a personal scroll inscribed by a priest-scribe for his own purposes and forgotten when he laid it aside or died; or a list of *torot* cherished at a particular shrine and brought to Jerusalem sometime during the preceding century, as local shrines were closed as part of a cult-centralization program, and forgotten. In either case, the scroll would have been the product of private initiative rather than of anyone's sense of sacred duty. It would have had no public standing.

CONCLUSION

The idea that Moses or Samuel or Amos or Isaiah may have been nonliterate troubles many people. But these were respected and wise men whose lives have served as models to a hundred generations of literate folk and whose teachings are held sacred throughout the West; we must not impose on them attainments appropriate to later times but not to theirs. Today literacy is a prerequisite for standing in the community, and there is a proven link between incapacity and illiteracy. In pre-exilic Israel, however, scribes were useful folk who could be hired by the day and paid piecework wages. Not everyone needed to master that skill, any more than everyone needed to be a smith or a potter. Many were learned but not literate. Literacy was not essential to the creative process. People composed in their minds and spoke their compositions; the audience absorbed what they heard. Developed as a tool of administration, literacy was not yet universally acknowledged as essential to civilization and personal advancement.

While literacy has proven a boon to civilization, civilization did not have to await literacy any more than the development of biblical religious thought had to await the publication of the *Sefer Torah*. Few periods in Israel's history were as productive as the seven centuries between Moses and Jeremiah. This was the time when the idea of monotheism surfaced, was refined and purified, when the wise and sensitive in Israel began to recognize God as not only powerful but dependable, not only as Creator but as Redeemer, not only as Lawgiver but as trusted Judge. This was the period in which Israel's prophets defined righteousness as a covenant-faithful way of life and developed a definition of religious obligation which went far beyond conventional ideas about placating the gods through sacrifice and shrine attendance. Poets composed in their minds moving hymns to express their needs and faith. A Promised Land was settled, and the concept of stewardship was developed as Israel's teachers warned the community that peace and prosperity depended not on power or might but on their careful management of their patrimony and their willingness to obey God's instructions. Wisdom balanced these doctrines with a down-to-earth prudential morality and a tendency to reflect seriously on the brevity of human life and the uncertainties that accompany every life.

Ancient Israel developed its religion long before it had a scripture. Traditions and teachings were inscribed in its people's minds and hearts. Later some began to write down on papyrus and parchment what they heard—a selection of writings that in centuries to come would be part of a published anthology millions would call scripture and declare to be inspired and sacred.

3

MEMORY BECOMES MANUSCRIPT: THE YEARS OF EXILE

> If you are willing and obedient, you shall eat of the good
> of the land; but if you resist and rebel, you shall be de-
> voured by the sword.
>
> —Isaiah 1:19–20

There are few inevitabilities in a people's life. For Israel, the emergence of a scripture was not inevitable. Neither Solomon nor Jeremiah looked to a sacred book as an ultimate source of authority. Neither the shrine priests of the early years nor the priest-theocrats after the return from exile sponsored convocations of scholars and scribes and charged them to assemble an authorized text. No one ever said, "Israel needs a scripture."

Though the centuries after Moses saw a steady increase in record keeping and interest in literature, Israel's culture remained predominantly oral, as did the surrounding cultures of West Asia. The concept of a scripture, a holy book(s), treasured because it contained God's teachings, was unknown before the fourth century B.C.E. None of the religions of the area read from a holy book during public shrine ceremonies. The prophet Zoroaster, roughly Jeremiah's contemporary (late seventh to sixth centuries B.C.E.), spoke his messages; and these were passed on by word of mouth for generations before being recorded. Many cultures possessed tablets or scrolls of venerated myths—Gilgamesh, the Vedas, the *Avesta* and sacred hymns— but none was treated as a sacred object. The concept of a book declared to be wholly inspired, whose every line, every word, was revealed, had not yet been born.

A scripture emerged by stages over nearly a thousand years. During the first part of this period, the seven centuries from Moses to Jeremiah, Israel's society was still largely agricultural and culturally homogeneous. Literacy was a special accomplishment. Authority resided in oral traditions which established custom and stability. Such written records as there were were useful but not for their evidentiary value. The seminal ideas of Judaism before the Exile were composed in people's minds and passed on from mind to mind—through recitations and storytelling—rather than from mind to writing to reader.

It was only during the Babylonian Exile (sixth century B.C.E.) that the books we know as the Pentateuch, the Prophets, and the Histories began to take shape. During the pre-exilic period, bits and pieces of the traditions had gradually merged, along with the growing recognition of the value of written records, but no coherent presentation was completed before the fifth century B.C.E.

External pressures had a great deal to do with the process. Under continuing attack by neighbors, the separate tribes slowly transformed themselves into a confederation and then into a nation. In one of their periodic attacks on the west, the Assyrians in 722 effectively eliminated Israel's northern tribes. Somewhat over a century later, Babylonian armies exiled the Judean élite of the south, captured Jerusalem, and destroyed the Temple (597,586).* Their fate

---

*In this book I use the names *Judah, Judea,* and *Palestine*—choosing them from among many others (Eretz Israel, Canaan, the Holy Land, etc.) that have been used to refer to the area west of the Jordan River in which some of the ancient Hebrew tribes settled and in which Jews have lived, more or less continuously (when not forced to leave it) ever since. *Judah* refers here

was different from that of the Israelites one hundred fifty years before. The community had suffered a catastrophic defeat. The capital and national shrine were destroyed. The altar had been pulled down and closed. Many of the priests and storytellers who knew the sacred lore lay in premature graves. Few remained who knew the traditions, which were in danger of being lost or becoming confused. Removed from their homes, their Temple in ruins, lacking the usual props of faith and community, these exiles began to set out the national traditions in written form. They wrote to organize and preserve Israel's memory. It was in the Exile that the effort to draw together and write down traditions began to take on significance. Priest-scribes during the Exile preserved and arranged the old traditions. Some drew together the nation's history, some set down beloved hymns, others compiled well-known maxims into Wisdom tracts. Of the many reasons for the spurt of record keeping, none reveal a conscious plan to provide Israel with a scripture.

THE SCROLL TRADITION

Hundreds of studies have attempted to describe how one or another of the volumes that emerged as scripture achieved its final form. The truth is that we really know precious little about that process other than that it was long and complicated. Many traditions circulated. Some remained oral. During the Exile, some appeared in both written and oral form. We are not even sure, after written records of the oral tradition began to appear, how selections were made, and how and when oral and written traditions were brought together. Sometimes a storyteller added new material he believed made his story more understandable, or an ending his audiences found more satisfactory than the original one. Various traditions were amalgamated into a single telling. There was continuity and there was

to the pre-exilic Davidic kingdom and its heirs. *Judea* is used for the area to which the exiles returned (with Jerusalem as its spiritual capital), which later became a Roman province. *Palestine,* used in its original adjective form by Herodotus ("the Philistine Syria"), denoted a larger Roman province of which Judea was the southern district; after crushing the Bar Kokhba rebellion (132–35), the Romans changed the name of the autonomous area of Jewish settlement to Palaestina in order to emphasize that the Jews had lost their homeland. There has never been a name in general use to denote the land in its entirety.

change, but the individual Judean, living within a coherent tradition, did not feel the force of the slow change that beset his way.

To the storytellers and scribes of ancient Israel, it must have seemed only natural to gather and present the sagas in historical sequence. This could not, of course, be done with the lists of *torot*, which, as we have seen, all came to be associated with a single moment in history. Such had not always been the case: some laws refracted the conventional legal norms of West Asia, many of them much older than Sinai. It is also likely that lists of Instructions had been associated with various early historical figures or were the cherished possessions of one shrine or another.

Only in late Hellenistic times (third to second century B.C.E.) was there sufficient interest in establishing a *textus receptus*—a "received" or "correct" text—that the central texts of Judaism achieved a final form. In some cases, oral tradition preceded the text by many centuries; in others, according to tradition, it was only a matter of hours or days as when, in a single day, Baruch wrote out Jeremiah's prophecies at the prophet's dictation (Jer. 36:18). Sometimes the layers are visible and apparent, but often we cannot tell with precision when and why one particular tradition came to be set down or how several distinct versions of the same episode were blended into a single account. The various lists of *torot* in the Pentateuch are clearly of independent origin. Deuteronomy presents a different version of the Moses years from that in Exodus-Numbers. Repetitions and inconsistencies are many, and this variety complicated the editorial process that sought to relocate and root all *torot* in the covenant experience at Sinai. Even in the final text, the received text, all the *torot* are not ascribed to Moses; some are ascribed to Aaron.

In the oral tradition, a variety of narratives about individual patriarchs indicated that each had received from God knowledge of a series of *torot*. Stray fragments of this tradition appear as late as the Hellenistic period in the Book of Jubilees (2nd century B.C.E.), which elaborates on accounts of the patriarchs and of Moses in Genesis and the early parts of Exodus, adding stories that are not a part of the received text. Early translations such as the Greek Septuagint include material not in the received text. Later rabbinic writings often cite ancient quotations that vary from those which became biblical—that is, "official."

At no time during the biblical period did the books we think of as biblical monopolize the field. Narrative traditions not included in the *Sefer Torah* continued to be accepted by one group or another and to find their way into manuscript. *Torot* other than those now included in biblical lists circulated; other scrolls of trusted materials were prepared. A catalogue of the Library of Qumran makes clear that any number of works circulated, including many that did not make it into scripture and yet seem to have been valued as sacred. The story, not included in the received text, that Terah, Abraham's father, made idols in Ur which the young Abraham tested and found impotent, and so broke into pieces, was as well known in Israel as any incident recorded in Genesis and was surely considered part of the "official" tradition (Ber. Rab. 38:13). Even when the Five Scrolls of Moses and many of the Prophet books emerged as recognizable entities about the fifth century B.C.E., they were not closed texts which could not be tampered with, nor were they immediately enshrined. Centuries would pass before the community's attitude toward these books changed from respect to reverence and from reverence to acceptance of them as a statement of God's will, powerful both as language and as a source of redemptive truth.

During the Exile and at least the first half of the post-exilic period, the biblical books were not enshrined as Bible. William Hallo and other students of ancient Near Eastern cultures have provided useful descriptions of the more or less parallel development of written collections of revered myths and sagas among Israel's neighbors in West Asia (Hallo 1980, 1988). The process of producing a written composition of any length took generations and was largely carried out by successions of individual scribes working in schools associated with the palace or royal shrine. This editorial work seems to have been more a matter of individual interest than a planned agenda sponsored by the authorities. The growing importance of records and written literature, together with the scribes' burgeoning literary interests, encouraged them to set down the community's traditions at some length. Since this work was not officially sponsored, there was no body or council interested in declaring one or another formulation as definitive, and it was not unusual for several versions of a text to circulate.

These scrolls played no role in shrine or royal ceremony. They were used primarily in schools where masters assigned them to students to copy and memorize. They were also useful to refresh the memory of storytellers and rhapsodists. Scrolls were to be found in shrine archives, which were repositories of all manner of rolls, as well as in private hands. Clay tablets could not be bound together, and papyrus and parchment scrolls consisted of individual sheets which, even if sewn together, often became frayed and separated. As a practical matter, therefore, lists were prepared of the opening words of successive tablets or sheets so a reader could know how to keep in order lengthy writings that covered a number of separate tablets or skins.

While the final table of contents of the *Tanakh*, the twenty-two books that constitute the Hebrew scripture, was not fully determined until the second or third century C.E., there is general agreement that portions of the *Tanakh*—the *Sefer Torah*, the so-called Five Books of Moses, for Jews *the* scripture, and the Prophets—were accepted as authoritative before the fourth century B.C.E. This editorial achievement is generally associated with the work of the Judean priest-scribe Ezra and his immediate predecessors and successors.

THE PRIEST-SCRIBES AND TORAH

Priests dominated Judean life during the exilic and post-exilic period and were largely responsible for the governance of Jerusalem when it was resettled. One theory holds that the priests prepared the Five Scrolls from oral traditions and available documents to provide Jerusalem, when it once again became a city governed by a Judean élite, with a constitutional document that clearly stated God's will. Ezra and his colleagues believed that obedience to such a document alone could guarantee God's generous protection. Post-exilic leaders accepted the teachings of pre-exilic prophets like Amos, Isaiah, and Jeremiah, who had driven home the lesson that the national fate depended on the people's loyalty to the covenant. These leaders looked on the Exile as deserved punishment. God had now forgiven the people; but to be secure, the nation had to be pure before God, obedient. To be obedient, the nation had to know what was required and to do it. A proper and complete knowledge of God's will was a matter of crucial national concern. Since many divergent practices claimed to be authentic, Ezra and the priests took as their first task to make clear to the community which specific *torot* must be obeyed.

Torah began to be used in both a singular and a collective sense, *a* law and *the* law, a special Instruction and the body of sacred rules God required the community to accept and abide. *Torah* came to be a general term to define teachings accepted as part of the community's sacred traditions. Several of the lists of Instruction which later would be patched into the received text were introduced with the phrase *Zot Torat,* "This is [God's] instruction concerning . . ." (Lev. 6,7; Num. 5:29, 6:13). Torah designated not only the rules accepted as divine instructions but venerable sagas about the founding fathers, explanations of creation, reports about the Exodus, Sinai, the Wilderness Trek, the Conquest, and much else. Torah was not yet limited to material that ultimately found its way into the biblical text, but designated any and all material the community held sacred.

In the early stages of their history, the Israelites, living within the envelope of an all-embracing tribal culture, had known what their way required, that their way was right and, if followed, pleasing to God. As they settled down, life became more complex. The tribes began to live cheek by jowl with those of other cultures and to recognize the need for a more specifically defined tradition.

In these years of Exile and return, as in earlier times, chance played its part in determining which traditions would become scripture and which would not. Earlier, it had been decided according to which tribe or group came to dominate a particular tribal assembly or which family of priests controlled the activities of a shrine. The various covenant-enabling ceremonies described—Sinai, Schechem, Gilgal —had played, or were held to have played, pivotal roles as occasions when confederations of tribes met and accepted a single set of obligations. Now, during the Exile, the traditions binding on the priest-scribes prevailed because their caste had gained political ascendancy. The priest-scribes were heirs of certain traditions that they began to write down as sanctified. They included many matters held in common with the whole community and others that represented their own priestly traditions. *Torah* became the term to define the emerging consensus and continues to serve that purpose to our day.

The term *Sefer Torah,* a scroll of divine instructions accepted as sacred and binding, appears only in the late layers of the biblical text. We find it used in the telling of the discovery in the Temple of a book of the law in King Josiah's day (*c.*621 B.C.E.); for the first time, more than six centuries after Moses, a written scroll of sacred traditions is described as playing a role in Israel's history. *Sefer Torah* appears again in the description of certain events of the fifth century B.C.E. when the chief priest-scribe, Ezra, is said to have brought from Persia a roll, probably of parchment, and to have read from it to the Jerusalem community a list of *torot* the community accepted as obligatory (see pages 112–21).

Much of the scripture's authority and functional value derives from the certainty that these are *God's* words and must not be trifled with. The text is fixed: "You shall not add nor subtract from it" (Deut. 4:2). Yet, in the centuries before Ezra and for some time thereafter, scribes routinely added or eliminated materials, juxtaposed separate lists of *torot,* and blended details from various versions into a single narrative. Thus, upon close examination, the received text seems more like a haphazard collection than a carefully edited text. In fact, the Torah is not a systematic law code or an inclusive chronicle but an anthology of myth, saga, and law which grew out of various texts deemed venerable or inspired, whose merit was that they stood for the entire range of Israel's ancient and sacred traditions.

Much of the tradition was not set down. One could not expect that this ocean of treasured traditions, as broad as the community's life, could be captured in a single volume or even in several. That a saga was not set down or a law not listed did not mean that it was not accepted as Torah, God's word. There seems to have been no urgency to get it all down in one place or to limit authority to a single form.

The important fact is that these scrolls were never intended to be exhaustive or complete. Inscribed texts were parts of much larger codes. The received text, for example, prohibits work on the Sabbath but does not define work. May someone travel on the Sabbath? Take care of livestock? Light a fire? Obviously, there were answers to such questions. There had to be. The community lived, and such living questions had to have answers.

It is highly doubtful, as some have argued, that the practice of reading portions from the *Sefer Torah* during public worship, *Keriat ha-Torah,* began during this time. If books were read at meeting times, and some may have been, it was a purely local custom. There is no specific evidence from the Persian period (550–330 B.C.E.)—when Judea was a dependency of the empire, and Jerusalem was governed by a priestly élite—of a conscious effort to equip Israel with a scripture or even of any apparent desire to do so. It is also doubtful that the widely separated communities—in the East, in Egypt, and in Judea—possessed similar sets of Torah scrolls. Jerusalem, from the first return of some exiles in 520 to Ezra's arrival several generations later, seems to have possessed no Torah scroll.

The records from the Persian period are few. Israel's priest-historians were not interested in recording a domestic history of the exiled community; nor were they, really, interested in Jerusalem and Judea, except to detail the story of the resettlement and the successful efforts of Ezra and Nehemiah to re-establish the authority of the priest classes over the altar and the capital.

There seems to have been a class called *soferim,* literally "scribes," who were Ezra's disciples and political heirs, but we know little about their activities. There is in the records no actual mention of scribes or editors working on a Torah document. Nor does the editing of the Torah seem to have been carried out to fulfill a direct royal command. The Torah simply grew. Popular interest and perceived need were the primary catalysts.

The process of compiling and editing was never centrally organized or coordinated. No one set out to examine all circulating traditions and texts and select those that met some predetermined standard of merit or authenticity. Scribes took what they found and added what they knew or what interested them. Naturally, traditions known and approved by the religious leaders, primarily other priests, had preference in the selection process. Researchers have found interpolations in various texts, designed to give added prominence to the priests. Rules governing the cult and the shrine occupy an extraordinarily large role in the lists of *torot;* but the result of these priestly efforts should not be seen simply as a triumph of a group of crafty and self-serving priests. These men did not invent. Tradition for them, as for the whole community, was a reflection of an ancient sacred body of obligations. Priest-scribes did much of the scribal work simply because they had the necessary skills and opportunity and interest.

They based their claim to authority on the God-appointed dynastic mission to serve at His altar. God had chosen Moses. God had ordered Moses to appoint Aaron, his brother, as high priest. The priests were Aaron's descendants. When Korah challenged Moses' right to the priesthood, God intervened to lay low the rebels (Num. 16). It was important to the priests that the sacred rules governing their services at the altar be set down in a way that made clear that their claims to authority went back to and derived from the original revelation—an end toward which they worked zealously.

Scribes with an archival bent compiled all the records they could locate or whatever ancient traditions they knew. Some presented the tradition as a storyteller would, with an eye to audience reaction. Some explained names or places. Some traditions were not recorded and disappeared from the text. One scribe may have tried his hand at turning several versions of a well-known episode into a single presentation, and another may have sewn together parchment sheets that contained quite disparate materials. Material was conflated, inflated, found, lost, kept for no apparent reason. None of the scribes busy recording the tradition felt that they had been set a divine task of preparing a scripture. They were simply memorizing, reciting, recording, and updating Israel's cherished traditions.

The scribes were not interested in being creative. They retained familiar story lines and much of the original language. Their work seems curiously unsystematic, part faithful submission to the authority of fixed recitation and part comprehensive editing which, by eliminating inconsistencies, stamped the material with a consistent point of view. Their work can be compared to wash hanging on a line, the scribes having hung it out and pinned to it unrelated blocks of long-familiar narrative and law. While the image has a certain appropriateness, these men did more than wash old clothes and hang them out to dry. They patched up some of the clothes with cloth taken from other garments or brightened them with ornamentation. They gave many of the garments style they had not had before.

There is no indication that these men worked with any sense of urgency, or felt awed or restricted by any presentiment that they were dealing with materials a later age would consider inviolate. There is no suggestion in the surviving texts that scribes working with the sacred traditions must be in a special state of ritual purity or use specially prepared or blessed writing implements or surfaces, or copy the material without change. It is unlikely that the scribes approached the work of transcription with any fear that if they tampered with God's words they might suffer the fate of Nadab and Abihu, those two priests who were incinerated by divine fire for having brought a strange light to God's altar (Num. 3:4). The material was, by and large, faithfully copied because that was how scribes operated in a traditional society. Traditions were marked "Handle with Care" but not "Danger, Explosive." Changes could be and were made.

Since preservation was always of primary interest, several inconsistent versions of the same episode were sometimes set down side by side or interleaved. The signal importance of Sinai is evidenced by the proliferation of versions that have gone into the received text. A single chapter of Exodus tells us that Moses went up to the Lord alone (24:2); that Moses was accompanied by his brother, Aaron, and Aaron's two eldest sons, Nadab and Abihu, and seventy elders (24:1); and that Joshua accompanied Moses on the climb "up into the Mount of God" (24:13). In one version, God Himself inscribes the stone tablets; in another, the task is left to Moses; and so on. All versions emphasize the importance and accuracy of these Instructions. They are God's own, stated exactly as God had intended. One senses that various editors simply piled up well-attested traditions about this crucial event because such traditions existed and no one knew how to choose between them. Nor was it important that a choice be made. Scribes who could not choose between one stream of tradition and another solved the dilemma by blending them. Thus, the Garden of Eden story, as we have it, weaves together at least two originally separate traditions: one that focused on the Tree of Life; the other, on the Tree of Knowledge.

Just as no attempt was made to produce a consistent and tightly edited narrative, no attempt was made to eliminate inconsistencies in wording. Even the foremost of all biblical passages, the Ten Commandments, is not presented in exactly the same language in Exodus and Deuteronomy. No scribe seems to have imagined that he was preparing a constitutional document or an all-inclusive and systematic law code. When a rule is presented in several places, there are almost always subtle but important differences in language and context; the Instructions, as set out, are anything but clear. One stipulation, for instance, requires that a husband who wishes to divorce his wife must give her a document, a *get,* "a bill of divorcement" (Deut. 24:1). There is no indication what specific matters that paper should address, how division of property issues is to be arranged, or how the *get* is to be drawn up and enforced. Though we are not told how or whether a woman may initiate a divorce, women had some say in such a procedure, or so many rabbinic interpreters of this text assure us; but the text does not specifically mention this fact. The rabbinic interpretation assumes that we acknowledge the existence of a more inclusive set of rules and regulations.

Nor was there any apparent effort to ennoble the text's central figures. The incident in which Moses forgets to circumcise his son, and is attacked by some malign spirit for that failure, is certainly not ennobling (Exod. 4:24–26). As a vignette of the great prophet, it was simply recorded. At the time, no one proposed to avoid mention of questionable actions by the great.

The process of amalgamation and editing proceeded slowly. Traditions were slightly reshaped by each retelling. A word or phrase might be added; an incident dropped or relocated. Working with venerable traditions which they completely believed, the scribes had no need to say, "This sounds better," or, "This is what we meant"; still, they consciously filtered traditions through their minds and presented them in ways that sounded right to them. Probably they could not have explained their standards had they been asked but, clearly, they respected the needs, interests, and beliefs of their audience.*

---

*This approach was updated just over a century ago by conservatives like Zacharias Frankel (1801–75) who, seeking a way to establish the structure of religious practice for a generation that no longer accepted on faith the right of the rabbis to set standards for the community, argued that community consensus and practice rather than the opinions and authority of individual scholars should define God's intentions. Frankel's argument was in many ways an update of an approach that had worked well for Israel in biblical times when accepted traditions emerged naturally from community consensus.

EXILE AND PROPHECY

Those who were marched off into exile by the Babylonians in 587–86 B.C.E. were not a representative cross-section of the population of pre-exilic Judah. Except for a sizable draft of artisans taken because they would be useful on imperial building projects, the exiles came mostly from the upper and urban classes, "the notables of the land," those who customarily employed scribes or were themselves scribe-administrators (2 Kings 24:15–16). Among them were certainly scribes and administrators whose work before the defeat had included preparing the royal chronicles and the lists of Temple deposits and records. Now, in exile, work on these records would have seemed not only a natural concern but also one of some urgency. The princes and priests needed copies of their genealogies and privileges that entitled them to tithes and other benefits. Cut off by defeat and exile from their estates and privileges, the leaders were almost certainly challenged by those who blamed them for the disaster. The élite must have felt it imperative to record and secure their pedigrees, which backed their claim to tribal leadership. Since they no longer held the power of effective office, they would have to prove their claim to authority if they or their sons were ever to reclaim their family's privileges. As a reminder of their past glories and future hopes, the royal family encouraged histories of their dynasty's founder, David, and his heirs.

But self-interest was not their only or overriding concern. The exiles were a decimated community, no longer confident that there would always be a Jewish presence; they needed reassurance that their traditions, and most particularly the prophecies of hope, would not be forgotten. In troubled times, people do what they can to protect their most valued possessions. Treasured heirlooms may be hidden. Sacred tradition must be protected. This was done by turning memory into manuscript.

There was equal need to preserve and to reassure. The Temple lay in ruins. The princes of David's dynasty were prisoners. People were reminded that various prophets had predicted the defeat, and declared that defeat and exile were a deserved punishment. Because of His special relationship with Israel, God had brought disaster since, despite repeated warning, the community had been faithless to the Covenant. The prophets had brought words of judgment and also, fortunately, words of comfort and encouragement. God had not completely abandoned His people: "Behold, the days come, said the Lord, when I will raise unto David a righteous shoot and he shall reign as King and prosper and shall execute justice and righteousness in the land. In his day, Judah will be saved and Israel will dwell in safety" (Jer. 23:5–6).

During the Exile, such prophecies assumed new importance because they held out hope to the defeated and exiled nation. Scribes recorded the words brought by trusted prophets counseling repentance and promising forgiveness, so that the community would not lose the hearing of them, particularly the certainty of God's promise that a repentant and righteous people would be redeemed. Since God's judgments are fair, a loyal and repentant community could expect better times. God rules the world in justice, and in His justice and mercy lay the nation's hope. Their hope lay in understanding the reasons for their defeat and correcting them. There is nothing like a disaster to rekindle the sense of urgency: a way, a teaching, must be found that will lift the spirit and give hope, for without hope what may be only temporary defeat becomes unredeemable disaster.

God had not abandoned them. Those who drew together the early sagas and the law provided a reminder of the people's origins, their covenanted ties with God, and the terms of obedience. Those who wrote down the prophecies helped to explain what had happened, and held out the promise of a better day. The scribes who began to edit the biblical chronicles were showing how God's providence would work out in actuality. They did not see themselves as writing what theologians today call divine history. Believing God controlled the destiny of men and nations, they and their histories explained events providentially. The nation would be, had been, punished by God when it deserved to be, and had prospered, would prosper, when it was loyal to the Covenant. A nation loyal to God's instructions could expect to live securely. A faithful community of exiles could expect to be restored and favored. Israel's history offered clear proof of God's providential and just care of His people, tangible evidence of the operation of the Covenant. God is dependable. An obedient nation can expect to be restored to its land. Thus was history written to encourage hope.

Among the records of prophecies, those that preoccupied the exiles, and consequently were recorded by their scribes, promised restoration and made known the terms of Israel's obligations to God and the rewards of faithfulness: "If you are willing and obedient, you shall eat of the good of the land; but if you resist and rebel, you shall be devoured by the sword" (Isa. 1:19–20). The contemporary prophecies that commanded lasting attention were like those of Ezekiel and Deutero-Isaiah which spoke of a time when "aliens shall rebuild your walls, their Kings shall wait upon you, for in anger I struck you down, but in favor I take you back" (Isa. 60:10); and taught that the original redemption, the Exodus, was not simply an event of the past but a portent and promise of the second redemption that would soon be.

Much that became scriptural achieved that status because it offered the community guidance and hope. The land assumed new importance: it was the goal, the exiled people's dream. History filled it with a gracious past, and memory lent enchantment to it—a land flowing with milk and honey. Later Jewish piety would also associate the dissemination of Torah with the Promised Land. The prophets insisted: "For out of Zion shall go forth Torah [The Law] and the word of God from Jerusalem" (Isa. 2:3; Mic. 4:2). The rabbis would associate the Promised Land with religious inspiration: "The climate of the land of Israel makes one wise" (b.B.B. 158b). The medieval poet-philosopher Judah Ha-Levi would argue that a prophet needed to be present in the land in order to hear God, even though scriptural history suggests otherwise. Moses received the original law in the Sinai wilderness. Ezra brought his scroll from Babylon. The process of collecting, inscribing, and editing the traditions and documents that ultimately became the *Sefer Torah* proceeded apace not in Canaan but in what is today Iraq, where the exiles were quartered. No matter. In Jewish thought, the primary identification of the land of Israel and Torah was never seriously challenged.

THE RELIGIOUS LIFE OF EXILE

The exiles were first settled in a number of villages in central Iraq in the general area of modern Baghdad, but many of the wealthy and well-born quickly managed to move into nearby commercial centers. Some members of the royal family, including apparently King Jehoiachin, became courtiers at the imperial center, where they were thrust into a far more sophisticated and cosmopolitan world than any they had known before (2 Kings 25:27–30). Commerce there was international. The capital teemed with scribes. The Babylonian emperors necessarily had organized an elaborate imperial administration to manage their interests; and the Persians, who would soon take over the empire (*c.*550 B.C.E.), followed suit.

The palace supported schools where the needed cadres of officials and clerks were trained. The court patronized rhapsodists, poets, astronomers, mathematicians, and philosophers. It was a liberal, urban, and urbane society. Babylon was the capital of a sophisticated and cosmopolitan world. Jerusalem had been the capital of a small provincial country.

The exiled Judeans found themselves in a world where palace and temple contained extensive archives which included, besides the inevitable administrative records, tablets and rolls on which were incised well-known myths, hymns, royal annals, Wisdom, legal texts, ritual and incantation lists, eulogies, even works of magic and medicine.

Literature was cultivated for pleasure as well as practical benefit. The Judeans quickly learned that writing played a far more important role in the East than it had back home, and Judean scribes quickly discovered that their new professional colleagues had developed far more advanced techniques than any to which they had been accustomed. These accomplishments appealed to the exiles, and Judean scribes adopted the script and many of the procedures of the imperial bureaus.

The upper classes, particularly the priests whose lot seems to have improved quickly and significantly, showed a new interest in literature. During the Exile, for the first time, we come across literary images drawn from that imperial world. The image of Moses in the later sections of Deuteronomy as not simply the prophet who speaks God's will but as the scribe who sets it all down in a book, may have first appeared at this time. Ezekiel says, "And when I looked, behold, a hand stretched out to me, holding a scroll, and it was inscribed on both the front and the back; in it were written lamentations, dirges and woes" (2:9–10). Ezekiel is not to read the scroll but to eat it: "Feed your stomach and fill your belly with this scroll and then go and repeat my very words to them" (3:3–4). The scroll, indeed, "tasted as sweet as honey" (3:3).

Why eat a scroll? When we digest what we eat, it becomes part of us. Presumably, the image of eating a scroll was a way to indicate that its contents have been fully digested and absorbed. What is to us a surprising and somewhat awkward image indicated to the prophet's audience that he had fully understood and accurately reported God's message. Apparently, it was not yet self-evident that the normal thing to do with a sacred scroll was to study it carefully or read it aloud.

During the early years of the Exile, the captives began to meet in assemblies (*Kinishtu*), from which came the later Hebrew *Keneset,* today used both for synagogue, *Beit ha-Keneset,* and for Israel's parliament. We know little about these meetings save that they were held, though many later commentators confidently describe Sabbath and festival meetings when psalms were sung and portions of a Torah scroll or a scroll of prophecies were read out or chanted. With the Temple in ruins, the priests could no longer officiate at the altar. So it is assumed that as a surrogate rite they chanted the hymns that had been used in the Temple during Sabbath and holy day sacrifices, and recited the Instructions, *torot,* pertinent to that day's Temple ceremony, in this way substituting intention for the act.

A community's religious life requires both shape and structure. One can argue with some logic that religious life requires a calendar, a visible public presence, and customary forms, and that the only way the exiles could have provided such essentials for themselves would have been to hold meetings on some kind of regular schedule, preferably one based on traditional sacred times; but to go farther and say that the exiles' religious life formed itself around meetings where traditional narratives and respected prophecies were recited and/or read is to move into the realm of speculation. Moreover, though we know a good bit about the sacrificial cult in pre-exilic times, we know little, if anything, about the role in it, if any, of recitation and prayer. We do know that nowhere in West Asia was there yet any formal tradition of reading from sacred books. If there were, it would help us understand one of the critical steps in the process which turned simple records of tradition into a sacred scripture. Records that were, from their first appearance, associated with a public ceremonial moment, would have had their sacredness guaranteed.

It is possible that shrines, not unlike the Jerusalem Temple, were set up in the Exile and sacrifices offered in them. It may be that there was specific mention of such shrines in the biblical materials removed after the Exile by the theocrats who gained control of religious life and of the Second Temple—who were determined, as we know, to protect their interests in the Temple's uniqueness and centrality. They gathered together and emphasized the *torot* that stipulated that Jewish life was to be centered on a single and unique sanctuary, controlled by its priests. During the pre-exilic period, Shiloh, Dan, Bethel, Gilgal, Mizpeh, Hebron, Bethlehem, and so on had been for Israel separate centers of pilgrimage, sacrifice, and worship; each had its own practices and probably worship, and probably its own list of *torot*.

The centralization of worship had developed gradually during the pre-exilic period, largely as a consequence of political circumstance, the most important being Assyria's defeat of the northern kingdom in 722 B.C.E.; but, while the community had accepted worship at the royal shrine in Jerusalem as appropriate, it had not taken readily to the idea that a single central sanctuary was a required act of obedience to God. Most local shrines were not shut down until perhaps a generation before the Babylonian defeat, if then; and Mizpeh retained sufficient sanctity to become the cult center of an active religious life for those Judeans who eluded being taken as captives into exile in 586 (2 Kings 25:23–26; Jer. 40:6–12).

During an exile they confidently believed would be only temporary, the former priests of Jerusalem preserved the traditions that had been cherished at the royal shrine with special emphasis on the role of the shrine priests. As priests, they operated within an institutional context that spawned records prescribing forms and precedents. It seems likely that during the Exile priest-scribes began to assemble a special scroll of *torot,* a list of rules dealing primarily but not exclusively with cult regulations. A late section of Deuteronomy, probably prepared by them at this time, has Moses endow Levi with a mandate to "teach Jacob Thy ordinance and Israel Thy Law" (33:10) and to promulgate laws: "Let your Thummim and Urim be with your faithful one" (33:8), using words—"Thummim" and "Urim"—that refer to oracles specifically revealed to priests but whose precise nature and mode of operation are now unknown. In the post-exilic period, the only new history of interest to those who determined the contents of the biblical records concentrated on the activities both of the priests who returned and began the reconstruction of the Jerusalem shrine, and of the prophets who prophesied there; indeed, this was the only history that really interested the generation of post-exilic priest-scribes.

Still, the histories, the prophecies, and the hymns that dwelt on the shrine, and loom large in the post-exilic literature, must not make us forget that Jerusalem was not the only shrine at which Jews then worshiped. Early in the fifth century, Judean mercenaries in southern Egypt dedicated a temple-shrine at Elephantine. There was an altar in Samaria built on Mount Gerizim by Sanballat, governor of Samaria, for his son-in-law, grandson of a Jerusalem high priest. In Hellenistic times, an altar in Jordan and another at Heliopolis in Egypt were maintained by some of Jerusalem's ancient priest families. The priest-scribes who inscribed the traditions and wrote and edited the histories that became scripture had every reason to choose not to mention such places; but the records of their existence, and that sacrifices were offered to God by pious Jews at these altars, are undeniable.

The priest-scribes who worked on the written compilations during the Exile evidenced little interest in describing other forms of religious life or even in preserving the records of the non-Jerusalemite Judean communities. Except for Ezekiel, who provided a vision of a glorious reopened Temple, and Deutero-Isaiah, who prophesied return, little of exilic life and thought has survived.

Of little interest were prophecy that did not focus on God's promise of redemption, and history that did not focus on Jerusalem and the Temple. We hear a bit of the fate of the first generation of exiles and somewhat more about those who returned to Jerusalem after 520 B.C.E., but little else. It's not quite clear why. Did all their concerns center on God's promise of return; on the necessary preconditions of return—obedience, repentance, God's decision to act for His own glorification; and on the fact of the return itself? If so, how then do we explain the fact that, given the chance to return, most exiles did not take advantage of it?

The surviving literature seems to be the work of a small caste of priest-scribes who returned and took over control of Jerusalem, and reflects their parochial interests. It may even be that they systematically eliminated records describing life in the Exile in order to heighten the importance of Jerusalem and the shrine. Still, the cultural interest of the exiles must have been of a high order—as evidenced by their interest in making records and editing traditions, and their involvement with such concerns as ritual purity and the oneness of God.

The few references to the religious life of the sixth-century exiles provide few specific details. Songs certainly were sung: some were lamentations (Ps. 137); others, songs of hope (126). Storytellers must have continued to practice their ancient and well-loved art. There were meetings where hymns were chanted and even sacrifices offered. Recitations certainly took place, probably as they always had, at local and family events. Traditions were kept alive, but there is no trace in the literature of a new ritual featuring the recitation of the Word of God as a central element of the liturgy. God still spoke directly to and through prophets and in oracles delivered by priests to whom people turned, as they had in the past, for help in determining an auspicious day for a marriage or for acquiring a home. In everyday life, the oral tradition continued to be determinative. No scroll was venerated. There was no tradition among Jews that encouraged chanting portions of holy books at public worship or formal study of such books. There is not a word about scrolls in Ezekiel's loving description of the architectural details of the rebuilt Temple which would replace the destroyed sanctuary, nor any indication that the priests were to handle, teach, or read such scrolls as part of their official duties. The Elephantine Papyri, which record some of the details of the activities of a fifth-century B.C.E. community of Judean mercenaries in southern Egypt, mention a shrine, sacrifices, altars, the Passover celebration, but not a word about sacred scrolls.

There is no indication that the priests who accompanied the first group of Zionists to return from Babylon in the late sixth century B.C.E., and served in the Temple until Ezra's reformation, brought sacred writings with them. When about a century later Ezra appeared, scroll in hand, it was a novelty—and Ezra's use of the authority of that scroll to challenge a number of current religious practices, an even greater novelty. No Jerusalemite is described as pulling out a scroll of his own to dispute Ezra's claims and question the new regimen. If the commentators who have suggested that the practice of *Keriat ha-Torah,* regularly organized scriptural readings, developed in the Exile, are correct, one would expect the first returnees to have introduced the practice into the ritual of the Temple or the city; but there is no evidence that they did so. Without scrolls, they had no texts to read. There is no creditable evidence of a ritual that involves the reading or chanting of portions of a holy book in the Temple for another five hundred years.

A CHANGE OF LANGUAGE: ARAMAIC

Just as the tribes had entered Canaan at a propitious moment soon after the alphabet had been shaped, so the exiles had the good fortune to find themselves among peoples who were making major improvements in all technical aspects of the scribal arts. The scribes of the imperial bureaus of the Babylonians, and particularly of their Persian successors, made significant technical improvements that made these skills easier to master. Clay was finally abandoned for papyrus or parchment—a shift that permitted, among other benefits, the presentation and preservation of longer texts. A clay tablet can be inscribed front and back but cannot be hinged to another tablet, while strips of papyrus sheets and rolls of tanned leather can be joined into sizable rolls. Parchment scrolls of the Hellenistic period up to twenty-eight feet long have been found (Yadin 1985).

After 550 B.C.E., the new Persian administration established Aramaic as the language of record for all documents dealing with government matters and commerce in the western part of the empire and adopted a formal script for official use. This script of squarish design, far more readable than cuneiform-influenced predecessors, was quickly adopted by Judean scribes. Recognizing its eastern origins, they named this new script, somewhat anachronistically, *Ashurit,* the "Assyrian script." It later became, and remains to this day, the standard for all liturgically approved Torah scrolls.

Linguistically, Aramaic is a near cousin to Hebrew. The languages, both related to Akkadian, share many words, employ essentially the same grammatical forms, and are written with the same alphabet. Bilingualism became increasingly common. By the time Alexander the Great's conquests ended the Persian period (late fourth century B.C.E.), Aramaic was well on its way to becoming the vernacular of most Judeans. The priest-scribe who some time in the fourth century prepared a history of the reforms Ezra had instituted in Jerusalem, a chronicle included in the Bible, felt comfortable introducing into his history several untranslated Aramaic documents purportedly issued by the Persian imperial bureau (Ezra 4:8–6:18, 7:12–26).

The increased use of Aramaic, particularly by élite, literate Judeans, increasingly allowed these former provincials to feel themselves part of an international literary world. The exiles found Aramaic a useful, even indispensable, tool in maintaining contact between them and their hosts. The increased use of Aramaic also exerted an unplanned pressure toward the creation of a Hebrew scripture. As more and more Judeans used Aramaic as their vernacular, the number who could readily understand recitations of the tradition diminished, and a bilingual audience (Hebrew and Aramaic) began to impose subtle, but important, changes on the traditional language in which the *torot* and the narratives were presented. While the need to be understood dictated linguistic change, there was at the same time a predictable conservative reaction determined to preserve familiar idioms and language.

One way to accomplish such preservation was to fix the material in written form. The population at large was, as it had always been, dependent on professional memorizers and reciters. Since fewer and fewer of the traditional Hebrew forms and idioms were part of everyday speech, even reciters began to refer to notes. This language shift tended to reduce significantly the average listener's ability to remember text with a full complement of original phrases and cadences. Understanding the reciter less, the audience exerted less influence on the storyteller who, in turn, gave his recitations more by rote. There is a law of cultural transfer that the more endangered an oral repertoire, the greater the felt pressure to record it. Memorization became, for many, a self-conscious effort.

The tradition would have lost all sense of being tradition had people used translations to bridge this growing sense of distance from the original material. Fortunately, they made no such attempt. To translate the tradition into Aramaic would have vitiated its power, which in the popular mind derived as much from its ancient phrases as from the ideas it contained. On the level of popular faith, the issue was not accuracy or understanding but the people's belief that the language of tradition possessed special power. Language is an essential element of tradition, and the best translation can only approximate the meaning and style of the original. Greek rhapsodists continued to recite the *Iliad* in the classic tongue long after demotic Greek had become the vernacular of their audiences who, though they no longer fully understood the words, recognized familiar cadences and, most of all, responded to the symbolic power of the words. In the Middle Ages, Muslim scholars routinely taught that a translation of the Koran was no longer Koran; and in modern times, non-Arabic-speaking Muslims in far places like Malaysia and Indonesia, where Arabic is little known, are routinely set the task of memorizing the Koran in the original.

Pre-exilic Hebrew, the ordinary vernacular of the tribes and the language in which the sagas had been formed, now begins its measured ascent into the status of *Lashon ha-Kodesh*, "holy speech." Hebrew took on a gravity and weight it had not enjoyed when it was simply the people's speech. A cloak of holiness was spread over whatever was written or spoken in the classic speech. The old words were seen as heavy with power. Since Hebrew had been the language in which the prophets had reported God's message, it followed that God spoke in Hebrew. Praise of Hebrew as a divine tongue would become a stock element of the rabbinic tradition: "Our Hebrew language is called the holy tongue because the Holy One brought it into being. . . . Its words are not accidental, but the result of a wondrous design and sublime wisdom, based on profound mysteries and meanings" (Delmedigo 1631). Over the centuries and until quite recently, Jews have found it difficult, though there are exceptions, to revere any work, however learned or pious, that was not written in Hebrew.

EZRA'S SCROLL

The scroll Ezra is reported to have brought up to Jerusalem from Persia some time in the middle of the fifth century B.C.E. provides an idea of what was written during the Exile and how those who wrote it conceived of their work. The story of Ezra's scroll, as told by later priest-historians whose efforts are recorded in the books of Ezra and Nehemiah, is significant because for the first time the community seems to have acknowledged that religious authority can lodge in a text. Little in the earlier biblical records foreshadows such a change. The first group of Judeans to return to Jerusalem (c.520) with the aim of renewing the cult had apparently not felt the need to bring a Torah type of scroll with them, as none is mentioned. In the intervening generations before Ezra's arrival, we hear of prophets who brought God's word to Judea (Haggai, Zechariah, and so on), of priests who were consulted about the oracles, and of the altar and its implements; but there is no mention that a scroll of any kind played a significant role, or any role, in the life of the community. Even later writers, like the rabbis of the talmudic period, who assumed that the *Sefer Torah* had been in existence since Moses' day, sensed the novelty and the importance of the event: "Ezra was worthy of having the law given through him to Israel had not Moses preceded him" (b. San. 21b).

The date of Ezra's mission is still in dispute—some scholars preferring a mid-fifth-century date, others placing it in the first decade of the fourth century—but what is not debated is that Ezra's activities and those of another contemporary official who came from the East, Nehemiah, represent attempts by the Judean aristocracy among the exiles, primarily the priests, to assert the authority of their views and practices over the Temple and the City of Jerusalem. Furthermore, both Ezra, a "priest and scribe of the law of God of Heaven," and Nehemiah, a nobleman who had served as a cupbearer in the royal court, seem to have been backed by the Persian court and to have come to Jerusalem on missions authorized by it.

The chronicle presented in Ezra and Nehemiah was edited, years after the events described, from several traditions that agree on the intimate involvement of Temple personnel, priests and Levites, in what occurred. The most dramatic event reported was a public ceremony held in Jerusalem. Upon Ezra's arrival, he read, or had read, to an assembly of tribal leaders from a scroll variously called "The Book [Scroll] of the Law" (Neh. 8:3), "The Book, The Law of God" (8:8), "The Book of the Law of YHWH, Their God" (9:3), and "The Book of Moses" (13:1). The absence of a precise citation suggests that, though this particular incident was well known, the specific scroll was not, and there were different traditions about it. This absence also suggests that the scroll was not identified as one of the received scrolls, one of the five that became the Pentateuch, for later editors would surely have been able to identify such a scroll.

Questions abound. What was the provenance of this scroll? What text did it contain? Did it contain narrative as well as law? Which, if any, of the five scrolls that make up the *Sefer Torah* did it approximate, and to what degree? Nothing is known of the scroll's provenance except that Ezra brought it with him. It cannot be identified as a scroll taken east by those who had been exiled in 586. We do not know for sure whether the scroll was available in 520 when the Persian court allowed the first small group of Judean nobles and priests to return to Jerusalem. The biblical record indicates that they brought with them to Jerusalem money, the "vessel of the House of the Lord," what was left of the booty taken in 586, and various genealogical records of the priests who would serve at the altar; but no mention is made of a scroll of *torot* (Ezra 1:7). It seems probable that

Ezra's scroll had been prepared in the East, probably sometime during the previous half-century, by scribes of the priest caste to which he belonged and whose interests he represented, but even this is not certain.

It would appear that this scroll was not a complete *Sefer Torah* or even some early version of that anthology. Every reference speaks of a single scroll. Although early in the post-exilic period the Five Scrolls came to have a special degree of authority associated with them, they were not inscribed as a single text on a single scroll until at least the first century C.E. Our information is too scanty for us even to be sure, though it seems likely, that "The Book of the Law" refers to an early version of any of the scrolls included in our Torah.

In spite of the two thousand years in which the *Sefer Torah* has been known and treated as a single entity, each scroll is distinctive in style and content. Genesis consists of a string of narratives more or less bound together by recurring genealogies: no author or source is indicated; there is almost no law and certainly no list of *torot*. Exodus opens with a review of a portion close to the end of Genesis (46:8ff.). Such review was a common practice developed by ancient scribes to indicate to a reader that the scroll he had in hand followed on another, since scrolls were not titled or bound. Exodus dwells at length on the Passover history and the Sinai covenant, providing along the way several short blocks of *torot*. Leviticus also presents lists of Instructions but in a more discursive way than Exodus, where the approach, particularly in cultic matters, is simply prescriptive. Both books end with summaries. Numbers hangs various blocks of Instructions on a framework that describes in some detail the stages of the trek made by the tribes as they passed from the Mountain of Revelation to the Plains of Moab, preparing to enter the Promised Land. Various Instructions are introduced that were presumedly given during the latter portion of the trek; the editors of Numbers seem to have been less concerned than those responsible for the other scrolls to make the point that all the *torot* were included in the climactic revelation at Sinai. Numbers also contains what must have been originally an independent novella which centers on a gentile prophet, Balaam, and the idea that, despite the power of prophetically uttered words, Israel need not fear the prophets of other nations. Deuteronomy presents itself as a series of valedictory speeches in which Moses, about to give up his office, reflects on what he has heard, taught, and seen. It contains its own version of many incidents and *torot* mentioned in Exodus-Numbers, and has long been recognized as having developed independently of the other scrolls before its inclusion in the *Sefer Torah*.

Ezra's scroll is called a *sefer*, which tells us only that the manuscript had been prepared following generally accepted scribal norms. The writing surface would have been specially prepared parchment sheets; the inscription, ink on skin. Once inscribed, the sheets would have been sewed together and kept as a roll. The text would have been consonantal, unvocalized, and probably set out in the new *Ashurit* script which had become the official script of the Jews who corresponded with the Persian administration. The scroll may have been wrapped, as was the custom, in a single linen slip to protect it from dust and sun. It may have been Ezra's own property, perhaps by his own hand, perhaps by the hand of another Judean priest-scribe.

Ezra is called "a scribe [*sofer*] skilled in the Law of Moses" (Ezra 7:6). Used in this way, *sofer* conjures up the image not of a humble notary but of a well-born and well-placed priest, a senior administrator who had acquired position and authority based less on his ability to handle a quill than on birth and rank as a senior member of the Judean priest caste.

At least two accounts of the public ceremony that accompanied the reading of Ezra's scroll are reflected in the present text. In one, Ezra mounted a platform set up just outside the Temple, opened a scroll, and read it in its entirety to the convened citizenry in a ceremony that lasted from dawn till noonday (Neh. 8:1–4). In the second version, Ezra convened the assembly, elevated and recited a blessing over the scroll, but did not himself read. A group of leading citizens, Levites, performed that task with care, "gave the sense," and "caused the people to understand the meaning" (8:3–8). The assembly then confessed their sins and made "a firm covenant" to obey God's instructions. Nehemiah then joined Ezra. Together they declared the day holy and informed the assembly that, although much of their practice had not conformed to God's instructions that they had just heard, they need not be downcast. They now knew what was expected of them. From now on, matters would be set right, and the day should be treated as festive rather than as a time for lamentations.

A sequel, or perhaps a fragment of a third version, describes another assembly, convened the following day, again outside the area of the Temple proper. No details describe how the scroll was handled on that occasion, but we are told that "they discovered written in the law" rules that required that every Judean dwell in booths during the Succoth festival. The community's response is described as immediate. Booths were quickly erected, and the community lived in them during the seven days of the holiday, a holiday celebrated by daily reading "in the Book of the Law of God" (Neh. 8:13–18).

Of the text inscribed in Ezra's scroll, we know only that it contained a number of discrete *torot,* and that one dealt with Succoth, and another with foreign wives. Whether the scroll also contained narrative we cannot say, though that possibility cannot be ruled out. While the priestly editor of this history tended to use *Torah* in the limited sense of divine instructions given to priests, the community had long been accustomed to presentation of the tradition that combined narrative and divine law. Law and narrative were often juxtaposed, as in accounts of the earliest covenant renewal ceremonies, which include, beside the list of *torot,* references to God's redemptive acts (see Neh. 9 and 10).

The priests who dominated Jerusalem's political life during the Persian period looked back to Ezra's ceremony as the covenantal act that confirmed their authority and set out the terms of their mandate. These were the men who imagined themselves in Moses' role writing down God's instructions. As Moses' stand-in, Ezra read or had read from "The Book of Moses," which as a *sofer* he might well have inscribed. The official histories present Ezra and his fellow officials as dressed that day in robes appropriate to a ceremony of covenant acclamation. The reading took place on the Temple Mount but outside the Temple precincts, "in the broad place that was before the water gate" (Neh. 8:1). The event is described in constitutional rather than liturgical terms.

The day turned on the scroll. Its contents are obviously of major

interest and concern, but the day did not end with the scroll's conse-
cration. The scroll was blessed, read, interpreted and/or translated,
but not enshrined. We are not even told whether it was placed in the
Temple archives: though that seems its likely fate, no further record
of consultation of Ezra's scroll exists.* A half-millennium later, a talmudic source named a few Torah scrolls it claimed were known to
have been kept in the Temple library before its destruction by the
Romans (70 C.E.); none is identified as Ezra's.

Some students of Jewish history have suggested that the synagogue's practice of reading publicly from the Torah on holidays and
the Sabbath derives from Ezra's public ceremony. Others argue that
Ezra's exaltation of the Torah, the presence of others on the platform, the recitation of prayers before the reading, and the addition
to the reading of an interpretation or translation, suggest that reading from the Torah during public worship was already in the fifth
century B.C.E. a well-established ceremonial routine, probably one
that had its origin in the emerging synagogue; and that the sole
unique aspect of Ezra's ceremony was the content of the scroll.

That the returnees accorded the scroll so much respect, although
many could no longer understand Hebrew, illustrates the power of a
sacred scriptural tongue to transcend its meaning. The scroll may
have been chanted, perhaps to a learning melody such as scribes customarily used to assist them in their work, adding sacred resonances
to the recitation, but also making understanding more difficult.
Scholars speculate that the phrase "and give the interpretation" may
mean that the Levites rendered the text intelligible by translating it
into Aramaic.

The accounts suggest that the scroll commanded respect, ultimately, because it was based on the emperor's authority, which Ezra
used to effect certain reforms in the governance of Jerusalem. Ezra

---

*While the Ezra-Nehemiah history suggests that Ezra's scroll is identical with the Torah text,
the *Letter of Aristeas*—a second-century B.C.E. text—casts doubt on this point. *Aristeas* is an encomium that purports to describe the preparation of the Septuagint, the early third-century
B.C.E. *Koine* (a popular Greek dialect) translation of the Pentateuch which became sacred to
Greek-speaking Jews. *Aristeas* reports that when the king of Egypt, Ptolemy II (*c*.280), requested the Jerusalem high priest to send a proper Hebrew text from the Temple archives to
Alexandria to be the master copy for an official translation, there was no indication that the
text requested was Ezra's scroll which that priest may have placed in the Temple archives.
Certainly, the high priest did not offer to send it.

apparently also used his scroll as a symbol of his mandate from God, almost as an oracle from God brought by a priest, and to buttress his claim that certain *torot,* which he and his caste affirmed, must be enforced if the community wished to be right with God. I suspect that Ezra was a shrewd politician. Where he might simply have recited *torot* and stipulated that they were authentic statements of God's will, he chose to heighten the drama of the occasion by emphasizing certain goals for the community. Apparently, he gained his ends. The community bowed to his will less in deference to the written "proof" he offered than to *force majeure,* the imperial mandate. Nonetheless, what was read out from the scroll had an aura of authenticity. The memories of defeat and exile were still fresh. No one wanted to take any chance that God might have reason again to punish Jerusalem.

During the post-exilic period, images of Moses placing inscribed tablets of stone in the Ark after the Sinai ceremony, and writing out a scroll of *torot,* began to be featured in literary re-creations of those ancient but critical events. Apparently, the familiar version that described the Sinai covenant as an encounter was no longer fully satisfying. People had become accustomed to written records of myths, dynastic histories, and laws as well as of treaties and commercial transactions. The community needed to know that their obligations were fixed, their past chronicled, and the future promise set down. They were to do the right in a culture where right and wrong were treated as definable categories. Many must have felt that the recent disasters were caused not so much by willful disobedience as by confusion over what it was that God required.

Though not a *Sefer Torah,* Ezra's scroll probably contained a substantial part of central legal sections of what became the Book of Deuteronomy. Why Deuteronomy? More than the other four scrolls, Deuteronomy emphasizes the relationship between covenant and divine judgment, a theme of particular interest to a community that had been judged and found wanting and now sought to reorganize itself on the basis of fidelity. Deuteronomy is also the Pentateuchal text that most emphasizes the importance and incomparability of a central shrine.

Also, while Ezra's ceremony apparently took place on Rosh Hashanah and laid specific emphasis on the proper observance of Succoth, there is no mention in the list of laws of Yom Kippur, the Great White Fast which falls between Rosh Hashanah and Succoth. During the post-exilic period, the period in which these chronicles took shape, Yom Kippur was the great day of the Temple year and deemed indispensable to remove the weight of sin from the nation and so assure its future. Its rites were elaborately conducted by priests and supervised by the high priest. Temple priests never ceased to emphasize Yom Kippur's importance and constantly elaborated its rituals. Since it is unlikely that Yom Kippur was not observed in Ezra's day, the most likely explanation of the absence of any mention of it in Ezra's reading is that it was simply not referred to in his scroll. Yom Kippur appears in two lists, Leviticus and Numbers, but is absent from the calendar of holy days in Deuteronomy 16. The absence from one law list of any instruction dealing with the Day of Purgation is not surprising since none of the lists pretend to be exhaustive on any subject. The code that became central in Deuteronomy may have been the source of Ezra's, since it is the one list of holy days that does not include Yom Kippur.*

A likely reconstruction, then, is that Ezra brought with him an anthology of *torot,* probably some version of Deuteronomy, probably one of the lists of *torot* that in our version became the central chapters of the received text. The major question still hangs in the air: What did Ezra think he would accomplish by bringing such a scroll and organizing such a ceremony? We know of no precedent nor of any development in the Persian environment which would have suggested to the Judeans that they should ascribe sanctity and authority to a sacred book. Though many of the Persian priests, the Magi, were literate and displayed what we today would call literary interest—some were, after all, administrators of wealthy institutions and masters of shrine and court schools where Wisdom was taught as well as technical skills—their religious activity focused on the

---

*A scroll that does not mention Yom Kippur might well have been an early version of Deuteronomy, which names Succoth as the Festival of Booths—precisely the title used by the editor of the Ezra histories. One could argue that the chronicler and/or Ezra felt that Jerusalemites observed Yom Kippur appropriately, and therefore there was no need to emphasize that day's proper observances, but in that case, Ezra's general charge of laxity of observance would be unwarranted.

conduct of public ceremonies, the sacrifices, purification rites, and the recital of sacred hymns and magic. Such records as we have of their activity make no mention of the chanting of portions of a sacred text or the adoration and study of a sacred book. Studies of libraries found at Persian shrines and palaces have revealed that they contain collections basically similar to the libraries of the previous millennium. An occasional tablet presents some well-known myth or a coronation hymn or dynastic chronicle, but most entries deal with administrative matters. Not until the second century B.C.E. is there a contemporary description, originating in West Asia, of the reading from a sacred book during a public worship service: the Greek geographer Pausanias described, in a passing note, a service he attended at which Magi read a portion of Zoroaster's teachings (Pausanias, Book of Elis, 27:6).

There is the possibility that Ezra presented the scroll to add significance to the moment and mute complaints about the measures he and his backers intended to impose. Armed with such a "witness," they could say, "It is God, not we, who makes these demands." Presenting the scroll highlighted the authority being demanded by the priest class, whose interests Ezra promoted. Heretofore, priests had served at the altar and consulted the oracles; apparently now they were beginning to claim a broader authority based in part on possession of books containing ancient and sacred traditions that defined the way the community must organize itself if it wished to please God. Those who possessed the records and the skills to consult these texts became God's interpreters, indispensable authorities.

Finally, we cannot, of course, rule out the slight possibility that there was no scroll, and that the record we have represents legendary embellishments of a crucial moment in the people's history dramatized by priest-historians who, in the century after Ezra, prepared such scrolls. If they could put a scroll in Moses' hand, why not in Ezra's?

It is clear that with Ezra's scroll something new was being introduced into, or had developed within, the Judean ethos. For the first time, a story appears that describes the written word being used for its authority. It may be that people simply responded with and to ancient and powerful phrases; but the history, as we have it, does not suggest that everyone ascribed magical power to these teachings. Ezra's accomplishment at the Temple Mount was one of constitutional import whose ends were practical: the plain sense of what was read led to immediate reforms.

THE SCROLL TRADITION AFTER EZRA

Events in the political arena played a large role in this emergence of scripture. Descendants of the royal family apparently incurred the wrath of the Persians by making a bid for power during the first years of the return. That experience suggested to Persian administrators that it might be good policy to send more compliant leaders to reorganize the troubled governance of Judea. Priests, men like Ezra and Nehemiah, who had knowledge of Israel's law and were recognizable figures of authority, filled the bill. Priests had political ambitions, but not kingly ambitions that might trouble the peace of the empire.

This powerful and literate priest group had developed its own version of tradition which it accepted as God's will. It now found itself with a chance to govern Jerusalem, the city where God dwelt as well as where the Temple was located, and which played a central role in the lives of Jews everywhere.

Because the scribal art had developed sufficiently to allow literate people to feel generally confident about reading a document with accuracy, trust in textual evidence grew. The language shift and the community's growing distance from the oral tradition paradoxically played an important role in this new emphasis on written texts. Because everyday life no longer reinforced the oral tradition, records were, for the first time, essential. The exiles, finding themselves in a world with significant literary interest and capacity, had begun to appreciate the larger world more than ever before. Moreover, the development of a scroll tradition was part of a process of bringing together the different traditions into an apparently united presentation which allowed the exiled community to feel that they knew what God demanded of them, how to repent, and how to gain God's forgiveness. The priests benefited from all these developments, as scribes, as interpreters of the tradition, and as leaders of the nation.

Conservative by habit as well as profession and eager to secure their authority against all challenges, priests began to suggest that the gates of prophecy had been closed. Remembering Hosea's and Jeremiah's challenges to priestly claims for the centrality of sacrifices at the Temple altar and the priestly role at those sacrifices, the priests encouraged the populace to see them as the guardians of God's law and to turn to them for its proper interpretation. They wanted Israel to consult God only through them and to break the popular habit of consulting wandering soothsayers or itinerant prophets.

God's speech was affirmed, but since it was generally limited to the distant past, how could God continue to be heard? God's speech could be heard in the books ascribed to Him. Since all reading was aloud, God spoke from the ancient texts whenever someone opened and read one of them. In a society increasingly comfortable with records, it must have seemed natural to argue that authority lay with those who had possession of venerable records, who could consult them and properly decipher their meanings. Records became "proof" against any challenge to priestly authority; and for the priests, possession of records became nine-tenths of charisma.

Here is a fascinating paradox: the priests sponsored continuing work on these scrolls but showed little eagerness to make ceremonial use of the results. The priests made no effort to enshrine the scrolls in some visible place in the sanctuary, nor did they introduce any regimen of readings into Temple ceremony. The scrolls were not publicly paraded. Priests did not convene a council to declare a particular scroll the authorized version, nor did they set scribes to work producing numbers of copies of a "final" edition to be made available for study or worship in communities outside of Jerusalem.

Perhaps the priests acted as they did because they knew of no divine instruction requiring the public presentation, exaltation, or chanting of a text. Or, since various traditions still circulated, the priests may have wanted to avoid debates over which version was the authorized one in order to concentrate on establishing their authority in other matters. Priests did not treat these works as reserved texts that they alone could consult. There seems to have been no attempt to deny public access to these scrolls. We know of no attempt made by priests to preclude others from making copies or from owning their own texts—an attitude that distinguishes them from similar priest groups in Egypt and Babylonia who carefully guarded the "secrets" of their cult, including the scrolls in which such secrets were inscribed. This attitude toward texts remained characteristic of Judaism. Evidence of this open approach to Torah appears in fourth-century iconography. In the Mithra Temple at Dura a central image is a magician with his sacred scroll closed in his hand (now in the Yale University Art Gallery, reproduced in Goodenough 1964, fig. 140). In the synagogue at Dura a man, without any sign of office and variously called by scholars "Moses," "Ezra," or "a laymen," is represented reading the open scroll of the *Sefer Torah* (reproduced in Goodenough 1964, plate 5). Still, the Torah books were of particular importance to Judah's priests not only in presenting the nation's literature but also in providing written certification of priestly rank and role.

The priests' power to define God's rules did not go unchallenged. Over the next century or so, writings appear attacking the thesis that God requires that gentile wives be set aside. The author of the Book of Ruth makes a heroine of a Moabite wife, a gentile, and rewards her loyalty to her Israelite mother-in-law not only with a happy second marriage to a well-to-do Israelite but by allotting her a place of honor in the ancestry of King David and, by extension, of the Messiah. Similarly, the poetry of Song of Songs celebrates a prince's love for a girl who is not one of the "daughters of Jerusalem" (1:5).

A major step toward the emergence of Torah as scripture had been taken, but Ezra's text was still more record than scripture. It was not enshrined or apparently consulted. Primary authority still lay in the oral tradition—as can be seen in many ways, not least the way phrases, ideas, and incidents appear and reappear, showing that they were clearly part of the living tradition. People knew the traditions. Jeremiah's prophecy of a return after seventy years of exile is cited in four or five different contexts. The famous litany Moses is said to have used at Mt. Sinai—"The Lord, The Lord God, is merciful, gracious, long suffering and abundant in mercy and ever true"

(Exod. 34:6–7)—appears in various forms at least half a dozen times in biblical literature. Tradition was cited, but there is no record from the Persian period of anyone citing a text directly from a scroll, and little evidence that scribes and rhapsodists felt the need for absolute accuracy in transcription. Any taboos there may have been against writing down the traditions had long since disappeared, but the reverse taboos which would protect the Torah's sacredness had not yet emerged. There were as yet no special rules governing the writing or handling of a Torah scroll.

For some centuries, during and after the Persian period, these scrolls played a larger role in the schoolhouse than in the sanctuary. Some scrolls may have been used at informal meetings, but if they were, the reading had no set form. Any readings on the holidays would not have been from an authorized text nor would they have followed a set form. In different places, Jews read from entirely different texts. There were not yet enough scrolls to enable every village to have one or more; manuscripts were growing more numerous but were still relatively rare and costly. Many readings, like those for the Passover, were undoubtedly still oral recitations.

But a new attitude was in the air, evident in the version that reports that Ezra limited his role to praising and exalting the scrolls and left to certain Levites the task of reading and interpreting them. On its face, this version is unlikely. Extensive and time-consuming preparation would have been required for the readers to get the reading right, yet we are told that Ezra had just arrived. Behind this detail there may be a reference to the fact that during the fifth century some Levites took on the responsibility to make known to the nation at large the increasingly unified tradition Temple scribes were recording. A tradition recorded in Chronicles describes the Levites as circuit-riding teachers who "taught in Judah having the Book of the Law with them" (2 Chron. 17:9). Morton Smith and other late-twentieth-century scholars have observed that the narratives of this period (Chronicles, Ezra, and Nehemiah) seem to be full of what look suspiciously like brief sermons which may reflect the work and the techniques of such teachers (1979, p. 258, n.42).

Indeed, the Persian age is full of literary interests: Chronicles-Ezra-Nehemiah (the so-called priestly history), Job, Ruth, Jonah, Tobit,

Song of Songs, and various biographies of the prophets and some psalms appeared at this time. By the late fifth century B.C.E., texts of the Five Scrolls of the Pentateuch and of the major prophets had achieved much the form with which we are familiar. Unfortunately, there is little available information about how these scrolls were used.

The community increasingly found in written records a source of certainty about their way of life: they were living as God intended them to live. The presence of such records, like the stones at Canaanite altars, served as witness to the power and presence of God's prophecies. The narratives "proved" His control of history, and the laws symbolized God's eternal covenant with Israel.

Increasingly, there were two sources of authority: the oral culture and the written word. Tradition and text were becoming separate categories of religious activity. The oral tradition continued to develop and to have force, particularly among the nonliterate portions of the population. The élite were coming to see parts of the oral tradition as folklore and to argue that only a carefully preserved text could be completely trusted. The text came to be used by the literate élite against the more flexible and less organized tradition of the populace as a means to enforce conformity. It is clear that intellectuals increasingly turned to texts—both those that became parts of the Bible and those that did not—for serious and sophisticated guidance; and it seems equally clear that, while the oral tradition continued in full force, in their limited ways the nonliterate, too, began to feel the significance of the nation's documents.

The biblical canon ends abruptly and confusedly with the events that centered on Ezra's career, the acceptance of the terms of the covenant he imposed, the development of a new basis of financial support for the shrine, and the purification of Jerusalem (that is, the separation of the alien wives). The priest-editors of the canon were interested in writing a history that would legitimize their claim to authority and assert and underscore their understanding of the "rewards and punishments" of covenant loyalty.

During the nearly three centuries after Ezra, much happened in Israel's religious development—almost all of it, unfortunately, hidden from view. During this time, Ezra's one partial scroll is replaced by five, which are fleshed out and broadly accepted as constitutional and inspired. By the end of the Persian period, Torah has become the *Sefer Torah,* but it is highly unlikely that any other scrolls had as yet gained uncontested authority as the authentic statement of God's will.

We know exasperatingly little about the details of life in Judea from roughly the middle of the fifth to the end of the third century B.C.E. After Ezra, only one name emerges, a priest, Simon the Just, whom the rabbis describe as the last of the *soferim.* Simon is extravagantly praised for piety, demeanor, and leadership (Wisdom of Ben Sirah, second century B.C.E.; 2 Macc., first century C.E.; Josephus; and the Talmud [b. Yoma 39b; Tos. Sotah 13.7]), but what he actually accomplished is never made clear, nor are the sources in agreement about his dates. We are not even sure whether there were one or two men of the same name.*

What little we know suggests that the religious leaders of the time, whoever they were, were, like Ezra, priest-magistrates; and that their authority was dynastic and Temple-centered, not book-centered. The altar was still primary. But a second front in the struggle for religious authority was beginning to open: During the centuries of Persian rule, the authority of the Jerusalem priest-scribes grew, and the scrolls they compiled began to gain a special place in Israel's religious life. Bit by bit, the psychological and spiritual foundations were laid for the acceptance of sacred scrolls as scripture. The simple fact that these scrolls existed gave them importance. That they could be seen and read aloud gave them standing. The scrolls became known as presenting venerable matters. They were written in the original language of the tradition, in classic Hebrew, which the community associated with its origin and knew as God's own language. Some portions claimed to be in God's own words. The text contained God's special name. An aura of magic began to surround these writings. No one doubted that God had spoken, or that His words could be heard again when

---

*Ben Sirah describes Simon as a high priest who fortified the Temple with high double walls, built stone houses and cisterns in the city to enable it to withstand a siege, and was a prepossessing figure when he served at the altar and a priest whose blessing was known to be powerful (Wisdom of Ben Sirah 50). A rabbinic tradition from half a millennium later mentions Simon as the last of the high priests actually to speak aloud the Tetragrammaton, God's miracle-working name.

these scrolls were read. They were identified in popular history with Moses writing down what God had told him at Sinai. Priests consulted them, and priest-scribes found reason to busy themselves with them.

Texts became a part of the sanctified tradition—a part, but not the whole. No one yet looked on these texts as the only authoritative statements of the tradition or as a complete statement of its fundamental teachings. Life was still governed primarily by edict and ancient custom. The ascription of an all-embracing holiness to these scrolls would come later, and with it the problem of defending a limited set of writings as all-inclusive and a particular set of formulations as normative.

A consonantal text of the books of Pentateuch and the Prophets in pretty much the form we know must have been in circulation by the time the Persian era ends (330 B.C.E.); but there were not insignificant variations of language, presentation, spelling, and even text, which would continue to trouble scribes for centuries. Books claiming plenary authority for their particular list of *torot* circulated. The lists and narratives that qualified as scripture clearly were accepted as part of the tradition. The existence of variant versions helps explain the numerous differences between the Hebrew text and the texts used as the basis for early translations into Greek (Septuagint, third century B.C.E.). Centuries later, rabbinic midrash would frequently cite one or another variant reading, of which some may represent scribal error but some had a long history as accepted variations. Standardization increased; but given the manuscript tradition and the fact that the scrolls were not used ceremonially in the Temple, there was little pressure to get it all straight. As texts multiplied and as respect grew for the written word, varying degrees of authority were ascribed to the separate works, but there was as yet no agreement on every letter or every phrase or even every sentence. Memory was becoming text, but text had not yet become scripture.

DEFINING THE
FIRST SCRIPTURE:
THE TORAH

Unveil my eyes that I may behold wondrous things from
out of your Torah.
—Psalm 119:18

Over the generations following Ezra's mission to Jerusalem, the five
separate scrolls we now know as the *Sefer Torah*, the scrolls attributed
to individual prophets, and the two extended histories edited by
priest-scribes largely in Jerusalem, were in approximately their present form and on the way to becoming the three-tiered Hebrew scripture. Portions and fragments of various Hebrew texts found in the
Dead Sea caves above Qumran suggest the process: some were destined for inclusion in the Hebrew scripture, and some were destined
to be set aside as the faith tradition was redefined. In Egypt, beginning in the third century B.C.E., there appeared Greek translations of
some Hebrew scrolls—the most important those that came to be

known under the umbrella label of Septuagint, which included the first translation of the *Sefer Torah* done in any language. Work on the translation of the biblical corpus seems at first to have concentrated on the Five Scrolls of the Pentateuch but soon extended to the whole published text as the work of definition continued over half a millennium.

THE GREEK DIASPORA

The communities of West Asia had been subject to Greek influences for some time before their conquest by Alexander and his armies in 330 B.C.E. But it was only after the Greeks established control over the area that their cultural impact became pervasive. The Judeans who had remained during the Persian period what they had always been, primarily an agricultural and pastoral community, now found themselves increasingly urbanized and engaged in commerce.

Jerusalem, the capital, grew substantially. Under Persia, Jerusalem had been a theocracy where activity was carefully regulated by Torah rules which the priests insisted were God's instructions. Since its reconstruction, the Jerusalem Temple had become the unrivaled religious center of the whole Jewish world. Every Jew, no matter where he lived, paid an annual half-shekel tax toward its upkeep.

Jews lived in Judea and throughout West Asia and Egypt. By the second century B.C.E., Alexandria, the new city built in Egypt by Alexander's generals, was well on its way to becoming the region's most populous and prosperous city of Hellenistic times (late fourth century B.C.E. to first century C.E.) and home to a sizable and increasingly prosperous and cultivated Judean population. Jews had lived there since the king's father and city founder, Ptolemy I, fearful of populating his new capital with potentially rebellious natives, had brought a Judean labor battalion down to Egypt to help build his city and protect his rule, and then had allowed them to stay. Alexandria was from the first a remarkable success, and the Jews flourished with it.

For the Greeks, with their lively interest in literature, books played a central role in the definition of culture. Besides numerous private collections, the Greeks established and lavishly endowed libraries in Pergamon (by the Attalids), Antioch (by the Seleucids), and Alexandria (by the Ptolemies). By some estimates, in the first century B.C.E. half a million parchment or papyrus items were available in the Museum Library of Alexandria and another one hundred thousand in its companion across the park, the Serapeum. Unlike the peoples of Asia, Greeks wrote books and signed their names to their works. Under Greek influence, for the first time West Asians began to recognize that a book could be a shaped and self-contained work presenting a consistent and individual point of view.

Greek scribes had refined the techniques of manuscript production and editing, and developed sophisticated techniques which enabled them to clarify the grammar and construction of classical texts, fix their presentation, and determine the most reliable of several manuscript traditions. "Authoritative" texts of many works were established, and scholia—marginal comments which discussed doubtful spelling, the meaning of unusual words and forms, apparent omissions or repetitions, and so forth—were added to the more important works. Measured by these standards, Judean editorial work was primitive; but stimulated by contact with the Hellenistic ethos, local scribes soon caught up, and a great age of writing and scroll production began.

The importance of the Greek alphabet's technical advance over the Aramaic and Hebrew, particularly its introduction of vowels, is evident in the greater number of works prepared for Greek-speaking Jews compared with those in Aramaic and Hebrew. Greek works were easier to edit and read. A translation service from Hebrew and Aramaic into Greek seems to have operated in Jerusalem, perhaps in the Temple itself. There is no record of a similar service designed to translate Greek scrolls into Hebrew or Aramaic. It was among the Greek-speaking diaspora population that the first tentative experiments with a vowel system for the Hebrew-Aramaic alphabet appeared.

Literacy spread rapidly among the Judeans, as it tends to do among people who move from farms and villages into towns, where commerce requires them to read contracts and do numbers. The available copies of well-known manuscripts increased significantly.* We begin to hear of scrolls written by a single author on such diverse subjects as medicine, history, astronomy, and even the esoteric meaning of a prophet's speeches. Early in the second century B.C.E., the schoolmaster Ben Sirah had an academy in Jerusalem which must have had a library of some size, as did the monastic community of Qumran. The Temple had a sizable archive, as did most shrines, where scrolls were deposited for safekeeping.

The Hellenistic ethos was, at least among upper-class Jews, highly literate, book-oriented, and inclined to endow classic texts with an aura of sacredness and to discover in them depths of meaning the original authors may well not have intended. Jews had entered an age in which the community, or at least its leading lights, were beginning to look to books for religious guidance and to assume that knowledge of what was in them provided a blueprint for community organization.

Torah in Hellenistic times meant law and, broadly, tradition. The prophetic books were trusted but read separately from the five books of *Sefer Torah*. Writings, sometimes ascribed to "the Fathers," seem to have varied. *Mikra*, the rabbinic term for *scripture*, does not yet appear in the literature; nor does the acronym for the three-tiered scripture, *Tanakh* (*T*=Torah, *N*=*Neviim* [Prophets], *K*=*Ketuvim* [Writings]), a concept of rabbinic times.

THE EDITORIAL PROCESS

About the use of scrolls during the informal meetings in those institutions that go by the awkward name of "proto-synagogue," we know too little to speak with any confidence. On Sabbath and holy day, portions from a Torah scroll, the Psalms, or perhaps a prophet's message may have been recited or read, but there was no formal schedule

---

*Writing in the first century B.C.E., a courtier of the Hasmoneans, who ruled Judea from the mid-second to mid-first century B.C.E., reports, probably inaccurately, that Nehemiah in the fifth century had established a library in Jerusalem in which he had collected "books about the kings and prophets, and the writings of David and letters of kings about votive offerings," but further reports, probably reliably, that Judah Maccabee also "collected all the books that had been lost on account of the war" (2 Macc. 2:13–14).

of readings; and where scrolls were chanted, practice must have varied from place to place. Such readings may have occasionally been taken from works that would not be included in the Hebrew scriptures. We simply do not know which scrolls Ben Sirah's grandson had in mind when he described his grandfather's curriculum as "The Law, the Prophets and other writings of the Fathers" (prologue).

The ordinary Jew probably knew that the Exodus story was central, and the story of Samson and Delilah less so, since he rehearsed the Exodus deliverance every Passover and heard about Samson only on the occasional visit of a wandering storyteller or professional reader. If he thought about it, as he probably did not, he might have sensed that there must be some gradations of authority among the scrolls. But he probably never saw all the scrolls finally included in the Hebrew scriptures, and certainly never in one place, bound together, and designated as scripture. In the way of laymen in all generations, he left these issues to the few who took them seriously.

The first solid evidence that any group of Jews had adopted a discipline centered on the study of venerated texts comes from the records of the millenarian sect whose headquarters were at Qumran (second century B.C.E. to first century C.E.): The congregation was to "watch in community for a third of every night of the year, to read the Book and study Law." Of the community council, one of ten was "to study The Law, continually, day and night" for the improvement of all (*Manual of Discipline* VI:4–8, in Vermes 1987). The purpose of this study was to uncover "hidden things," a term that seems to have included both the sect's special interpretations of the Torah laws and its understanding of God's plans for redemption and End Time. This sect sometimes called itself "the men of truth who are doers of the Torah" (*Commentary on Habakkuk* VII:10–11).

During this period, the Prophets had a status equal to the Pentateuch as a source of ultimate truths and were avidly studied for their secrets. That the prophetic speech witnessed to God's justice and set forth the sacred promises in Hebrew, God's own language, commanded respect. Prophecy recorded God's original bond with the Jewish nation, proved His just treatment of its people, and stated God's promise of national redemption. Obedience was crucial: "If you agree and give heed you will eat the good things of the earth but if you refuse and disobey, you will be devoured by the sword" (Isa. 1:19–20). The Teacher of Righteousness who in the second century B.C.E. founded the monastic community of Qumran drew his special knowledge primarily from his inspired understanding of the work of such prophets as Isaiah and Habakkuk. He and his followers thanked God, for God had "caused me to know Thy wondrous mysteries" (Hymns IV:27–28).

In respect to the two histories (the Deuteronomic Joshua-Judges-Samuel-Kings and the priestly Chronicles-Ezra-Nehemiah), their editors made no claim to be setting down revealed or inspired material. The histories had been shaped to make the point that all that had happened to Israel and Judah was explained by the operation of the covenant. Israel's history was set forth as an object lesson in the value of covenant faithfulness. God's justice and mercy were revealed through His control of the destiny of Israel and the nations; as He had promised, so it had happened. God's dependability gave Israel reason for hope. God had told the people the consequences of covenant disloyalty, and Israel had been punished; but God had also promised the people that His anger would not burn forever, and they would be redeemed. The histories told them they could also depend on that promise.

As during Hellenistic times an increasing number of Jews outside the priest class became literate and were able to study the writings, new issues arose: Who had authority to interpret those texts? Which texts were authoritative? How much authority was to be reserved for community practice, the unwritten tradition, what we would call common law? For example, not all groups had the same writings. The Sadducees, a conservative landowning group, accepted as authority—in addition to the Law, the Prophets, and other writings—a Book of Decrees of which unfortunately no trace remains. The Pharisees, a table fellowship who had set for themselves particularly stringent standards of purity and tithing and thought of themselves as another priestly élite, accepted the Law and the Prophets and a limited number of writings together with an oral tradition based largely on text interpretations shaped in their circles. Groups of apocalyptics had their own understanding of the Prophets, and their *torot* differed in part from those in the received text. Ascetic communities like the Essenes had, in addition to the *Sefer*

Torah and the Prophets, their own scrolls, such as the *Manual of Discipline*. Variety rather than uniformity was the hallmark of the age; and, paradoxically, the emergence of accepted texts encouraged greater variety of interpretation. As modern literary critics have shown, a text can be construed to mean almost anything.

The Jewish historian Josephus revealed his hopes and those of the Pharisees among whom he had trained, rather than the actual state of affairs in first-century Judea, when he wrote: "We have not an innumerable multitude of books among us, disagreeing from and contradicting one another [as the Greeks have], but only twenty-two books which contain the records of all the past times, which are justly believed to be divine and of them five belong to Moses which contain his laws and the traditions of the origin of mankind till his death" (*Contra Apion* 1:8). In fact, there were many texts, with more appearing all the time. Some were simply other versions of well-known narratives and oracles. Others were entirely new. An occasional work like Tobit floats outside the scope of scriptural narrative, but most of the story scrolls that were not canonized were somehow connected to the biblical text. Susanna provided another illustration of Daniel's wisdom, as did Bel and the Dragon. The Prayer of Azariah and the Song of the Three Young Men, with their theme of religious loyalty, were placed between two verses in the third chapter of Daniel. There is no way to know why such material as the prose biography of Jeremiah was canonized and the Epistle of Jeremiah was not: perhaps it was simply that one tradition came into the hands of the right scribe at an appropriate time, and the other did not. Some judgments reflect the seriousness of the material involved; others were simply serendipitous. Contrary to most modern assumptions, the decisions to include or exclude were sometimes made for reasons as superficial as a scribe finding empty space available at the end of a scroll he had just copied, and filling it with something he liked.

Sometime in the third century of the Common Era, the rabbis finally settled on a table of contents for scripture, whose order to this day governs the masoretic text. This table of contents numbered twenty-two books, with Judges-Ruth and Jeremiah-Lamentations considered as two, rather than four, books. It seems to have been desirable to have twenty-two books in the Hebrew scriptures to correspond to the twenty-two letters in the Hebrew alphabet. Since the alphabet was seen as containing all the building blocks out of which the universe is constructed, and served also as Israel's numeration system, this equation suggested that all knowledge was to be found in these texts.

No one could play such a numbers game until there was a consensus on which books were accepted as scripture. Agreement was fully achieved only after the rabbis emerged as the leaders of a reconstructed Judaism in the period after the destruction of the Second Temple in 70 c.e. Until then, there were many books in existence, all that became scripture and all that did not.

A first-century c.e. scroll, 2 Esdras, describes how Ezra, under divine inspiration, produces a copy of all the sacred books after they have been incinerated in a fire. Ezra, we are told, dictated to secretaries ninety-two books. Ezra is instructed: "Make public the twenty-two books that you wrote first and let the worthy and unworthy read them: but keep the seventy that were written last in order to give them to the wise among your people for in them is the spring of understanding, the fountain of wisdom, and the river of knowledge" (14:45–47). For the author of Esdras, as for the Essenes' Teacher of Righteousness two centuries earlier, the most precious knowledge, essentially that which deals with eschatology, lay outside the twenty-two books that became scripture.

Even as late as the early talmudic period, there were still debates about whether certain scrolls should be included or excluded from a collection that had not yet been named or defined. Editorial consistency is one hallmark of an active push for a text's unity, yet editors still apparently felt no need to remove or resolve all divergent descriptions of the same event or different presentations of the same speech when these appear in the Deuteronomic and priestly histories. Even the Ten Commandments appear in slightly different forms in Exodus and Deuteronomy, as in their separate explanations for the rules of Sabbath observance. Nor do the scrolls present the ten Instructions in the same order: "You shall not murder" precedes "You shall not steal" in the masoretic, Samaritan, and Qumran texts, and in Josephus, but follows it in the Septuagint and Philo.

Studies by J. A. Sanders of Dead Sea psalm manuscripts found in the Qumran caves give us an idea of the editing and publishing process as it operated at a fairly late stage in the development of the Psalter (1967). Several psalms appear that are not found in our Psalter. There are differences in the brief programmatic notes that preface psalms, variations in the order in which the psalms are presented, and slight textual variations in language between versions. A number of the Dead Sea texts, like that of Psalm 145, reproduce a congregational refrain after each verse ("Praised be the Lord and praised be His name forever and ever")—a practice only occasionally followed in the received text. Sanders argues that a broad consensus governing the presentation of the Psalms was in place by the first century B.C.E., but that scribes still felt free to make additions, elaborations, or even revisions. Scrolls were formed but not yet fixed.

Variations are even more apparent in the sectarian literature and in individual works not accepted into the canon. Jubilees presents a different version of the narratives of Genesis and of the early sections of Exodus and differs from the canon text in many details, most dramatically in certain *torot* and in describing a lunar calendar that varies considerably from that of the accepted text. Its Sabbath laws are more detailed and stricter than the *Sefer Torah*'s, and are described as having been revealed to Abraham rather than to Moses (20:4). The fact that portions of several copies of Jubilees were found in the Dead Sea caves, along with portions of the Pentateuch, suggests that these versions were accepted as complementary.

Late in the Hellenistic period, the Pharisees, whose way of faith depended on precision, would begin to press for a more rigorous definition of the acceptable and the unacceptable. But most Jews of the time were not particularly involved; as long as dues were regularly paid to the Temple and the cult was in operation, most were satisfied. Still, the idea that Judaism could be defined by holy texts was beginning to emerge—for example, in the writings of the Essenes, who reserved their secrets to the initiated and looked on any outside their circle as blind to the saving truths. In such sectarian circles, conflicting claims to Torahic authority could lead to bitter dispute. In one of the *Hodayot*, or hymns of the Qumran community, the author speaks of "Teachers of

Lies" who scheme to entice believers "to exchange the Torah engraved on my heart by Thee for the smooth things which they speak to Thy people" (Hymns IV:10–11).

The *Damascus Document,* which served as the constitution of the Qumran community, openly challenged the claim that the lists of Instructions in the Five Books contained the full text of revelation: "He (God) made His covenant with Israel for ever, revealing to them the hidden things in which all Israel had gone astray" (III:13–14). When the Qumran texts praised the *Osey ha-Torah,* those who follow the Torah law, they were referring to those who followed their Torah and calendar rather than the general run of Judeans who knew and obeyed only the generally accepted text.

Samaritan leaders cherished the Five Scrolls of the Torah and only those scrolls. Their text was similar to that of the Judeans but included in the Ten Commandments a requirement that an altar be built on Mount Gerizim and sacrifices be offered there. It also changed Mount Ebal to Mount Gerizim (Deut. 27:4) as the place where the first altar was to be erected in the Promised Land—a change that made the Judeans consider the Samaritans schismatics because it cast doubts on the primacy of the Temple in Jerusalem.

The recently published *Temple Scroll* (second century B.C.E.) included *torot* sacred to the Dead Sea community but unknown to the received text: animals could be slaughtered only by priests in the Temple, and all sexual intercourse was banned in the holy city. It also required that priests celebrate an annual ordination festival and participate in several otherwise unknown agricultural festivals: one celebrating the first fruits of the vine; another, the first fruits of the orchard; and another, the first waving of a newly cut barley sheaf. Unless we dismiss the narrative and law traditions of various groups as deliberate forgeries or the idiosyncratic writings of some "inspired" individual, it is at least apparent that religious attitudes of one or another group of Judeans are reflected in such texts.

The decisions to include or exclude were ultimately determined by extrinsic as well as intrinsic factors. The Law, the Prophets, and the Psalms were the heart of the tradition and the first to be accepted by all. Other scrolls were judged by other criteria. That the canon turned out as it did was not a resolution of conflicting claims about which version God preferred, but a reflection of the fact that certain scrolls were cherished by the group of sages who ultimately gained sway. In the end, those sages limited the library of venerated work to the texts they found fully acceptable.

Minor textual variations could become significant. The Israeli archeologist and scholar, Yigael Yadin, in his careful analysis of the *Temple Scroll*, has shown how the author quotes from a text substantially similar to the known text but at times in a slightly different mode (1983). Such "slight" differences must not be overlooked since a different text inevitably led to interpretations other than the normative ones. The *Temple Scroll* declared that the king may not marry more than one wife, and insisted that his wife be from his father's tribe and family, a rule apparently based on the textual tradition that also lies behind the Septuagint rule (Lev. 21:13) governing the marriage of a high priest: "He shall take to wife [*wife*, not *wives*] a virgin of his own people [not from another family]." The rabbinic tradition based on Deuteronomy 17 would rule that the king "may choose for himself wives, of the daughters of priests, Levites or Israelites"—in short, any Jewish woman (Tos. San. 4:2).

Scrolls circulated that contained versions of the early narratives and variant lists of *torot* as well as speeches and biographies of the prophets. Several chapters at the end of the scrolls of Jeremiah and 2 Kings concerning the last days of the kingdom of Judah are in all respects identical. Isaiah 2 and Micah 4 present an identical end-of-days oracle. The scrolls that include such repetitions seem to have developed independently and circulated independently.

In many cases, there were still open questions about which text tradition of a particular scroll was the preferred one. Corrections made by a scribe to one of the Dead Sea Scrolls are almost all in the direction of the version that became the accepted text; corrections made by another scribe to a scroll of Deuteronomy take it further away from our text. Our Jeremiah text differs considerably from scrolls that served as the basis of the Septuagint translation. A psalm scroll from Qumran divides some of the poetic units differently from the accepted text and contains several hymns not included in the one hundred fifty presented in the Psalter. The two Isaiah scrolls found in cave 1 at Qumran differ from each other and from our text not only in script—one was written in the old *Ketav Ivri*; the other, in the newer, square *Ashurit*—spelling, and grammar but also in content. Such variations testify to an active interest in literature and to an attitude that did not yet consider such works sacrosanct. These distinct textual traditions were not yet sufficiently disturbing to prompt the community to appoint a commission to declare one scroll authorized and another suspect. Scribes and readers chose whichever version appealed to them, or perhaps simply whatever text was available. While the talmudic "history" written later must be rejected as anachronistic, there was by late Hellenistic times broad acceptance of a particular textual stream for the *Sefer Torah* scrolls and the prophetic books, and acknowledgment of their special role in the community's life. A faith that had been essentially bipolar—tradition and the Temple—was becoming tripolar: tradition, Temple, and text. Two of these three poles, Temple and text, were controlled by an élite, disparate but nonetheless an élite: those who were born to the priestly caste, and those who could read and took the effort to master the texts.

Besides the Law, the Prophets, and the Psalms, scribes in Hellenistic Judea worked on histories, Wisdom, and, increasingly, on apocalypse (Daniel, the last half of Zechariah, Enoch, Esdras). Apocalyptic interests peaked during the Maccabean revolt and the early Roman centuries when the belief was widely held that the millennium was at hand and the kingdom of God just beyond. Apocalypse presents the history of the future and deals with such themes as the ultimate fate of Israel and the nations. It generally took the form of a report by someone who had been allowed to enter heaven and read there from the book of the future, or who had heard from some heavenly personage revelations about the future. Apocalypse might also be presented as an esoteric commentary on some well-known prophecy that revealed the *razim*, secret information about End Time. The Essenes treasured scrolls of *Pesharim*, eschatological interpretations of biblical material (Habakkuk, Isaiah, Nahum, Micah, Hosea, and Psalms) in which the sect's founder, the Teacher of Righteousness, passed on esoteric explanations of textual meaning. The scrolls containing these secrets were zealously guarded by the Essenes lest their secrets be revealed to the unworthy. Had this material been of critical interest to the later rabbis, some of it would undoubtedly have been included in the scriptural anthology.

For the first time in Judea and the diaspora, writings were authorized or composed by known contemporaries: Ben Sirah, the Teacher of Righteousness, Artapanus, Ezekiel the Tragedian. Histories appear (the Hasmonean Chronicles, Artapanus) as do collections of Wisdom (Ben Sirah), novellas (Tobit, Judith), and hymns (Qumran's thanksgiving hymns).

The Hellenistic world delighted in moralistic biography, books designed to provide readers with upright and virtuous heroes whose lives could serve as compelling examples of noble character. In addition to Daniel, Judith, Hannah, and the Maccabees, the patriarchs were generally portrayed costumed in nobility. Abraham is zealous for God even to the point of burning down an idolatrous shrine (Jubilees 12:12). He meets every test of loyalty to God with patient endurance and is often depicted, as are the other patriarchs, giving high-minded advice to his family gathered about his deathbed.

Interest in literature was evidently even greater in the Greek-speaking Egyptian diaspora than in Judea. Philo devoted a whole volume to a panegyric to Moses (*Vita Moysis*). There historians (Artapanus, Eupolemos), philosophers (Philo), and even playwrights (Ezekiel) plied their trade. The Greek-speaking world produced histories, books of Wisdom, novellas, testimonies, and extensive commentaries.

Not all contemporary lists of venerated scrolls are identical or even complete. The Greek-speaking diaspora developed its own table of contents, known as the Septuagint. The sectarians at Qumran also developed their own consensus over several hundred years.

There was as yet no agreed-on formal method for the presentation of venerated writings. Most scrolls were set out in the new square script (*Ashurit*), but others continued to be written in the older *Ketav Ivri*. Still, the scrolls had achieved a recognizable role in the life of the community. Among the scribes and those who cared, there was now heightened interest in establishing a "correct" text. Many questions of orthography, spelling, and word division were resolved. Versions were compared, and decisions made. Issues of particular concern included syntax, spelling, word division, and pagination as well as scribal glosses or corrections which had mistakenly entered into the body of the text, often resulting in a conflated reading.

During Hellenistic times, the scribes who worked on these scrolls did not feel constrained from making minor changes in spelling or orthography, even from deleting sentences. Torah and Prophetic rolls found in the Qumran caves included letters that had been struck out and words inserted above other words. The Law, the Prophets, and the Psalms carried a large and increasing measure of authority but, in these pre-rabbinic centuries, had not yet fully graduated to the rank of scripture, in which it is crucial that every word and every letter be presented accurately and copied faithfully. Rabbinic Judaism would later require that a scribe who made an error in copying a single letter of a Torah scroll carefully erase it and get it right; mortals are not allowed to tinker with God's words.

Judean scribes began to develop a Masorah, a tradition of proper scriptural presentation under careful editorial supervision; and soon Hebrew scholia began to appear on textual matters, spelling, word division, and meaning. Although no text of the early Masorah survives, some of its methods can be deduced from Qumran scrolls surviving from this period and from comments on masoretic issues that found their way into rabbinic writings; in reading aloud, certain traditions had developed that were incorporated into the written text, such as the observation: "*Ha-Er* is written, but we read *Hatzer*" (b. Eruv. 26a to 2 Kings 20:4). Researchers have discovered among the various manuscript fragments of the *Sefer Torah* in the Qumran materials evidence of textual and orthographic variations, although most of the Qumran manuscripts were written with care and represent a single text tradition. Editorial judgment comes into play. Rather elegant theories of textual criticism are discussed. Scholarly and literary motivation play increasingly important roles in what can for the first time honestly be called a literary enterprise.

The five scrolls of the Law and the scrolls of the Prophets were among the first on which this effort was concentrated. Great care was taken to establish their correct texts. The Talmud describes *Magihei Sefarim*, investigators of texts, who were responsible for examining Torah scrolls to ensure that they were free from error, and suggests that these scribes were paid from Temple funds (b. Ket. 106a). Such detail puts a bit too much of an administrative gloss on what was certainly a less than formally organized process, but editorial work was in progress. Hebrew scrolls were beginning to get the attention Greeks normally gave to written documents. Indeed, several legends surrounding the "officially accepted" Torah translation into demotic Greek, the Septuagint, suggest a felt need among Jews to confirm that they treated their books with at least the same care as the Greeks.

TORAH IN GREEK: THE SEPTUAGINT

It is hard to assess how much Greek assumptions about the importance of a constitution affected the emergence of the Five Scrolls as pre-eminent within the Jewish tradition. In the Greek-speaking diaspora *Nomos*, "law," was the term most often used to translate *Torah*. On the one hand, *Nomos* suggested a narrower range of meanings than Torah: law rather than tradition. On the other, it extended the meaning of Torah by associating it with the idea of a constitution. Constitutions were much prized in the Hellenistic world. In providing the basis of a human community that conformed to the laws of the universe, they defined the right and set standards for every citizen. To have a constitution was proof that one belonged to a civilized community. Having become in a relatively short time both numerous and prosperous, Alexandrian Jewry needed a constitution for practical political reasons and for cultural self-respect.

In the apologetic literature, we find Moses pictured as a Hebrew Solon and the claim, which seems to have satisfied the Jews who made it, that they possessed not only a constitution but *the* constitution, God's own. Jews could and did say not only, "We, too, have good laws," but also, "Our law is older and better." Apologetes knew few limits to their enthusiasm for the law. One claimed that Moses taught law to Plato. The philosopher Philo took the matter more seriously. His depiction of Moses in *Vita Moysis* as a paragon embodying all the accepted virtues was a way of underscoring the unique virtues of the law itself. Moses' law was a reflection of his moral and spiritual perfection. Philo also made the somewhat inconsistent argument that the Torah's superiority derived from its author—not, like Solon or Lycurgus, mere mortal, but God.

The author of *Aristeas*, too, translated Torah as *Nomos*, "law"—a practice followed in most of the Greek writings by Jews. *Aristeas* describes how an authoritative translation of the Five Books of Moses into demotic Greek was completed in Alexandria during the reign of Ptolemy II (285–47 B.C.E.). This translation of the Five Scrolls is commonly called the Septuagint on the basis of *Aristeas'* report that seventy-two scholars had worked in separate cells on the translation, and that their individual efforts had agreed in every detail. It became for the Jews of the Egyptian diaspora the equivalent of Solon's laws, a divinely appointed constitution for their community.

The account of *Aristeas* is legendary, probably written in Judea rather than Egypt well over a century after the events it claims to describe. The author seems to have had several purposes in mind: to validate the miraculous accuracy of the translation against all challenges; to suggest that it contained all meanings and, therefore, shared the authority God had placed in the Hebrew original; and to praise its value as a constitution so Jews need not feel culturally inferior to the Greeks to whom a constitution was the absolutely indispensable foundation of any civilized community. Indeed, Jews could legitimately feel superior because their constitution alone was divine.

Aristeas reports that the court of Ptolemy was urged by one Demetrius, the founding administrator of the famous Museum Library, to request a translation of the Five Scrolls. Demetrius, we are told, informed his royal patron that the library needed a Greek language version of the "Book of the Law of the Jews," presumedly to give the court access to reliable information about the laws of the Jews, a sizable and flourishing segment of the Alexandrian community. Demetrius asked for translators "who have led exemplary lives and are experts in their own law . . . so that when we have examined wherein the majority agree the work of making an accurate translation can proceed" (I:32). His letter indicates that the library owned manuscripts of the Five Books "written in Hebrew characters and in the Hebrew tongue . . . committed to writing somewhat carelessly and not adequately" (I:30). In short, Hebrew manuscripts existed but did not meet the standards Greeks expected of major manuscripts.

The meaning of "not adequately" is unclear. It may suggest scrolls written in the old, hard-to-read *Ketav Ivri* script; or that the manuscripts in the library's collection were, for one reason or another, suspect. Whatever the explanation, the unreliability of the existing scrolls is taken for granted, with anxiety about the inadequacy of a translation based on such a text.

According to *Aristeas* more than a century after the event, the king passed on his librarian's request to the Jerusalem high priest, Eleazer, who, as Ptolemy's subject, was quick to do his overlord's will. He dispatched Temple scribes to sort out textual problems and prepare a usable translation. A skilled courtier, Eleazer dispatched not merely the requested scholar-translators, six from each of the twelve tribes, but sent along several scrolls that could serve as a secure textual basis for the translation. There is no indication that the scrolls he sent were handled in any special way or treated as sacred objects. In Alexandria, the scrolls were "uncovered" and "unrolled" in the king's presence so that his curiosity about them could be satisfied. *Aristeas* shows no concern about a violation of ritual purity— that is, the exposure of a holy object to contamination by contact with those who were ritually "impure," or non-Jews (I:176–78), which would have horrified later generations. Eleazer requested that his scholars be returned, but there is no mention that the master scrolls should be.

There are many problems with this version of events, not the least that Demetrius did not hold the librarianship under Ptolemy II; and that when the translation was completed, it was not shelved in the library but proclaimed by the Jewish community as their law. The library, after its initial efforts, seems profoundly indifferent to the work it had commissioned. It seems likely that a dependable translation became possible and was, in fact, accomplished when Alexandrian Jewry finally acquired a clear text, possibly an *Ashurit* scroll. Scrolls in this square script were prized for their legibility. A sage quoted in the Palestinian (Jerusalem) Talmud explains that *Ashurit* has the meaning of "the even writing" (j. Meg. 1:71b).

The Greek-speaking diaspora seems to have accepted a version of the Septuagint Pentateuch as constitutional; to have used copies of it in their schools; to have accepted it to be what their religious leaders told them it was—a translation as good as the original; and to have used it as such.

In the translation that became normative, attempts were made to pick up some of the nuances of the Hebrew original. "I" is, in Greek, *ego*; in biblical Hebrew, *ani* and, in rare cases, *anochi*; in the Septuagint *ani* became *ego* and *anochi*, *eim*. Such uses opened many interpretive possibilities; at the least, they suggested the importance of attention to language. No wonder Philo called these translators "prophets and priests of the mysteries, whose sincerity and singleness of thought has enabled them to go hand in hand with the purest of spirits, the spirit of Moses" (*Vita Moysis* II:VI.41).

If the original purpose was to develop a Greek translation useful for administrative and constitutional purposes, the existence and popularity of the Septuagint ensured that it would be seen not simply as a translation but as a primary text which included the original speech of God. Many Jews in the diaspora must have believed that God spoke Greek. The Greek diaspora came to prize this translation, lavishing effusive praise on it. The Septuagint Pentateuch played so central a role in the Greek-speaking diaspora that the elaborate legends (such as *Aristeas*) told about its translation were apparently meant to defend it against Judean detractors who objected to the various ways it differed from their understanding of the Hebrew text.

Despite such pious legends as *Aristeas*, the facts suggest that several translations circulated until one version gained widespread approval and became in the diaspora the basis of schooling, storytelling, ceremony, and preaching. Analogous in its impact was the King James translation of the Bible, which became after its appearance in the seventeenth century not only the authentic word of God, who many in the Anglican Church assumed spoke English, but the standard for centuries of English style and speech.

THE LANGUAGE OF SCRIPTURE

In a world where no one read silently, it was only natural that scribes should think first of how a text would sound rather than of how it looked. In this early stage of the effort to establish a written text, it was therefore natural that one significant purpose was to ensure that it would be properly chanted. Since books were always read aloud, the Hellenistic Jewish world instinctively associated the written and the spoken word. In many of the Qumran texts, the word *adonai* was written above God's name, *YHWH*, to ensure that the reader would not utter God's most powerful name. A typical early masoretic effort inserted weak consonants in words where their presence would help the reader properly sound the unvocalized text: the *Vov* was used to indicate *o*; the *Yod*, *i*. These so-called *matres lectiones* made for accurate pronunciation but did not provide a full-blown system of vowel notation, and none was developed during the Hellenistic centuries. An uninstructed reader could not be fully confident of his recitation; still, much had been accomplished. The Greeks had significantly improved the usefulness of the alphabet when they introduced, perhaps in the sixth century B.C.E., vowel signs into their texts. Vowels so markedly reduced the uncertainties in sounding phrases that a person could pick up a voweled text and be fairly sure of being able to read it aloud accurately.

THE USE OF GREEK AND ARAMAIC

Koine, the popular Greek dialect, became the vernacular of the large Egyptian-Syrian diaspora and was even spoken by some in Judea. Jews who could write and read Greek could take advantage of Greek books and culture. Perhaps *Koine*'s widespread use was one of the reasons literary interest was more highly developed in the diaspora than in Judea. A knowledge of everyday Greek was, however, no guarantee that a person could read the *Iliad* or Plato in the classic tongue. Philo's catholic knowledge of the classic Hellenistic curriculum was, as far as we know, unique among diaspora Jews; but there can be little doubt that the intelligentsia of the large Jewish community of Alexandria had access to that city's libraries and were influenced by Greek literary forms and interests and even by the contents of the Greek classics.

By the second century B.C.E., there is little doubt that most diaspora Jews could no longer speak or understand Hebrew. For a Greek-speaking Jew to have mastered the Hebrew texts would have been a significant accomplishment, requiring learning not only an unfamiliar alphabet but also the sounds of a language rarely heard or used. Greek translations were an absolute necessity. Despite the claim of the *Letter of Aristeas* that the Ptolemaic court had ordered the Septuagint translations, there is little, if any, evidence that the Greeks of West Asia were interested enough in the sacred literature of their oriental subjects to have any of it translated. This was a task for Jews.

Hebrew was losing out on all fronts. Aramaic was becoming the vernacular of Jews in Judea as *Koine* was for Egyptian and Syrian Jews. An editor of the priestly history has Nehemiah say that on arrival in Jerusalem he found among its citizens many whose "children spoke the language of Ashur . . . and could no longer speak the language of Judah" (Neh. 13:24)—one of several texts that point to the spread of Aramaic as a vernacular among the Jews in Judea. Besides the Aramaic material that found its way into the Bible, Aramaic texts found at or near Qumran include fragments of a prayer ascribed to the Babylonian king Nabonidus, sections of Tobit, Enoch, the Testament of the Twelve Patriarchs, a translation of Job, and the Genesis Apocryphon. There is also in Aramaic a *Megillat Ta'anit*, a small scroll listing thirty-six days on which fasting is prohibited, which some scholars regard as a document of a rebel party fighting Rome, apparently written in haste and for popular consumption, shortly before the Temple's destruction in 70 C.E. Josephus wrote the text of *The Jewish Wars* in Aramaic and then arranged for its translation into Greek (introduction).

THE USE OF HEBREW

Despite the dethronement of Hebrew as the national vernacular, schooling and custom ensured that familiar hymns, stories, phrases, and idioms in the old speech remained part of an active universe of discourse. But the oral tradition in its original form was no longer of a piece with the community's daily speech, a change that served to spur interest in written texts. As contemporary culture no longer reinforced the classic tradition, the study of Hebrew texts increasingly became the preserve of a segment of a literate élite who, increasingly and sometimes without consciously planning it, found themselves determining and shaping tradition through their ability to interpret the revered texts.

Any text requires interpretation, if only to put the bare words in some appropriate context. Who but a well-informed commentator could provide that understanding? Those who knew Hebrew were obviously the only ones who could provide background and context and also derive from the texts written in Hebrew new levels of meaning. During late Hellenistic times, Hebrew became for Judean intellectuals what Latin was for Europe's best and brightest during the Middle Ages: a proof of status, a means of self-conscious academic communication, and the basis of a claim to religious authority.

Men wrote in Hebrew for many of the same reasons but particularly to associate their words with God's speech, to dress them in holiness. The *Temple Scroll*, Jubilees, and the *pesher* on Habakkuk were written in Hebrew. So was the Wisdom of Ben Sirah; so were Tobit and Judith. But the existence of a work in Aramaic was not a compelling reason for exclusion (the Aramaic portions of Ezra-Nehemiah and Daniel) or a work in Hebrew for inclusion (Ben Sirah, Judith, and Tobit).

One bit of evidence from rabbinic times of the synagogue's emergence as *mikdash me'at*, a small sanctuary possessing some of the redemptive power once associated with the Temple, was the deliberate retention of some Hebrew in the worship service and the requirement of public readings from the scrolls in their original Hebrew. Theoretically, one could pray in any language—there were Aramaic and Greek prayers; but the sense of power and mystery associated with Hebrew tended to outweigh more practical considerations. Hebrew was, for the most part, deliberately kept alive in the house of prayer. Much of the power implicit in the liturgy lay in the participant's use of God's language. Hebrew was the language in which God had addressed Israel and in which Israel felt it proper to address God. Though it is not generally considered in this light, the rabbinic ritual of *Keriat ha-Torah*—reading the Torah as part of synagogue worship, for which every male was trained—was shaped to be a rite of communion. A reader read God's own phrases in God's own tongue.

THE BEGINNINGS OF LITURGY

The Jew worshiped his God in a special way. In pre-exilic times, levitical choirs recited psalms for liturgical purposes in the shrines. The Shema and a few other rubrics were already well known. In its first stages, the rubric was simple: "Hear O Israel, the Lord is our God, the Lord is One." In concise, parallel phrases, it taught the Jew theology: God is, God is singular, God is active in our history and our lives and near to us. Later the rubric was built on and became far more complex: Torah readings added commands to love God "with all your heart, with all your soul, with all your strength," and petitions asking for a quiet and confident trust in God's redemptive power. The history of Jewish liturgy is a history of accumulation.

The Levites had sung their psalms in Hebrew, which became the language of worship. Prayers were always in the first-person plural. These characteristics—the deliberate use of Hebrew and a collective expression of faith—meant that the liturgy was shared by all Jews, whatever vernacular they spoke and whatever community they lived in. It made the liturgy independent of circumstance and history and served all Jews equally wherever they went.

By the end of the second century C.E., a fixed form and a fixed order of prayers had been established, reflecting the growing authority of the sages. At first the prayers were not written down; their specific wording was not yet defined, but their general content was known and accepted.

TORAH READING AND TEMPLE PRACTICE

Readings had played no role in the ancient cult. Though Temple scribes worked on Torah texts and were encouraged to do so by the hierarchy, the texts had not been used liturgically. The rabbis had a tradition they codified in two Mishnah texts (early third century C.E.) which indicate that portions from the Torah had been read during certain Temple ceremonies. The Mishnah was edited over a century and a half after the Second Temple was destroyed, and some of its historical notes reflect not eyewitness testimony but "recollections" of what Temple practice was imagined to have been by men confident that their own practices were based on sacred precedent —in this case, the belief that Torah readings on a holy day had been a Temple practice.

The two Mishnah texts—Yoma 7:1-5 and Sotah 7:7—describe an elaborate Yom Kippur rite in the course of which the high priest presumedly read certain Torah portions to the assemblage. According to the Yoma description, the high priest, clothed in white linen garments, conducted this reading at a time that coincided with the most important Yom Kippur sacrifice, an offering of a bullock and a he-goat on the high altar. The reading is said to have taken place at some distance from the altar so that a spectator could not see both the activity around the altar and the high priest reading from a Torah scroll. The reading was surrounded with ceremony. Three officials—the *Segan*, the *Rosh ha-Keneset*, and the *Chazzan ha-Keneset*—handed the scroll from one to the other. The last of the three presented it to the high priest, who received the scroll while standing and read it standing. The reading consisted of sections from Leviticus that describe how the Yom Kippur rites are to be observed (Lev. 16, 23:26–32). When the reading was completed, the high priest rolled up the scroll, put it in its case, spoke a formula, "More is written than I have read out to you," and recited by heart a short list of Yom Kippur laws taken from another section of the Torah scroll (Num. 29:7–11). He then completed this section of ceremony by reciting eight blessings listed by title in the Yoma description.

Profusion of detail is, of course, no proof of authenticity. Nor does the appearance of an apparently historical note in the body of the Mishnah guarantee its facticity. There is no reference to such a ceremony in any of the surviving literature written during the period when the Temple was still standing. A careful examination of the Mishnah's description also raises doubt about its accuracy. The rituals of Yom Kippur were carefully choreographed: "Every ceremony of Yom Kippur was carried out according to prescribed form. If one act was done out of order it lost all its force." (M. Yoma 5:7). Yet we are told: "Those who saw the sacrifice could not see the reader and those who saw the reader could not see the sacrifices" (M. Yoma 7:2). It is hard to believe that priests would have organized the drama of Yom Kippur in such a way to prevent those in attendance from observing two of its most important moments, since these would take place at the same time and at some distance from each other. But the most intractable barrier to accepting the text is that it requires the high priest to be at two different places at the same time: he simultaneously presides at the sacrifice and reads the Torah portions. The only explanation possible is that two high priests were involved. In late Temple times, the title of high priest seems to have been both specific to the priest who had effective authority over the Temple and an honorary title borne by those who had served in this office and by other senior members of Zadokite families, from which the high priests were chosen. But there is no suggestion here or anywhere else in the literature that on Yom Kippur any but the current high priest conducted the rituals crucial to the nation's future.

The description in M. Sotah 7:7 also deals with a Yom Kippur reading, though it focuses more directly on the portions of the Torah law that govern the conduct of that holy day (Lev. 16, 23:26–32; Num. 29:7–11) and on the specific blessings to accompany the ritual. The impression is inescapable that the purpose of this section was to enhance the emotional power of the Yom Kippur reading in the synagogue by attaching to it a precedent in the practices of the Temple—a habit not uncommon in rabbinic thought.

Immediately following this paragraph in M. Sotah is a report (7:8) of a public reading of the Torah in the Temple, which describes a reading by "the king" said to have taken place on the first day of the festival of Succoth during successive sabbatical years. According to the Mishnah, a temporary wooden platform was built in the Temple court, the scroll to be used was ceremoniously handed to the king by four officials (*Chazzan ha-Keneset, Rosh ha-Keneset, Segan,* and high priest); the king received the scroll standing but read seated; the reading consisted of certain portions from Deuteronomy, concluding with the same eight blessings which the high priest is described in Yoma as using on Yom Kippur. A specific instance is cited: King Agrippa had participated in such a ceremony.

This ritual may have been observed, albeit in not quite so elaborate a form and not necessarily regularly. Unlike the high priest's reading on Yom Kippur, the Succoth practice has some support in the Torah. In Deuteronomy, Moses instructs the priests that during the Succoth Festival in a sabbatical year, "You shall read this teaching aloud in the presence of all Israel" as long as "they [your children] live in the land which you are about to cross the Jordan to occupy" (31:10–13). This tradition may lie behind the association of Ezra's reading with Succoth and the ruling, also in the book of Ezra, that such readings should be repeated each sabbatical year. The Tosefta (late third century C.E.) specifically quotes Nehemiah 8 in this connection and goes on in some detail about the trumpet flourishes and royal pomp with which the ceremony was managed.

According to Chronicles, Ezra's reading took place on a temporary platform erected on the Temple Mount but outside the Temple proper before the water gate. The Mishnah places the king's reading outside the sanctuary proper in the Temple court. The corresponding Tosefta speaks only of some place, undesignated, on the Temple Mount. The septennial reading was a political, not a priestly, ceremony. No special rites of purification are indicated as required of the participants nor are we told that special vestments were worn (Tos. Sotah 7:8–9). The ceremony as described lacks all the distinctive elements of shrine ritual, including the most important of all— location in the shrine itself.

The purpose of this septennial ceremony seems to have been the desire to sanctify two political pieties: "the king derives his authority from God's law," and "the king must obey God's law." For a Hasmonean or Herodian dynast, this ceremony would have been of practical benefit as a way of validating both title and authority. The portion he was asked to read includes: "After you have entered the land that the Lord your God has given you . . . you shall be free to set a king over yourself, one chosen by the Lord your God" (Deut.

17:14–15). To gain this cachet, he need make only a symbolic submission to God's overriding authority: "to observe faithfully every word of this teaching . . . to the end he and his descendants may reign long in the midst of Israel" (17:19–20). Kings find acts of symbolic submission to God infinitely preferable to actual constraints imposed by public law or a constitution.

An unlikely list of Temple personnel are listed as playing minor roles in this ritual. The *Segan*, like the high priests, was a Temple official; but the other two bear titles that derive from synagogue administration. The *Chazzan ha-Keneset* role is unclear, but his title implies he was specifically associated with the synagogue. The *Rosh ha-Keneset* was the synagogue's paid administrator who, among his other functions, had charge of preparing the scrolls, bringing them into the synagogue from the chests where they were stored, and selecting those men in the Jewish community who were to read (j. Meg. 75b ff.). Neither official needed to be a priest or a Levite. I find it hard to imagine that a high priest would share Yom Kippur—the great day, Israel's most momentous occasion—with officials of a non-Temple institution or allow nonpriests to play a significant role in the ceremony.

Some scholars explain the presence of these officials by asserting that the Temple complex included a synagogue, that in the synagogue the Torah scrolls were kept, and that these officials were involved because they were the keepers of the scrolls. Those who describe such a synagogue offer as evidence the list of synagogue officials found in this Mishnah. There is no other evidence. Scholars suggest how the legend developed that a synagogue had been located in the Temple. A portico that surrounded the Temple Mount on all sides included meeting rooms used for various purposes. Scribes taught and worked in some of these rooms, and work on the Torah scrolls must have been carried on there. Since the definition of the synagogue was not yet specific, and the early synagogue included study rooms—and places to eat and rest as well as for worship—any of these spaces might well have been identified by later generations as a synagogue, a place of meeting and reading.

The argument that synagogue officials lent their scroll to the Temple for this ceremony makes no sense. As the national archives, the Temple possessed its own Torah scrolls. *Aristeas* assumed that the high priest possessed the most accurate scrolls. The priests had long supported scribal activity. Had a scroll been needed for the Yom Kippur ceremony, the Temple had its own. Temple worship was elaborate and highly formal. Great care was lavished on the shrine's apparatus. Utensils used during the sacrifices had to be without blemish and in a state of purity. Surely, if shrine ritual had required a Torah scroll, the priests would have had one of appropriate sanctity and would not have used a scroll whose sanctity they could not vouch for. The priests would not have had to borrow a synagogue's scrolls.

TORAH READING AND THE SYNAGOGUE

Debate over the synagogue's origins is unresolved. Some trace it back to informal meetings presumedly organized during the Babylonian Exile. Some locate it in the *ma'amadot*, the local groups raised in the towns of Judea after the Exile when it was their turn to provide the Temple with a delegation to assist at the altar. Some locate it in the need of the communities outside Jerusalem for institutions more intimate than the national shrine. As we have seen, already in the late Persian period Levites traveled through the villages of Judea carrying scrolls and teaching the law. Some of these men may have read from their scrolls during local meetings and followed the reading with an explanation in the vernacular. It is evident that meetings of various kinds developed in different locations as Jews sought ways to keep their customs alive, satisfy God through worship, and renew their knowledge of and attention to sacred customs and lore. When there were at last scrolls considered sacred, reading and recitation of them inevitably played an increasingly important role at such meetings.

Whatever form these meetings took, they differed from those in the Temple in that they were not the responsibility or province of the priests. The ancient priestly traditions make no mention of them. Priests organized the sacrificial cult; the synagogue had no altar. Strict rules of ritual purity surrounded the lives of the priests.

Such rules did not necessarily apply to those who led whatever worship took place in the synagogue. Familiar hymns could be sung, and traditional narratives could be retold. Someone might read from a text that had somehow come into his hands, or recite a list of *torot* that applied to the Sabbath or a holiday. The same worship calendar was observed as in the Temple, though the religious exercises appropriate to the Sabbath and holy days differed.

The public reading from the Torah on Sabbath, holidays, and market days seem to have its origin somewhere in the early history of the synagogue. Here was a way to immerse oneself in God's instructions and listen again to His words without intruding on the religious forms that the priests declared to be reserved for the Temple. As the synagogue's familiar name, *Beit ha-Keneset*, "place of assembly," suggests, the meeting rather than the building came first. The synagogue came into being to fill a community need for a local gathering place where political or guild issues could be discussed and religious practices given an intimacy the magnificent ceremonies of the Temple could not provide.

There is a possibility that the Torah scrolls first began to be read publicly in the Greek diaspora as part of an organized ceremony. As we have seen, Greek-speaking Jews in the diaspora were unlikely to understand or to use classic Hebrew, which cautions us against any confident assertion that the origin of the ritual of regular Torah readings from the original Hebrew texts can be located in the proto-synagogues of the diaspora. Yet the final scene of *Aristeas'* little drama describes a public reading of the newly completed translation of the Septuagint to the "community of Jews," their acclamation of the text, and the uttering of a curse against anyone who would in the future alter it in any way (I:308–15).

While the Temple in Jerusalem was sacred to Alexandrian Jews who paid their annual dues toward its operation, day-in-day-out local practice in the diaspora developed its own ritual forms independent of Temple practice. Religious life was organized around prayer halls (*proseuchai*) and informal meetings. By the turn of the millennium, we hear of buildings set aside for public worship. Subjects relating to various Torah texts seem to have been discussed in sermons in these early versions of the synagogue, though it is not clear whether there developed a formal schedule of public readings from the Septuagint.

Much depends on how we interpret Philo's comment:

> So on each Sabbath there stand wide open in every city thousands of schools of good sense, temperance, courage, justice and the other virtues in which the scholars sit in order, quietly, with ears alert and with full attention, so much do they thirst for the draught which the teachers' words supply, while one of special experience rises and sets forth what is best and sure to be profitable and will make the whole life grow to something better. But among the vast number of particular truths and principles there studied, there stand out particularly high above the others two main ones: one of duty to God as shown by piety and holiness, one of duty to man as shown by humanity and justice.
>
> (*De Specialibus Legibus* II:62–63)

While Philo was speaking of a sermon rather than specifically of a Torah reading, it is reasonable to conjecture that such sermons were linked in some way to a reading or recitation—as were, in fact, his own sermons. This certainly became synagogue practice.

We do not really know why and when the practice of the public reading from a Torah scroll began. Qumran's *Manual of Discipline* (first century B.C.E.) describes a practice of that community which may go back to the second century B.C.E.. A member of the order was appointed to read aloud at certain convocations, perhaps during meals, but it is not clear whether such readings were limited to the Five Scrolls of the Law, whether other texts were read, or whether any prescribed order was followed.

Philo's description of the Jewish monastic sect, the Theraputae, may reflect a similar discipline though it is not clear that he is describing a public function:

> They read the whole law book and seek wisdom from their ancestral philosophy by taking it as an allegory, since they think that the words of the literal text are symbols of something whose hidden nature is revealed by studying the underlying meaning. They also have writings of men of old, the founders of their way of thinking who left many memorials of the form used in allegorical interpretation and these they take as a kind of archetype and imitate the method in which this principle is carried out.
>
> (*The Contemplative Life* 28,29)

Defining the First Scripture: The Torah

LITURGY AND THE TORAH SCROLLS

During these centuries, the regulations that would govern the liturgical presentation of scripture were sorted out and firmly established.
The Judean (Palestinian) communities adopted a three- or three-and-
a-half-year cycle for reading the entire *Sefer Torah*; the Eastern (Babylonian) communities adopted a one-year cycle which, after a
considerable period, became Judaism's universal practice. Weekly
portions were determined; they were read or, more accurately,
chanted during morning and afternoon services on the Sabbath. Selections from the weekly portion were also chanted at services on
market days, Mondays and Thursdays. On the festivals, fast days, and
the new moon, special readings were chosen because of their thematic
or prescriptive relevance to the occasion. At first, some communities
took literally the idea of a continuous reading of the Torah and read
successive sections of that week's portion on Monday and Thursday,
concluding it on the Sabbath; but it became the rule that the complete
weekly portion would be read each Sabbath morning and short sections from it on Sabbath afternoons and market days.*

The *Tannaim*, the sages of the second and third centuries, successors to the Pharisees after the Second Temple's destruction, were
aware that there were still unresolved textual questions, and that
flawed scrolls were in circulation. Among the five things R. Akiba
(second century) is said to have taught R. Simeon b. Yohai was
"When you teach your son, teach him from a corrected scroll" (b.
Pes. 112a). An uncorrected Torah scroll should not be kept for more
than thirty days (b. Ket. 19b). The *Tannaim* proposed the general

---

*During later talmudic times, it became the custom on the Sabbath and holidays to add to the
weekly portion of the *Sefer Torah* a section from the Prophets or Writings (*Haftarah*), probably
to make clear that these scrolls, too, were deemed inspired. Selections varied considerably
from place to place; in some locations, the custom was for the portion to be chosen by the congregation or a local preacher. By the eighth or ninth century, a defined pattern of such additional readings had been established, and the portion selected was related thematically or by
some midrashic tradition to the Torah portion mandated for that occasion.

Somewhat later still, the custom developed of reading one of the five short scrolls known as
megillot on specific holidays and fasts. The recitation of the scroll of Esther on Purim is already
assumed in the Mishnah. In Amoraic times (third/fourth to sixth centuries), the practice developed of reading the Song of Songs on the last two nights of Passover, the Book of Ruth on
Shavuot, and Lamentations on the Fast of the Ninth of Av (Sof. 14, 18). The fifth is
Ecclesiastes.

rule that, in deciding controversies about a particular text, if two scholars differed a third was solicited and the majority opinion prevailed. The same standard was said to have been used when two Torah scrolls shelved in the Temple archives were found to contain variant readings: a third scroll was consulted, and the majority reading was considered the authoritative version (Sifre Deut.:356; j. Ta'anit IV, 65a; Soferim VI; A.R.N. ver. B 46).

It was the desire to fix the tradition and assert its dependability that made for popular pieties emphasizing that dependability. For instance, that the accepted version had remained unchanged since Moses: "Moses received the Torah at Sinai." Ezra's contribution was redefined as a limited one: placing diacritical marks above some ten passages where a word or words were to be omitted during the public reading to avoid any unwarranted or offensive assumptions about God's oneness, goodness, and power.

INSCRIBING A *SEFER TORAH*

There was a well-established form for the inscription of a *Sefer Torah*. Some histories ascribed to Ezra and/or the *soferim*—the priest-scribes of the late Persian period, the so-called Men of the Great Synagogue—the standardization of the chants for the reading of Torah and the proper form of text presentation, how the text should look on the parchment sheets. Each scroll was to be prepared from the skin of certain clean animals. Writing was to be done with a special quill and ink. The block letters of the *Ashurit* script were to be used, and aligned under rather than on the line. The presentation of other *Tanakh* scrolls, with certain exceptions, particularly the Psalms and Esther, was less formally prescribed; but care was taken with all. All scrolls were written on parchment or leather and left unvocalized. Particular attention was paid to certain scribal niceties; for instance, some held that a scribe setting down the names of the sons of Haman in the scroll of Esther should write one above the other, as if they were half-bricks laid on half-bricks, to suggest a badly built and unstable wall—a cautionary visual lesson that those who scheme against Israel will fail and their plans collapse. In contrast, the "Song of the Sea" (Exod. 15:1–19) was to be inscribed "Two bricks over one brick": that is, one line of two strophes separated in the middle above a line with a single strophe set in the middle. The two lines were said to represent the layers of brick the slaves had been forced to lay in building the storehouses of Pharaoh. As bricks laid in such an alternating pattern create a solid wall, so the promises of redemption in this hymn are solid and dependable.

The work of writing out sacred texts came to be seen as a sacred obligation, *Melechet ha-Kodesh*; and a class of professional Torah scribes came into being. Not all sages had a good hand, and one could rise to the rank of scholar without being able to write with ease or skill. Still, some rabbis held that as an act of piety every man should write a Torah scroll, which explains the otherwise surprising prescription in the Talmud "that a scholar should learn how to write" (b. Hul. 9a).

Writing a *Sefer Torah* required considerable technical skill and training. Around the sixth century, the rules and customs that had developed over centuries to govern such work were collected into a treatise known as *Masseket Soferim*, "A Treatise for Scribes." A précis of this work also appeared, *Masseket Sefer Torah*. Both guidebooks circulated widely and were included as appendices to editions of the Talmud.

EDUCATION AND RITUAL

The *Tannaim* were responsible for establishing and strengthening the elementary educational system that had been begun during the preceding centuries. Elementary education had a narrow focus: the ability to read and chant properly the *Sefer Torah* as part of synagogue ritual. Though by the fifth century cursive script was the accepted way of writing letters and business documents, a Jewish boy continued to be introduced to the solid block letters of the *Ashurit* script because it was the script used in the Torah scroll. He learned these letters one by one, then in combination; then he was set short Torah texts. All reading in the elementary school, *Beit Sefer*, was done aloud, and every phrase and sentence was chanted over and over again until the student had it down pat. Little concern was shown for any but the most rudimentary comprehension.

After several years, the quicker students knew most of the *Sefer Torah* by heart; what they knew were phrases and sentences they accepted as God's own and as basic elements of their faith; but the how and why of such connection could not have been clear to most of them. They took the value of the Torah for granted. The environment reinforced its importance and sacredness. If the student did not understand what was read, he knew that the sages did.

Students were taught that there were no primary or secondary texts in the *Sefer Torah*. No one said to them, "This text is critical, that one only illustrative"; all were accepted as essential parts of God's message. Where a modern may see an inconsistency or simply a bit of trivia, the rabbinic mind saw the possibility of meaning. This kind of education conditioned the student to accept an exegesis that binds together sentences and phrases apparently connected only in that they include a similar term or an unusual grammatical construction.

READING FROM THE TORAH

The obligation of *Keriat ha-Torah*, "reading from the Torah during public worship," allowed the worshiper to participate vicariously in the moment of revelation, Sinai, and so acclaim the covenant and rejoice in Israel's election. By speaking the words God had spoken, the worshiper reaffirmed the Covenant and drew near to God. The *Keriat ha-Torah* ceremony developed rules of its own. A specific number of readers were required: seven on the Sabbath, three on Mondays and Thursdays. A man of priestly descent was to be called first, then a Levite, then those of less distinguished birth. Technically, those called to read were to read; but the unvocalized Hebrew text and the trope were beyond the competence of most, so the custom became that a man fulfilled the duty of *Keriat ha-Torah* when he recited the designated blessings that preceded and closed the Torah readings, blessings everyone knew by heart. One better trained than the rest chanted the Torah text.

Care was taken with the reading and the chant. The chant, which developed out of the learning songs used in schools, helped to separate long and short syllables, suggested the proper division of phrases, and was an aid to pronunciation. Specialists, called masoretes, would continue to work for many centuries preparing a standard text which analyzed and approved every vowel and trope sign. The folio texts prepared by these grammarians were not used in worship, where only an unvocalized scroll was considered appropriate, but guided those who set the standard for all who performed the duty of *Keriat ha-Torah*.

The masoretes also designated those few texts where the accepted reading differed from the written text (*Ketib u-Keri*) and where a word was not to be read (*Ketib ve-lo Keri*). The existence of such problem texts suggests that after a certain point in time, probably as early as the first century c.e., scribes would no longer revise a text for grammatical reasons as their predecessors had freely done. By now, the Torah text was well known and seen as holy. Who knew whether God might not have intended the text to be read as it appeared, even if that reading seemed no more than a common scribal error. Perhaps the "error" was deliberate. Perhaps God intended it to convey some important meaning.

The sages appreciated the value of *Keriat ha-Torah* as a spiritual moment and as a means of keeping alive knowledge of the tradition. They encouraged Torah study and created mechanisms like the *targum* to ensure that the Aramaic-speaking community understood the Torah properly. Over time, some of these rituals became accepted customs which continued even when, as in the case of the *targum*, the rite no longer served its original purpose. *Targum* was originally simply an extemporaneous paraphrase into Aramaic, the community's everyday speech; but when Jews in the seventh and eighth centuries ceased to speak Aramaic, opting instead for Arabic, the language of the new empire, the *targum* became a memorized relic retained only by the innate conservatism of religious life. The trove of documents found in the last decade of the nineteenth century in the storeroom (*Genizah*) of the synagogue of Palestinian Jews in old Cairo contained letters that indicate that, long after Arabic had replaced Aramaic as the people's vernacular, youngsters were taught Aramaic *targumim* and much applauded when they recited the appropriate *targum* in the synagogue.

THE HOLY SCROLL

Torah scrolls were now available in every synagogue, and scrolls of the Prophets and Writings must have been available in most communities. Individuals could own scrolls. There is a good bit of discussion in the Talmud about dividing scrolls among heirs or for sale. A Torah scroll could not be divided. Scrolls of other than Torah books might be separated at the seams under certain conditions. Synagogue scrolls were kept, at first, outside the prayer room in a cabinet, *tevah*, where they were laid in bins and bound, as manuscripts generally were in antiquity. It is not clear whether scrolls other than the *Sefer Torah* were kept in the early *tevah*; but by the fifth century, when the ark became a permanent architectural feature of the prayer room, only the Five Books of Moses were kept there. In front of the ark was a curtain which in purpose and name, *parochet*, recalled the curtain that had fronted the Holy of Holies in the Temple, where the ark containing the Tablets of the Law was said to have been kept in pre-exilic times, and where in the Second Temple there had been an empty space filled with God's presence. Curtained in this way, the *Sefer Torah* was understood as God's immanent presence. Men bowed when they crossed in front of the ark and rose when it was opened, because of its sacred contents. Popular veneration of the *Sefer Torah* sometimes bordered on idolatry. Oaths were taken before the scrolls resting in an open ark. For some Jews the scrolls became a source of miraculous power, independent of the words they contained.

The *Sefer Torah* had become revelation, resplendent in divine mystery, symbol and substance of God's wisdom, the source too holy to be handled with any but the most reverent humility. Every letter had its purpose and was a vehicle of revelation. The Midrash is full of interpretations that turn on a single word or letter. Sermons and traditions emerge unexpectedly. R. Huna bar Nathan asked R. Ashi: "What is the point of the verse 'Kinah and Dimonah and Addah?'" (Josh. 15:22). R. Ashi replied: "The verse simply lists some towns in the land of Israel." R. Gebihah from [Be] Argiza understood the names this way: "Whoever has cause for resentment (*kin'ah*) against his neighbor and yet holds his peace (*domem*), he who abides for all eternity (*ade'ad*) will espouse his cause" (b. Git. 7a).

The sages derived meaning not only by logical extrapolation but from peculiarities of language and style, irregularities in syntax, or unusual spellings. Not only the letters but the spaces between them had meaning. Akiba is said to have described the Torah as black fire, the written words, on white fire, the spaces between the words. Since Hebrew had no separate numeration system, using the alphabet for that purpose, a Torah sentence was both a set of ideas and a sum which might suggest when the Messiah would come. The Torah was brimful of meaning; indeed, its wisdom could never be exhausted.

Gradually, the assumption of the divinity of the *Sefer Torah* meant that no one dared touch or tamper with a *Sefer Torah*. Between the first and the tenth centuries, the masoretes provided the text with vowels, punctuation marks and trope, musical notations, and drew up thousands of brief notes explaining usage, etymology, citing other examples of a particular word, noting unusual terms, and the like. Their careful notes were entered on the margins of folios, never in a *Sefer Torah* text intended for synagogue use. The classic Ben Asher codex (ninth century), which became *the* masoretic text, the standard for all subsequent Hebrew texts, is a monument to centuries of patient scholarship and a triumph of manuscript art, but it was not intended for synagogue use any more than were those beautifully illustrated Torah manuscripts that were inscribed and painted for wealthy patrons, particularly in Spain during the fourteenth and fifteenth centuries. A folio like the Ben Asher codex was used for research and to check out the accuracy of scrolls. The Torah scroll carried a special degree of holiness and was reserved for worship.

BOOK LEARNING AND BEN SIRAH

No one confronted a manuscript as we do a book, as a silent, inert object. As oral tradition became written text, it was known as *Mikra*, "that which is heard." Reading was never a silent activity. To those who read aloud, manuscript and speech were intimately identified. In his extensive commentaries on biblical texts, Philo never cited a particular Septuagint translation; rather, he quoted from memory, as did the sages cited in Mishnah and Tosefta, where most citations begin, *She-ne-emar* ("as it is said"), rather than, *Ka-Katuv* ("as it is written").

As writing became easier and swifter, and parchment easier to come by, scribes allowed themselves greater latitude in descriptive phrases and detail. Some literature begins to show the signs of being just that. The priestly chronicles are expansive and full of lists. Novellas like Esther are verbose. In Job the poet's imagination exceeds any need for compression.

A partial comparison of a late rewriting like the *Genesis Apocryphon*, a midrashic elaboration found among the Dead Sea Scrolls, with the biblical account of Abraham's visit to Egypt is revealing:

> There was a famine in the land and Abram went down to Egypt to sojourn there, for the famine was severe in the land. As he was about to enter Egypt he said to his wife Sarai, "I am well aware that you are a beautiful woman. When the Egyptians see you, they will say, 'She is his wife,' and they will kill me, but let you live. Say then that you are my sister, that it may go well with me because of you, and that I may remain alive thanks to you."
>
> (Gen. 12:10–13)

> Now there was famine in all this land, and hearing that there was prosperity in Egypt I went . . . to the land of Egypt. . . . I [came to] the river Karmon, one of the branches of the River (Nile) . . . and I crossed the seven branches of the River. . . . We passed through our land and entered the land of the sons of Ham, the land of Egypt.
>
> And on the night of our entry into Egypt, I, Abram, dreamt a dream; [and behold], I saw in my dream a cedar tree and a palm tree . . . men came and they sought to cut down the cedar tree and to pull up its roots, leaving the palm tree (standing) alone. But the palm tree cried out saying, 'Do not cut down this cedar tree, for cursed be he who shall fell [it].' And the cedar tree was spared because of the palm tree and [was] not felled.
>
> And during the night I woke from my dream, and I said to Sarai my wife, 'I have dreamt a dream . . . [and I am] fearful [because of] this dream.' She said to me, 'Tell me your dream that I may know it.' So I

began to tell her this dream . . . [the interpretation] of the dream . . . that they will seek to kill me, but will spare you. . . . [Say to them] of me, 'he is my brother, and because of you I shall live, and because of you my life shall be saved.'

(Genesis Apocryphon, col. XIX.)

Prolixity and—what cannot be seen from the translation—the fact that the work was in Aramaic rather than in Hebrew, are dead giveaways that the work was set down at a time when the art of reading had become relatively common. The author clearly wrote for readers and not for listeners who needed to memorize his story.

In fact, most scrolls composed and written in Aramaic or Greek during the Hellenistic period seem to have given little weight to the necessity of memorization. They not only tend to be wordy but make less use of mnemonics, alliteration, word play, and the other techniques used in oral cultures to ease memorization. Increasingly, written works are attributed to specific authors and claim attention not because they were inspired but for the force of their ideas and the reputation of their author.

By contrast, the Hebrew writings of the Pharisees and early rabbinic sages show little, if any, evidence of the changes that occur when an oral culture is transformed by the introduction of writing. Far from being verbose, their writings consist largely of discrete axioms marked by economy of phrase and mnemonic devices. The few statements cited in *Pirke Avot* (third century B.C.E. to first century C.E.) in the name of sages of the second and first centuries B.C.E. are so terse as to appear gnomic. The earliest statement attributed to any of these men—"be prudent in judgment, raise up many disciples and make a fence for the Torah" (M. Avot 1:1)—characteristically can be read in any number of ways depending on the context the reader assumes. The Mishnah is a collection of compact sayings, statements of law, briefly noted incidents, and cryptic references to scholarly debates presented in the updated mishnaic Hebrew without elaboration or connective tissue. It can be said of the literary legacy of the Pharisees and their successors, the rabbis of the talmudic age, what

165

critics have observed of the Shaker settlements, that on no building they erected could you find a trace of ornamentation.

Theirs was, however, not the unselfconscious compression used by storytellers and earlier teachers who expected and desired that their words become a living part of the national memory. It is the tribute of the sages to the specific details of the covenanted life and to their responsibility to represent and maintain a tradition that is to be memorized—literally, taken to heart. This was Torah: material that should be in the forefront of every Jew's mind because it reveals to him what he must do to please God.

Schooling in Judea remained during the mishnaic centuries as it had been—tutorial, conservative, concerned with imprinting the classic traditions and consensus values on a youth's mind: "Train up a child in the way that he should go" (Prov. 22:6). As since time immemorial, most children did not learn to write or read. Imitation of the ways of their elders and immersion in an embracing and distinctive culture provided most of the young with the skills, conventional wisdom, and value system they required. Only well-born or extremely fortunate young men were given the opportunity of a formal education beyond basic literacy.

Most learning consisted primarily, as it had for centuries, of simple repetition until certain rudimentary texts were firmly fixed in the mind. We can describe only one school of this period, the early second-century B.C.E. academy for the sons of Jerusalem's well-to-do, whose headmaster, Joshua Ben Sirah, took the time—fortunately for us—to set down his favorite observations about morals and the nature of life for the benefit of his students and posterity. An Egyptian grandson later translated Ben Sirah's Hebrew book into Greek and added several paragraphs of prologue about his grandfather's school and methods.

While Hellenistic schools for upper-class Greek youths were often situated in a campus-like setting which included various buildings for lectures, athletics, and communal eating, Ben Sirah's school undoubtedly was not so grand. Apparently, Judean schools met out of doors. The term *yeshivah*, which became the designation for what we would call a secondary school or college, comes from the root "to sit" and suggests that students met wherever the teachers were, perhaps where they lived. The master, not the building, was the school. Even in winter any public place could do.

We do not know what Ben Sirah called his school. In his prologue to the book, his grandson called the school a *Beit ha-Midrash*, literally a "place for the exposition of venerated traditions," and described a curriculum that aimed to provide students with considerable proficiency in the correct reading and understanding of "the Law, the Prophets and other writings of the Fathers" (prologue). That is the wisdom that provides enlightenment. Ben Sirah's commonplace book contains observations on ethics, the arts, morals, manners, and the rules of literary interpretation.

Ben Sirah considered a proper education the key to the good life. He insisted that only education can implant the best thoughts in a person's mind, and appealed to his students, sons of privilege, to recognize and appreciate their advantages. Farmers, tradesmen, and craftsmen have their necessary place, but their tasks deny them the opportunity "to study the law of the most high." A scholar's wisdom depends on ample leisure. If a man is to be wise, he must be relieved of other tasks. It is a given that literacy confers authority: "They, the peasantry and city laborers, are not sought out for the council of the people. They do not obtain eminence in the public assembly. They do not sit in the Judge's seat, nor do they understand the sentence of judgment" (38:33).

He taught his students to read properly the texts that he believed any educated Jerusalemite should know. He seems to have believed, as did many Jews and non-Jews at the time, that a person is, and only can be, what the ideas he carries around in his mind allow him to be. Maxims were assigned because they were memorable and useful as discussion starters; and, more important, because they presented ideas that ought to be imprinted on the mind. Having the right thoughts was essential to the development of good character.

His assumptions about the value of memorizing good thoughts were consistent with other ideas held in his day. The practice of using certain traditional affirmations as mantras was common. Already in pre-exilic times, the Shema—"Hear O Israel, the Lord our God, the Lord is One" (Deut. 6:14)—may have served in this way. During the Hellenistic period, this practice of reciting key paragraphs from the tradition was expanded to include, beside the Shema, other and longer sections from the Five Books (Deut. 6:4–9, 11:13–21) and the Ten Commandments, which many Jews recited twice a day. Unlearned people used such recitations to fix key ideas in the mind and so to try to stay on the right path, and also as talismans, protective formulas, to ward off evil thoughts and evil spirits.

Ben Sirah would have none of this. He concentrated on ideas and values that would help his young scholars make their way in the world and lead effective and responsible civic lives. In tune with Hellenistic pedagogical practice, he offered, besides good thoughts, a selection of role models. His book closes with a series of thumbnail biographies of the heroes of the past which highlight their civic virtues. Abraham is presented as a model of faithfulness. Joseph is omitted; presumedly his youthful egotism might have suggested to the boys that self-centeredness was a virtue. Ben Sirah often only suggests an incident in the lives of his heroes, clearly expecting that his charges could fill in the details—another indication, if one is needed, of the community's broad familiarity with its early traditions.

Since books were still expensive, few homes had them, and Ben Sirah's pupils had to memorize them. Learning required reading aloud and being corrected by the master—listening and repeating, listening and repeating. "Wisdom is known through speech and education comes through the spoken word" (Ben Sirah 4:24). Even with improved scribal techniques, books could not be instantly read. Ben Sirah must have used long-familiar methods to teach students the correct reading of a manuscript. Though his goal was the mastery of a text, he probably gave an occasional lecture on ideas suggested by the reading—though in Hellenistic Judaism there was no systematic interpretive methodology.

Ben Sirah's student is to "investigate all the wisdom of the past": to study the prophecies, preserve the sayings of famous men, and penetrate "the intricacies of parables and the hidden meaning of proverbs. . . . Prepared in this way he will give sound advice and dispense knowledge, . . . he will disclose what he has learned from his own education and still take pride in the law of the Lord's covenant"

168

(39:1–3). Knowledge, as Ben Sirah offered it, comes from inspired texts, experience, the intellectual deposit we call Wisdom, and probably from a variety of ideas that had simply caught his fancy. His book presents itself not as a commentary on any scroll or set of scrolls but as an independently wrought synthesis of Torah and Wisdom. Though his language is replete with familiar biblical phrases, he does not provide proof texts to support his teachings. The value of the whole tradition, oral and written, is assumed. Truth comes from many sources, not just one, certainly not just one book.

CONCLUSION

In the mishnaic centuries (first century B.C.E. to third century C.E.), the sages for the first time begin to acknowledge the authority that texts have come to bear, and consciously design texts to exert authority. Certain essential features of a scriptural tradition have emerged, the basis of the later rabbinic teachings. Since, at least symbolically, a scripture serves as the court of final appeal on all issues that concern the basic requirements of a community's religious life, it must be understood as pregnant with good thoughts and examples. Essene commentators went to great lengths to protect the good name of the founders of the Davidic dynasty who, they believed, would rule again in messianic times. God Himself had promised that "the scepter shall not depart from Judah" (Gen. 49:10), and "that shoot will grow from the stump of Jesse" (Isa. 11:1). David and Solomon were not only renowned and successful kings but founders of the messianic dynasty: yet, in violation of Torah law, both men had taken gentile wives. Apologetes explained that the Torah had not been available to the great kings ("David read not in the book of the law"), for from the time when Israel had sinned with the Golden Calf, the Torah books had been sealed and placed in the ark, and that seal was not broken until the time of the high priest Zadok (*Damascus Document* V:2–5).

In Hellenistic times, those who dealt with texts did so primarily in cult and academic settings, where texts were looked at, studied, and interpreted as a way to understand God's design for the religious life of His people. Some, like Qumran's Teacher of Righteousness, examined certain prophetic texts to understand their teaching about End Time. Some, like the Alexandrian scholar-preacher Philo, read the law allegorically and in so doing dressed Judaism in philosophical clothes. Some, like the Pharisees, developed an intricate exegetical method, *derash*, to extricate from the texts all that they knew God had placed there. It would take some generations for the Pharisees to convince the community that their interpretation of Torah was the only acceptable one; but history—in the form of the failed rebellions against Rome of 68–72 and 132–135—came to their aid by demonstrating that Jews needed clear disciplines and a fully articulated way of life.

It was not pure logic that carried the day. The Pharisaic sages had followed the advice of their early leaders and raised up many disciples. Confident of their approach, they were ready and willing to fill the power gap that opened after the revolt of 68–72 was crushed and the Second Temple destroyed. Their midrashic technique was not unlike contemporary Greek techniques used in interpreting Homer—ingenious, sometimes elegant, ways to discover meanings that were not self-evident. The Pharisaic way would ultimately be the Jewish way.

The prophetic texts are seen as containing apocalyptic teachings and millenarian secrets. In this sense, they are the heirs of the biblical writers who reinterpreted the seventy-year oracle spoken by Jeremiah so that it referred to later events (25:9–12, and 2 Chron. 36:19–23; Zech. 1:12, 7:5; Daniel 9:2, 24–27). The men of the Hellenistic age and the talmudic sages after them looked on certain books as their forefathers had looked on certain oracles—as predictions of events yet to happen.

Accustomed to print and the linear, matter-of-fact thought patterns that silent reading imposes, we tend to assume a text is no more or less than it presents itself to be. To these men, a written text was frozen speech. They never saw it without hearing it read. Hearing speech is a happening, an event full of surprises. We hear with our eyes as well as our ears. We listen creatively and sometimes surprise ourselves in the way we respond. The language in which these men begin to talk of the meaning of the venerated texts is revealing: one who knows the texts "pours out teaching and prophecy"; the psalmist asked God, "Unveil my eyes that I may behold wondrous things from out of Your Torah" (Ps. 119:18).

Rabbinic Judaism would assume the primacy of the *Sefer Torah* over the other books of the three-tiered scripture. Only the *Sefer Torah* is kept in the synagogue ark. Only the Five Scrolls of Moses, the *Sefer Torah*, are read through annually as an essential element of the Sabbath liturgy. To this Torah reading ritual, the rabbis later added selections from the other books (*Haftarah*), but these are not used systematically or exhaustively.

The authority of the Five Scrolls rested on their being accepted as God's own words. While most researchers have taken for granted that in the early Hellenistic period primacy of place was already given to the Torah scrolls, we really do not know which scrolls were on the meetinghouse shelves nor is it clear that the rabbinic doctrine of Moses' absolute superiority as prophet was yet broadly held.

The rabbis of the talmudic period (second century to sixth century C.E.) would insist that since Moses' day the Torah had been fully shaped, the text carefully controlled, and its proper interpretation broadly acknowledged. They insisted that Talmud Torah, the obligation incumbent on every Jew to read and interpret the Torah, had always been fully recognized; that the reading (really, chanting) of the Torah during synagogue worship, *Keriat ha-Torah*, was already established ritual; and that on Yom Kippur, the holiest day of the year, sections from the Torah were read out as part of the service in the Temple—in short, that the *Sefer Torah* was, and had always been, acknowledged and revered as scripture.

While there are occasional references in the Hellenistic period to the study of the Pentateuch and other scrolls, there is no evidence that a regimen of reading from the *Sefer Torah* during synagogue worship was widely acknowledged, and every reason to believe that Talmud Torah, the obligation of all Jews to study Torah, had not yet been clearly enunciated or widely accepted.

The text had a virtue peculiar to Judaism. The scrolls were available to anyone who could read. The power that accompanied the interpretation of texts served well the religious concerns and ambitions of many in the growing literate sections of the community. In understanding the emergence of the *Sefer Torah* as scripture, we must recognize the almost inadvertent role played by the conservative formalism of the priests. Priests tend to be jealous of their prerogatives; and Egyptian and Babylonian priests withdrew books of sacred magic and lore from circulation. But Israel's priests had no interest in using these scrolls in Temple liturgy; their open-handedness assured the scrolls' availability to the general community.

History is full of paradoxes. One of my favorites is the proposition that, if Israel's scripture had had a more exalted birth, the text probably would have been shut away as a prerogative of the priests; but since the texts had begun life simply as records of well-known oral traditions or as garden-variety histories, no one tried to monopolize them. Since no one at first had associated these writings with divinity, there was no reason to secrete them. By not being one of the Temple's sacred implements, the *Sefer Torah* could be seen as "the inheritance of the whole household of Jacob," as the Reform prayerbook reformulates the biblical phrase. Anyone could read a scroll, own a scroll, or study it and was, in fact, encouraged to do so.

5

ISRAEL'S SECOND SCRIPTURE: THE TALMUD

These are things for which no measure is prescribed:
cleansing, first fruits, the festal offerings, deeds of loving
kindness, and *Talmud Torah* equals all of these.
—M. Peah 1:1

In the two centuries following the disastrous rebellions against
Rome (68–72 and 132–135 C.E.), the final selections were made of
those scrolls that became the Hebrew scripture as we know it. The
Palestinian leaders in these years made the final decisions about
which scrolls to include (Ezekiel, Esther, Ecclesiastes) and which to
exclude (Ben Sirah, Wisdom of Solomon). At first the general term
Mikra, "that which is read," was accepted as an appropriate label for
the Hebrew scripture; but it was supplanted, by the fifth or sixth
century, by the defining acronym *Tanakh* (from *Torah; Neviim*,
"Prophets"; *Ketuvim*, "Writings"), probably because *Tanakh* not

only defined the anthology but also reflected the descending degrees of authority accorded the separate divisions. The *Tanakh* suggests not a single anthology of scrolls treated as equally significant but a three-tiered work. A single folio volume of the *Tanakh* would not appear until the sixth century.

In these centuries immediately after the destruction of the Second Temple, a strange thing happened in Jewish life. A community in which books of various kinds had been important, a community that had easily adopted the literary interests of the Hellenistic world, turned its back on most of the literature its literary folk had produced, with the exception of the twenty-two scrolls that were accepted as scripture. It tried to create a bookless culture. Christian literature of the times offers a striking contrast: the Gospels are novellas, "bios," accounts of singular human beings; Paul's writings are literary; many of the anti-Nicene fathers, the Christian writers before the Council of Nicaea (325 C.E.), proudly signed their names to their books.

As far as we know, after the generation of Philo and Josephus—for perhaps seven centuries—no sage wrote or signed a book, be it history, apologetic, or code. Just before the rebellions, there were several Jewish historians like Josephus, but for centuries after him, not one. None of the literature of the period—Mishnah, Tosefta, Talmudim, halachic Midrashim, and so on—were books in the sense of material presented by a single author on a predetermined theme; rather, these are simply collections of formulas and memorized notes which emerged over several generations, collected and set down as guides to action rather than as shaped literature. Jews not only stopped writing books but apparently lost interest in much of their literary patrimony. The sages did not bother to read, teach, or copy literature produced by diaspora Jews, though we know that some of the rabbis, and certainly the diaspora communities, spoke Greek. Nor was their indifference limited to books in Greek. A similar fate befell most of the scrolls written in Hebrew or Aramaic that were not included in the *Tanakh*.

But the sages were not idle. One of the paradoxes of Jewish history is that at the very moment when Hebrew scrolls were being transformed into a scripture, another body of teachings Jews would also call Torah was being organized. This other body of teachings, the Mishnah and its later commentaries, the two Gemaras (Palestinian and Babylonian), came to be known as the Talmud and in a surprisingly short time replaced the *Tanakh* as the primary source book to which Jews turned for knowledge about doctrine and duty. Though they would have denied with every breath in their bodies that the Mishnah was a second Torah, it was just that. Indeed, they sometimes conceded, *Mishnah Me'Kademet le Mikra* (j. Hor. 3:8), "Mishnah can take precedence over scripture," which they applied in certain practical matters.

THE CONTINUING ORAL TRADITION: MIDRASH

The oral tradition remained very much alive. It had to. Many Judeans still could neither read nor write. The growing importance of the Torah text did not mean that the oral traditions were cast aside or even reduced to the legendary. The historical writers of the first century C.E.—Eupolemus, Artapanus, Josephus of Tiberias, and, of course, Flavius Josephus—used the oral tradition with the same ease and sense of reliability as they used the written texts.

The emphasis on orality goes back at least to the Pharisees. There were no Pharisaic sages among the many Jews who wrote books during the last centuries before the destruction of the Temple. All that we have of even the best-known Pharisee, Hillel, are a few gnomic sayings, not all of which can be validated as originating with him. It is a peculiar feature of the Pharisaic movement—one that, unfortunately, the Pharisaic teachers did not explain—that they did not leave to posterity any programmatic explanation of their work. Their emphasis on orality may have been part of the Pharisaic effort to promote themselves as the new priest class. Since the law was not published, anyone who wanted to know the law must consult them; they wished to dispense Torah as the Temple priests had presented God's oracles.

Toward the turn of the millennium, Philo had felt it appropriate to make clear the importance and force of the unwritten tradition:

You shall not move your neighbor's landmark, set up by previous generations (Deut. 19:14). This law applies not merely to allotments and boundaries of land ... but also to the safeguarding of ancient customs. For customs are unwritten laws, the decisions approved by men of old, not inscribed on monuments nor on leaves of paper which the moth destroys, but on the souls of those who are partners in the same citizenship. For children ought to inherit from their parents, besides their property, ancestral customs which they were reared in and have lived with even from the cradle, and not despise them because they have been handed down without written record.

(*De Specialibus Legibus* IV:149–50)

In this age of intellectual ferment, new ideas were circulating: about the afterlife, personal immortality, and the individual's fate—as well as the nation's; about the messianic promise, martyrdom, and the secret, deeper meaning of certain cherished texts. Midrash—that massive interpretive effort through which Jews examined every aspect of their scripture and, in so doing, changed its thrust and nature—begins here. Midrash emerges as a full-blown discipline which required ingenuity and intellectual legerdemain since the texts were old, in a sacred language, dealt with limited subject matter, and sometimes seemed at odds with the needs and sensitivities of the cultural milieu in which Jews now found themselves. The ingenuity of Midrash inspires awe and sometimes bemusement, but we must not forget that at its heart lay the conviction that the sacred texts meant more than they seemed to mean. There was more in them than context, logic, or common sense readily suggested: in other words, even as Jews began to accept the concept of a holy scripture, the leaders pressed vigorously to ensure that the community accept these texts in a proper light—theirs. The sages did not rewrite the texts: they reinterpreted them. They held the texts sacred, but nonetheless read into them unexpected meanings.

If anything, the emergence of divergent texts intensified the importance of the oral customs, ancient practices, and familiar precedents which enveloped the text. Various groups used elements from the ocean of the oral tradition to make sure a text was understood in a particular way. (This approach is in sharp contrast to the later Protestant insistence on each individual's right and duty to approach scripture with an open mind.) To allow individual interpretation of scripture invited division within the community and ran counter to the biblical belief that God had specifically laid out what Israel must do. A text might have many legitimate levels of meaning; but at each level, only one interpretation was acceptable. The Pharisaic habit of thought, which became dominant in the centuries after 70 C.E., emphasized the careful definition of texts. Thus, with the spread of literacy and the acceptance of a particular set of sacred writings—the Torah, the Prophets, the Psalms, and the Writings—a critical shift in perspective began: the written text, once largely a repository of tradition, began to be seen as the place where investigation and discussion started, the source from which the tradition flows. Scribes and others began to study the texts for a full understanding of doctrine and discipline and for their secrets. The texts began to shape tradition.

It was the change from an oral to a manuscript culture that changed people's perceptions of what the early narratives meant.* The change was first manifested among the literate who cared about religious ideas, had access to the texts, and valued them. Trained as editors and scholars, they gravitated naturally to the analysis and the interpretation of texts; and, inevitably, not only new insights but differences of opinion began to emerge. Philo and the Pharisees drew different theologies and definitions out of the same text.

This change of perspective appears first, as we have seen, in the use of various biblical prophecies as sources for messianic and millenarian expectations. Qumran's Teacher of Righteousness took this approach to sources in the *pesharim* on various prophetic books he prepared for his followers. The Essenes venerated their founder, the Teacher of Righteousness, as an inspired interpreter of the Torah and prophets: "God had made known [to him] all the secrets of the words of his servants to the prophets" (Commentary on Habakkuk VII, 4–5), meaning that he had examined the texts of various prophets and been inspired to discover in them eschatological information. His *pesharim* developed the esoteric truths that sustained his followers. They studied the commentaries and writings and other

---

*Victor Hugo understood this transformation; in his *Notre Dame de Paris* (1871), he portrays a scholar, examining the first printed book he has ever seen, who looks up from his desk toward the cathedral and muses, "*ceci tuera cela*" ("This will kill that") (Vol. 1, p. 255).

books they considered "biblical" to understand what the teacher had uncovered when he had "digged the well of plentiful waters" (*Damascus Document* III:16), and to make sure that they kept the law of God as it should be kept. As they studied the original Torah and its prophets, they discovered "every matter hidden from Israel" which they would make known to their brothers and sisters but not to outsiders (*Manual of Discipline* VIII:11–12).

TWO FORMS OF MIDRASH

Two different midrashic techniques were adopted quite early by all groups: *peshat,* a straightforward contextual analysis of a passage's implications which made reasonable deductions from the text, filling in details and making connections between one text and another; and *derash,* a more imaginative and artful approach, and in early rabbinic times (second and third centuries C.E.) a more important one, using imaginative etymologies, assuming connections between homonyms or meaning in sentences containing the same word which otherwise have nothing to do with each other. *Derash* provided detail for sparsely sketched incidents and assured that the ancestors' actions were put in a good light. The Pharisaic sages did not invent these two forms of Midrash; both were already in the Bible. For example, there are two scriptural versions of the slaying of the giant Goliath: in the Deuteronomic telling, David does the deed with his trusty slingshot (1 Sam. 17); and, contradictorily, a soldier, Elhanan, is credited with the slaying (2 Sam. 21:19). A priest-interpreter resolved this contradiction by breaking up the words that name David's victim—*Hallahmi-et-Golyat* ("the Hittite Goliath") —to read *Lahmi ahi Golyat* ("Lahmi, the brother of Goliath") (1 Chron. 20). Thus, two different dead Philistines figure in what has become two different stories.

Derash transcends logic. *Derash* uses verbal casuistry to make the text yield what the interpreter knew ahead of time it must yield. Later the rabbis promulgated a set of rules for *derash,* but there is no doubt that the ultimate test of such interpretation was the rabbinic community's judgment that a particular midrashic analysis resulted in a fit interpretation. Some interpreters felt themselves to be inspired. Some spoke of a *Bat Kol,* a heavenly voice not unlike Socrates' Daemon, who whispered inspired interpretation to them. Interpretation, when it hit the mark, was not simply human speculation: it was linked somehow with the holy spirit.

The emergence of commentary significantly enlarges the authority of tradition, defines a particular stream of meaning, and is strong evidence that we have entered a world where the books of the Bible have begun to be seen as constitutive. Later, in rabbinic times, instead of asking priests to consult the oracles, people will ask their sages to ascertain God's will from holy texts.

THE PERSISTENCE OF ORACLES AND PROPHETS

During Hellenistic times, the texts were only one source of authority. Until the Temple altar was forcibly closed in 70 C.E., people continued to consult the priests for oracles. Philo reports that the Theraputae, a group of Egyptian Zenobites, sometimes spoke prophetically in their sleep. Daniel, which was probably written during the Maccabean revolt (168–65 B.C.E.), describes its hero as one "who had understanding of all visions and dreams" (1:17). God reveals to Daniel the context of Nebuchadnezzar's dream and then interprets its meaning. In his prayers, Daniel thanks God "who gives wisdom to the wise . . . and reveals deep and mysterious things" (2:21–22). Daniel is both sage and seer whose knowledge comes equally from the mastery of texts and from purification and prayer. He eats only pure foods, fasts regularly, and prays three times a day. He interprets well-known traditions, such as Jeremiah's prophecy that the Judeans would return to Jerusalem after seventy years of exile, even as he receives knowledge of other secret things. Visionaries like Enoch are pictured entering heaven to receive the knowledge of the future available there. Leaders of all groups claimed divine inspiration for their views and their interpretations of sacred texts.

Although the rabbis would later insist that prophecy had ceased in Israel soon after the Exile (b.B.B. 12a), it had not. While people turned to texts more often than to prophets, prophets continued to

179

speak and to be consulted on public and private matters. The rabbis understood that no one could predict what a latter-day prophet might claim to be God's will, while the text was solid, fixed, reliable. In post-exilic times, therefore, there are numerous references to what had been said before. The editors of Chronicles had the Deuteronomic histories in mind. Jubilees knows Genesis. Jonah is a novella built around a well-known prophecy concerning the destruction of Nineveh and a known historical figure. Increasingly, texts provided a place from which the rabbis could draw their definitions and extensions of the covenanted way of life.

THE MISHNAIC LANGUAGE

The Judean sages who developed the "oral law" wanted to associate their formulations with Torah, but some could not use the classic language, scriptural Hebrew, with ease. To remedy that lack, they developed an updated Hebrew dialect, which we call mishnaic, whose grammar, syntax, and vocabulary show significant Aramaic influence and include also some Persian and even more Greek words. It is not clear to what degree those who spoke mishnaic Hebrew could understand a recitation in the classic tongue, any more than a Greek speaker in Ptolemaic Alexandria who used *Koine* could understand a rhapsodist reciting Homer. *Targumim,* popular Aramaic translations of various scrolls, begin to appear in Judea. The original Hebrew speech became *Lashon Ha-Kodesh,* a sacred tongue, powerful because of its association with God's speech, revered for its identification with the ancient tradition and for its use by the priests when they conducted Temple ceremonies—all associations that helped raise the chosen Hebrew scrolls to the rank of scripture.

It is not clear whether the preachers and religious teachers of the Greek diaspora could manage classic Hebrew. There is a long-standing scholarly argument whether Philo, the best-trained Jewish scholar of the period, could read Hebrew: Philo's commentaries are seen to be based entirely on the Greek Septuagint, which he apparently quoted from memory. That such a question is raised about the most scholarly preacher-teacher of his age, and is still unresolved, suggests the distance between Greek-speaking Jews and their Hebrew traditions. Indeed, if sections from the Hebrew scrolls were chanted during worship in the prayer halls of the Egyptian diaspora, the congregation must have felt quite at sea. For most diaspora Jews, understanding the Hebrew text required translation. The rabbinic rule that a Jew may speak his prayers in any language suggests the need to accommodate monophones.

Scrolls were probably read only in translation in most early diaspora synagogues, though not usually in Palestine. Since Aramaic and Hebrew use the same alphabet, Aramaic speakers could sound out a Torah text and make intelligent guesses at the drift of what was read—not an easy task. Jews who spoke only Aramaic must have understood the Hebrew scripture's sentences much as a modern English-speaking audience hears and "understands" Chaucer or Marlowe.

It was likelier for Palestinian Jews to be bilingual in Aramaic and Hebrew. A *targum,* an Aramaic translation or paraphrase of the synagogue reading, was necessary to give most audiences a full understanding of the text and not only, as some later scholars would argue, to impose a particular interpretation of the text. We see here the separation of symbol from substance which will to some degree characterize all subsequent treatments of scripture. The *targum* was to be read aloud. It was not a sacred writing but a device to heighten understanding. *Targumim* were never encrusted, as the Septuagint was, with legends designed to establish their perfection and thus their use as a primary resource.

THE AGGADIC LITERATURE

Stories that circulated in Hellenistic times, in both oral and written form, were widely credited and would be so for centuries. History was still seen largely as story; and many imaginative products of this age, particularly the early *aggadah,* can be understood only as story. *Aggadah* is the nonlegal part of the postbiblical oral history embracing narratives, legends, parables, allegories, poems, prayers, theological and philosophical reflections. The Midrash literature, devel-

181

oped over more than a millennium, consists almost entirely of *aggadah;* and much of the Talmud is aggadic.

Several examples will stand for many. According to Jubilees, when Abraham's father, Terah, is born, the satanic angel, Mastema, unleashes a plague of ravens against his birthplace, the city-state of Ur, in the planting season. Ravens eat the seeds before the grain can grow, and the community faces starvation. There is no relief for many years, until Abraham grows up and comes to the rescue. Abraham has developed special powers, acknowledging the one true God and becoming a shaman. When the flock of predator ravens returns, Abraham stands in the fields and orders the birds "to return from whence you come." The birds turn tail. Farmers hear of Abraham's accomplishment and ask this all-powerful sorcerer to protect their fields. He plies this trade successfully and profitably for a year; but, not wanting to spend his life as a sorcerer-scarecrow, Abraham invents a mechanized substitute for his presence, a dispenser that fits on the front of the plow and drops the seed directly into the furrow, setting the seed safely in the ground before the birds can get at it (Jub. 11).

Midrashic versions of the early life of Abraham departed radically from the official narrative tradition. Jubilees, for example, offers two explanations for how Abraham came to acknowledge the one God. In one, Abraham simply thinks out the idea, and God rewards him by having the Angel of the Presence reveal to him theological secrets. And in the other, Abraham, noticing the irregular circuits of the stars moving through the heavens, reasons that if they were gods they would have arranged comfortable symmetrical circuits for themselves; consequently, their movements must be controlled from the outside. Man, Abraham reasons, should worship the controller, not the object controlled. Incidentally, in this period, Abraham had quite a reputation as an astronomer: Josephus reported that on his visit to Egypt, Abraham had taught Egyptian priests the astronomical knowledge of the Chaldeans (*Antiquities of the Jews* 1:7,8). Also, Pseudo-Philo's *Biblical Antiquities,* a free-wheeling first-century C.E. retelling of parts of the history of Israel from Adam to David, dates the beginning of Abraham's career to the generation that tried to build the Tower of Babel. In the course of the story, Abraham is cast into a fiery kiln for having acted as he believes God wants. God protects His faithful. He sends an earthquake. The kiln cracks, and its flames spread in all directions, killing those who stand about. Like Daniel, Abraham emerges unscathed. After these events, Abraham is rewarded with land and covenant and settles in Canaan, while the generation who built the tower are scattered abroad (VI.1–VIII.1, in Charlesworth 1983). The tale, again like that of Daniel, appealed to a generation that had to endure the harsh repression of Antiochus IV against whom the Maccabees rebelled. The story, though pure invention, is, like most ancient inventions, not without some link to tradition. Someone had noticed the similarity in sound between Ur (Abraham's birthplace) and Or (light, fire). Abraham emerges safely from Ur-Or, having given proof that his faith is alive.

Many portions of the written literature reveal the imprint of an oral culture's training in the use of memory aids. The frequent repetition of phrases, even of whole segments of a story, a prominent feature of biblical narrative, was one way storytellers helped their audiences fix the story in their memories. Here was a way audiences could hear the salient details they had missed the first time around. Certain psalms (111, 145) are organized on an acrostic pattern as are the first four chapters of Lamentations and the encomium to the "woman of valor" that closes Proverbs. The chant was a traditional aid to memory: rhyme, rhythm, and melody help fix words in the mind. Hebrew poetry, following familiar West Asian poetic styles, depends on a pattern of parallel lines which develop or contrast related themes, and on alternating stressed and unstressed syllables. Alliteration and word play, common stylistic elements, also helped memory. The economy of much biblical language is remarkable, considering its frequent use of repetitive patterns and word play.

THE MISHNAH

The Mishnah was organized by men who never contemplated its publication but, rather, composed and compiled the growing bulk of official rabbinic teachings into a manual of practices, processes, and instructions. The language of the Mishnah and the two Gemaras bears all the characteristics of oral tradition: a spare, compressed style, forms of argument designed to ease the burden of memory as much as to clarify logical relationships, and mnemonic devices. Indeed, in its early development, every section was taught orally.

Perhaps the most surprising fact about the Mishnah is that the decision to keep it oral was conscious. The *Tannaim* were legal folk, used to setting out their carefully reasoned and neatly sculpted arguments; and manuals of law are, after all, reference works to which a sitting judge or a legal counsel can turn for precedent and citation. Nonetheless, the Mishnah was not written down and made readily available because, despite appearances, it was not intended to be a law manual.

Mishnah presents the requirements of Jewish life, Torah, as understood and organized by several generations of *Tannaim*. Mishnah is a collection of discrete traditions organized into six thematic divisions (*sedarim*), arranged according to topics with little if any attention drawn to how these rules derive from the written Torah. While today the Mishnah is a book, it began as a process, a way of arranging material, a way of looking at the law. The rabbis compiled in their minds lists of statements of law together with spare dissents and comments, ordered them topically, and required their students to memorize these compositions as basic statements about God's requirements for Israel's religious and communal life.

The Mishnah's lists of tannaitic instructions lack any apparatus linking them to the Torah text. Rabbinic statements are generally presented on their own authority. The written Torah is rarely cited and then usually in connection with a story from the *aggadah* or in an aggadic context. The Mishnah has broken free of the Torah text. Its six thematic units were, as far as anyone knows, a major Pharisaic-tannaitic innovation.

When I present the Mishnah to students and we analyze a page or two, they immediately type it as a law code. It contains law and, like any code, tends to arrange the laws topically. The Mishnah contains law specifically described as sacred traditions received by Moses at Mount Sinai but not included in the *Sefer Torah* (*Torah le-Moshe mi-Sinai*), as well as law promulgated by contemporary and earlier authorities as far back as the *soferim,* the little-known religious leaders of the Persian period. Where the original Torah relates law to one event in Israel's past, Sinai, the Mishnah cites laws on the authority of generations of sages beginning with the Pharisaic leaders of the second century B.C.E. and running through the *Tannaim* of the second century C.E. Some rules are presented without any citation of authority; others, on the authority of a particular sage or group of sages.

As a law code, Mishnah fails in one major respect: it is not exhaustive or conclusive. It assumes many practices and rules without specifying them; it may cite two conflicting statements without reconciling them. Throughout the text are a small number of biblical interpretations and anecdotal illustrations not always apparently relevant to the topic at hand. In brief, if Mishnah is a code, it has been sloppily edited.

MISHNAH AND MIDRASH

Once it came to be believed that the written Torah could not be revised or amended, the only way to keep Torah relevant to the times was to bend every energy to its interpretation and enlargement. There were, of course, being developed at the time scrolls of legal exegesis, in which a wide range of rules and practices were drawn out of the biblical text. Indeed, Midrash was the customary way of interpreting scripture, and the sages assumed that all Jewish practice ultimately had its source in the written law. A Midrash scroll might relate to the written text, might extend biblical law, or might stipulate a rule not immediately apparent in the Torah text. Such Midrash scrolls were apparently being worked on at the same time and by the same men who worked on the Mishnah. The great exegetical undertaking of Midrash continued during and after the centuries of the creation of the Talmud. Copies of verse-by-verse compendia of rules relating to laws in books of the Torah— Mekhilta (Exodus), Sifra (Leviticus), and the two Sifres (Numbers and Deuteronomy)—were being compiled; and though researchers still debate when these texts were actually published—the jargon term is *reached closure*—there is general agreement that a major part of each was developed by the *Tannaim*.

The rabbis prized Midrash but evidently found that its verse-by-verse arrangement following the biblical text had many limitations. It is difficult to know where to look for a special midrashic source, for the biblical text is repetitive: its three different calendars of holy days (Exodus, Leviticus, and Deuteronomy), for instance, do not always use the same terms. Laws relating to similar themes are recorded in several places in slightly different language. The Torah text did not deal with a whole area of real estate law, an issue of great concern to a community such as Judea where there had been significant expropriation of property by Romans in recent times. There is no text establishing the permissible limits of Sabbath travel. The rabbis were fully aware of the problems involved in proving the dependence of the entire oral law on the written law:

> The law concerning absolution from vows [by a sage] hovers in the air. They have no text or scripture on which they can lean. The laws of the Sabbath, festival offerings and sacrilege are as mountains hanging by a hair. There is little scripture and many laws. The laws concerning civil matters, the Temple cult, purity and forbidden degrees [in respect to marriage] have scripture on which to depend. Both the former and the latter [all these rules] are essentials of the Torah.
>
> (M. Hag. 1:8)

Some long-accepted practices had no apparent base in Torah text, or at most an extremely tenuous one. The rabbis evidently felt the need for a more readily accessible and more authoritative statement of the specific rules that should govern Israel's religious practice.

THE AUTHORITY OF THE RABBIS

The men who promoted the Mishnah's agenda as the rule of community life were a learned élite. No one had elected them to any office. In fact, during most of the second century they held no official positions. Their authority was *ad hominem,* derived from the fact that they were learned men, confident of their views and intense and meticulous in their practice at a time when defeat and uncertainty hung heavy in the air. In troubled times, there is a natural human tendency to defer to those who somehow remain confident. These sages, the *Tannaim,* showed their confidence by giving themselves a new title—"rabbi." Today *rabbi* suggests an expert in rabbinic law or a congregational minister. Then it suggested the authority of learning and special knowledge about God's will rather than diligent scholarship or the shepherding of a flock. *Rabbi* comes from a root best translated "master."

The Pharisees had developed the idea that all Israel must become a kingdom of priests and a holy nation, and claimed that the concept of priesthood was not limited to a particular caste but included anyone who accepted the priestly rules of purity and served God with devotion and care. Where in Temple days priests had learned God's will through oracles and divination, the lay "priests" of the Mishnah schools did so by consulting the Torah, claiming that piety, learning, and the Holy Spirit had opened the Torah's secrets to them. The right to teach and lead was based on learning, sacred learning. The rabbis did not see themselves, nor did their disciples regard them, as simple teachers satisfied to spend their lives introducing students to texts. The rabbis taught their Torah on the Torah's authority *and their own,* and claimed the right to define the *halacha,* the way God intended His community to live.

The years of defeat after the failed and costly rebellions against Rome were desperate times. To provide Israel with a sure way to understand what was required of it was, the rabbis felt, their first and gravest responsibility. Life had fallen apart for the Jews. Urbanization, Hellenization, Roman authority, the appeal of the mysteries and millenarian cults had somehow culminated in the tragedy of 70 C.E. That cataclysmic event had given force to the belief the Pharisees had long espoused: that everyone needed to be sure of what God's instructions really were, so that there could be no question of what was right, so that the community could do the right and be guaranteed God's favor. A set of formal, highly articulated rules had governed Temple ritual. Now a similar formal, highly articulated set of rules would govern and redeem the life of the survivors.

After the defeats of 70 and 135 C.E., the synagogue stood on its own as a *mikdash me'at,* a replacement sanctuary. The *Tannaim* of the first generations after the destruction of the Temple attached to the synagogue certain rites that heretofore had been reserved to the Temple: the blowing of the *shophar* on certain occasions, the handling and blessing of the *ethrog* on Succoth, and the burning of incense. Worship was called *avodah,* the same word that had been applied to Temple ceremony. The community now met and worshiped in synagogues, a purely local institution which existed wherever Jews lived, with no authority over the whole community and few legislative powers. The rabbis recognized these limits and did not attempt to use the synagogue as the institution through which to exert authority. For that purpose they turned to their schools and the courts.

The schools were used to develop the law; the courts, to enforce the law. Through their control of school curriculum and court procedures, rabbinic law slowly and inexorably became the operative law of the Jews. The Mishnah's purpose was to draw together into thematic blocks the entire range of discrete statements about law and practice, brief case citations, equally brief references to differing legal opinions, variations of custom and community practice.

The sages gained standing during those desperate years when "Things fall apart; the centre cannot hold;/Mere anarchy is loosed upon the world,/The blood-dimmed tide is loosed . . ." (W. B. Yeats, "The Second Coming"). After the year 70, most Jews simply hunkered down and tried as best they could to survive. The Temple, the priestly venue, lay in ruins. Local government bureaus were in disarray. Some practical men undoubtedly treated with the Romans for permission to rebuild their lives and the sanctuary. Simple folk went about their work as best they could. The local synagogues were a help, but people still needed to be with and draw strength from strong and confident leaders. Even in the terrible confusion that followed on defeat, people needed to regulate their lives. Rules, laws of personal status—marriage, divorce, and inheritance—needed to be administered, and the rabbis, armed with the necessary knowledge, were available to administer what they affirmed as a God-mandated set of rules. The tannaitic masters were the only such group who had an articulated agenda. There was simply no authority other than the rabbis for people to turn to for advice, permission, or judgment. The sages were notable not only because of their piety and learning but because of their confidence in their teaching.

Reconstruction inevitably follows defeat. Victims organize to take advantage of whatever opportunities exist. In time Rome found it expedient to allow the Judeans to govern themselves in domestic matters, and turned authority over to a noble family that had not been implicated with the rebels. A member of this family was named patriarch, an official nominally responsible for the maintenance of law and order and the collection of taxes. It happened that this family, descendants of Hillel, had longstanding ties with the Pharisaic sages and their successors, the tannaitic rabbis. Rome, quick to recognize the value of the rabbis in maintaining law and order, made no protest when the patriarchs turned to *Tannaim* for administrative help as law officers and members of the various courts of appeal. No other group had sufficient status, learning, and commitment to restructure the community's religious and cultural life, to bring order out of confusion, and to offer hope and clear direction. As the *Tannaim* were co-opted into the system, their theoretical deliberations increasingly had practical consequence. That the rabbis broke new ground shows how eager the leaders were during this period of defeat, confusion, and turmoil to find a way to express clearly their purposes and commitments.

The rabbis recognized that a brief moment of opportunity was offered by the power vacuum following the defeat, and that this opportunity might be lost unless they moved quickly to impose on the community their vision and their way and to make that way clear and understandable. The rabbis do not seem to have been unassuming men. They knew what they were about. They called themselves rabbis, "masters," a term that carried intimations of authority. They recognized the mastery that such a body of knowledge gave them. They wanted to become the religious authorities of Jewish life, believing that only by following their way could the community be right with God.

Retaining close control over this emerging body of knowledge locked others out, if you will, but they were not interested only in monopoly. Tradition, as always, played its role. Many of the traditions they espoused had circulated orally for centuries. Religionists, notoriously conservative, they certainly reasoned that whatever the religious leaders of the past had done had been right; as their predecessors had acted as God wanted, they loyally followed suit.

Had the rabbis continued to use exclusively the midrashic method of line-by-line and phrase-by-phrase commentary, many Jews might have recognized just how tenuous were the relationships between the original Torah and what the *Tannaim* taught as Torah. Whatever their reasons—a desire for comprehensiveness, a desire to close off any doubts about the authority behind their program, or some other reason—the sages began to organize their teachings in the unique way we call Mishnah.

The Mishnah quickly became the foundation stone of a reshaped Torah tradition. Take, for example, the opening paragraph of the whole Mishnah:

> From what time in the evening may the Shema be recited: From the time when the priests enter (The Temple) to eat of their Heave-offering until the end of the first watch. So R. Eliezer. But the Sages say: until midnight. Rabban Gamaliel says: Until dawn. His sons once returned (after midnight) from a wedding feast. They said to him, "We have not recited the Shema." He said to them, "If the dawn has not risen you are (still) bound to recite it. Moreover, wherever the Sages prescribe 'Until mid-night' the duty fulfilment lasts until dawn." The duty of burning the fat pieces and the members (of the animal offerings) lasts until the rise of dawn. Why then have the Sages said: Until midnight? To keep a man far from transgression.
>
> (M. Ber. 1:1)

The Shema is a series of texts chosen from the *Sefer Torah* as representative of the basic commitments and hopes of Jewish life. By this time, it had come to be an extended declaration of faith. The elaboration of texts from the Torah had been matched by an elaboration of obligation—which is not derived from Torah. Nowhere in the Torah is there any mention of an obligation to recite the Shema daily. As this *mishnah* states—in characteristic, apodictic style—such rules were rabbinic formulations.

The rabbis did not look on themselves as innovators: the law was already in their minds and hearts. But the mishnaic structure and method were new: it was arranged by subject categories and its prescriptions for Jewish practice were based on rabbinic authority. The sages were confident that they were being Torah-true; but from our perspective, the reordering and recasting of texts they introduced is striking.

Everyone admits that the Mishnah represents something new under the Jewish sun, but the rabbis would have argued that things have not been so much changed as reorganized, a matter more of style than of substance. Laws supplementing the written Torah had existed since Sinai, and the *Tannaim* believed they had merely drawn together what had always been present. Religious reformers almost always claim that they are not breaking new ground but going back to the original revelation and providing a fuller understanding of it.

Still, these sages knew that their extensive rules—such as the elaborate dietary regulations—were a mountain hanging from a single scriptural thread; and that they taught Torah that included material that could not be derived directly from the written Torah: "R. Zeria said in the name of R. Yohanan: 'If you come across a *halacha* [a statement of God's law by the rabbis] and if you do not know its scriptural source, do not set it aside for many laws were dictated to Moses on Sinai [independently of Scripture] and all of them are embodied in the *Mishnah*'" (j. Hag. 1:8; j. Peah 2:4).

Although proof texts are generally missing, the Mishnah is not indifferent to the Bible. In fact, the Mishnah contains at least a quotation or two from every book of the Bible except for five of the minor prophets, and it is impregnated with the biblical text. The sages of the second century simply assumed the scriptural connection. They did not claim that what they taught was an elemental part of the Sinai revelation—that claim would come later—but clearly assumed that agreement among them on a particular position established the position's validity and had binding force. Authority lay with the sages and derived from their understanding of Torah.

Most manuals indicate that soon after the year 200 a wealthy and powerful Palestinian patriarch, Judah ha-Nasi, authorized one version of the Mishnah. We do not know when the first written manuscript of Judah's Mishnah appeared, though recent scholarship suggests it is more likely to have been shortly before the end of the third century. The Mishnah ascribed to Judah, which became the standard version, was based on the work of tannaitic predecessors who over the previous three generations had developed its topical arrangement and much of its material as elements in the curriculum of their academies. Actually, no one person wrote the Mishnah, and no one person edited it, nor was it intended to be a book. While Judah did not publish the Mishnah, he seems to have lent his authority to one of several formulations of Mishnah being developed in the various rabbinic schools, and thus effectively ended the prospects of other arrangements. Some masters arranged the blocks of law one way; others differently. Judah's motive appears to have been administrative. Like any good administrator, he was eager to reduce several choices to one and thereby reduce the chance for confusion.

The Mishnah did not become Israel's second scripture when Judah authorized a particular text. Many Jews of the time probably did not know of its existence. The rabbis were still few, and old ways disappear slowly. The Mishnah's authority expanded gradually as the rabbis extended their prerogatives, aided by their association with and support from the office of the patriarch, the delegated civil leader of the Palestinian communities. In those early centuries, it was not the text that was central but the teachings and the teachers. Indeed, the Gemara rarely quotes text: it is *tanna*, "he taught," not *katav*, "he wrote."

EDUCATION IN TORAH AND MISHNAH

One of the major functions of the received Mishnah was to provide the schools with a basic curriculum so that men who trained for religious leadership would share the same basic knowledge. The sages had a special fear of religious division, which they believed had been a major factor in Judea's defeat by Rome and the destruction of the Temple. One sage who lived in those fearful years before the destruction had commented that the community was rent apart and "two Torahs were formed" when the disciples of Hillel and Shammai had not followed the example of their masters, early first-century Pharisaic sages who could dispute without creating friction (b. San. 88b; b. Sotah 47b).

Insofar as we can re-create their thinking, the rabbis seem to have felt that the tragic rebellions against Rome were misjudgments, in part the result of the weakening of Jewish life by intellectual confusions and religious division engendered by misplaced confidence in misleading texts and ideas. God, the *Tannaim* seem to have believed, had been displeased by false doctrine and improper practice. To regain God's favor, Jews had to pay careful attention to the "right" way. The curriculum must focus on Torah and its proper interpretation—that is, on the Torah the rabbis accepted.

Elementary education was the province of the *Beit Sefer.* Here, as we have seen, the young student learned little beside his letters and the proper way to chant the *Sefer Torah* text, perhaps how to translate it. The school's goal was to train the student to participate in the ritual of reading and chanting the *Sefer Torah.* Elementary learning aimed at minimal control of the text of the *Sefer Torah* so that every male could participate in the rite of *Keriat ha-Torah.*

Higher education was carried on at the *Beit ha-Midrash.* Matriculation at this level was open to students who could show mastery of *Sefer Torah* and Mishnah: "At five the age is reached for *Mikra,* at ten for Mishnah, at fifteen for Talmud" (M. Avot 5:24). Matriculation depended on the recommendation of a *Tanna.* The later literature suggests that teachers assessed a student's competence by testing his ability to finish a Torah or a Mishnah verse when given only its opening—a test not of knowledge but of memory. The Mishnah was the set text students had to master before they were admitted to advanced study. Its text determined what was discussed in the schools. The term's assignment would be a particular tractate, one of the Mishnah's sixty-three units, to be gone through thoroughly and systematically. On the basis of these discussions, specific questions about practice were answered. Issues raised but not finally answered were, for the most part, on matters of minor detail.

At its upper levels, the Jewish school system was highly decentralized. A *yeshivah* was simply the place where the master sat; his class consisted of those disciples who gathered around. Akiba taught at B'nai B'rak; Eliezer B. Hyrakannus, at Lydda; Ishmael at Kfar Aziz. Most teaching was done out of doors. We hear of masters teaching in a vineyard, in the shade of a dovecote, in the open field, under fig and olive trees, and even in the marketplace. Apparently, concern that the untrained might be misled by conversation they overheard but did not understand, or be disturbed when they discovered that the rabbis did not always agree among themselves, led Judah ha-Nasi and a few other sages to prohibit open-air sessions. But buildings were at a premium, and some schools continued to be held out of doors. However, there were also school buildings. A few years ago in the Golan, a late second-century lintel was found that had been inscribed: "The school of Eliezer ha-Kappar." Think of low benches built into the wall rather than shelves, books, and desks. Some wealthy teachers (Halaphta at Sepphoris and Hananiah b. Teraydon at Sikkin) even maintained dormitories for their disciples.

In the early rabbinic years, there was no fixed curriculum and no governing body that could have established one. Schools were autonomous, both geographically and in respect to their interests; inevitably, several versions of certain topical units developed. One reference speaks of thirteen Mishnah versions. Masters who shared a particular vision and a general approach to tradition probably agreed on the topical divisions and the major terms of discussion, but not always on detail. The received Mishnah contains references to text that had been rejected (*Mishnah Rishonah*), and the Gemara of the Palestinian Talmud contains Mishnah texts and formulas called *Baraitot* that are sometimes different from those in the "official" version; so does Tosefta, also an expansion and alternate version of the Mishnah.

Even after the first written manuscript of the Mishnah appeared, students intending to pursue advanced Jewish studies generally did not read it but memorized it. The student went to a teacher whose first responsibility was to repeat the text again and again until the student had it letter-perfect. The Gemara usually introduces quotations from the Mishnah by a formula indicating that the sage was quoting his Mishnah from memory. Neither the Babylonian nor the Palestinian Talmud ever cites a book called the Mishnah or suggests that a citation is being quoted from a book. There is even an incident, certainly apocryphal, in which Judah ha-Nasi himself, asked about the wording of a particular rule in his Mishnah, could not immediately remember it. He turned, not to a library shelf, but to the professional memorizer attached to his court, who quickly reminded him of the quotation's full text.

Limiting advanced study to direct contact between master and student and keeping the texts oral contributed significantly to the success of two key elements of the rabbinic agenda: it concentrated interpretive authority in the hands of the masters and prevented the growth of any significant challenge to their agenda and authority. The sages controlled not only the subjects discussed in the schools but the terms of any debate. There were sages who challenged another's authority, but apparently no challenge resulted in any debate about the authority of the second scripture.

The impact of these schools depended upon the charisma of the master, who was generally recognized both as head of the school and as a holy man. We hear of masters healing the sick, writing protective amulets, and organizing prayers for rain during periods of drought. These schools radiated surprising power even though they had no statutory authority and teachers are seldom seen as powerful people. But, in the century after the defeat of 70, when the traditional sources of authority had been decimated and dismantled by the Romans, someone had to take charge, and they did. Indeed, the rabbinic schools were the first institutions to reassert themselves, which they could do in part because the Romans did not associate most of the masters with the rebels.

The *Tannaim* presented their Mishnah in Hebrew—specifically, in a contemporary dialect we call mishnaic Hebrew which retained the look and flavor of the classic tongue but differed from it in several areas of grammar and syntax and included words that were new or had taken on new meanings. The use of Hebrew was a conscious choice. Though Aramaic was at this time generally spoken by Palestinian Jews, the choice of Hebrew for the Mishnah was the *Tannaim's* way of saying: "This is Torah, no mistake." God had used Hebrew at Sinai. The priests had used Hebrew in the Temple, when they spoke God's protective blessings and recited the sacred formulas at the altar. The Talmud calls Hebrew *Lashon ha-Mikdash,* the "language of the sanctuary." The Mishnah was holy, the instrument through which Israel could become a "kingdom of priests and a holy nation" (Exod. 19:6)—the condition the *Tannaim* most devoutly longed for.

While the Mishnah was in mishnaic Hebrew, as is tannaitic literature generally, the Gemara was not. Commentaries on the Mishnah
developed in the schools of Palestine and the East. Beginning in the
late third century, the attempt to maintain all this commentary material in Hebrew was largely abandoned, and various Aramaic dialects became the language of instruction. I suspect that the language
change was prompted by the vast amount of learning and memorization involved as well as by a growing linguistic deficiency among
the teachers. It is also true that, since by the end of the third century
the Mishnah had already established itself as the central operative
document of Jewish life, there was no longer the same need to reinforce symbolically, in commentaries on it, the idea that this was
Torah.

The Mishnah had been completed without anyone setting pen to
parchment. Teachers drew together in their minds blocks of material on a certain subject and taught them as a unit to their students. A
student's first assignment was to memorize the block; and, if discussion developed, additional material of interest might be added. In
general, the process was one of formulation—as brief as possible—
then recitation, repetition, addition, and memorization.

THE PREFERENCE FOR THE SPOKEN WORD

As children of a skeptical age, we seek motives of power and privilege behind all human activity. Cynics will, with some fairness,
point out that reserving the Mishnah tradition and the sole right of
its interpretation was a way for the rabbis to monopolize power and
prestige. Trade secrets are a source of profit, prestige, and power—
temptations to which the rabbinic mind could not have been totally
immune. But I submit that such crass goals were not as important to
the sages as the power to control the definition of Torah. Only
trained minds could master the Mishnah as an oral document. One
could learn Torah only from a knowledgeable teacher, who was not
likely to accept or train students whose attitudes were suspect. Mo-
nopolizing the memorized Mishnah, as they did, the rabbis inevitably gained a degree of control over the tradition.

The sages' preference for orality may also have been influenced by the habit, particularly of Greek and Roman rhetors and lawyers, not to publish interpretations of their legal codes. A student in the Roman law schools had to memorize the law even when texts were available.

Perhaps the rabbis did not want to allow anyone to challenge their texts with other texts. More likely, they wanted to make sure that their texts were correctly understood: each text consists, for the most part, of a few bare-boned statements which need to be fleshed out and provided with context. Many talmudic sayings warn against those who know texts but have not "served the rabbis": that is, who have not been taught the accepted implications of the texts by an accredited master (b. Sotah 22a). By making it difficult for anyone to learn the text simply by memorizing a book in which it appeared, the sages built into their system an extra safeguard against misunderstanding and division. No bright and untrained rebel could get hold of a text and "prove" that the sages had made the text say what it clearly did not. The goal of Talmud Torah was not to develop a critical literary spirit but to gain and ensure acceptance of the rabbinic point of view as normative. In the twelfth century, Maimonides, with his usual acute perception, recognized many of the issues that must have been involved:

> *Words that I have communicated to you orally, you are not allowed to put down in writing* (b. Git. 60b). This precept shows extreme wisdom in regard to the Law. For it was meant to prevent what has ultimately come about in this respect: I mean the multiplicity of opinions, the variety of schools, the confusions occurring in the expression of what is put down in writing, the negligence that accompanies what is written down, the divisions of the people, who are separated into sects, and the production of confusion with regard to actions.
>
> (*The Guide of the Perplexed*, p. 176)

It is easy to understand how the rabbis came to believe that what the God of Israel wanted was for Jews to obey the text. Scripture seemed to require it. There was Exodus 34:27, which they translated: "The Lord said to Moses, write these laws, for from My mouth are these laws." By separating the two final clauses, they gave this text the meaning "that laws given to you in writing are not to be translated orally and laws transmitted orally are not to be set down in written form" (b. Tem. 14b; b. Git. 60b), the interpretation that Maimonides later praised. There were also all manner of later rationalizations. Some sages suggested that God wanted to keep the Mishnah oral to reserve these documents for Israel's sole benefit (Tanhuma, Vayera 5). Someone else reported that Moses had asked for permission to write out the oral law, but God had refused, knowing that gentiles would translate the written Torah into Greek and claim it for their own, saying, "We are Israel." God is made to say, "Only they are My children who possess My mysteries. That is the *Mishnah*" (Urbach 1975, p. 305, n.63).

A GUIDE FOR COMMUNITY LIFE

History suggests that there are two kinds of thinker: romantics, who delight in golden words like *justice, peace, beauty;* and realists, who argue that such terms are meaningless unless understood within a specific context. Romantics tend to dismiss realists as nitpickers and spoilsports. They admit that legal analysis is useful but find it, for the most part, spiritually unsatisfying. The soul should be able to soar above the constraints of qualifying clauses. Some rabbinic spirits may have soared to the heavens, but their labors on the Mishnah were concerned with precision and academic definition. Mishnah prescribed an almost endless series of specific and detailed structures for religious and community life and devoted little space to mystical or messianic fancies. Consequently, a searching soul would not pick up a Mishnah to find consolation and encouragement. Indeed, this is generally true of the second scriptures of all traditions. Though canon law may be neatly argued, as a guide for a troubled soul seeking spiritual encouragement, it is inadequate. For spiritual sustenance, each religion turns to its original scripture. For the definition of doctrine and practice, it turns to its second scripture.

The Mishnah's style is presumptive. "Cases concerning property are decided by three judges; cases concerning theft or personal injury by three, claims for full damages or half damages, two-fold restitution and claims against the idolater, the seducer, and 'he that hath brought unto an evil name' [are decided] by three [judges]—so R. Meir. But the sages say, 'He that "hath brought an evil name" [must be judged] by three and twenty, for there may arise therefrom a capital case'" (M. San. 1:1). Where the written Torah includes references to ordinary courts and courts of appeal, the principle that the seriousness of the penalty to which a person may be exposed shall determine the number of judges required to hear a case clearly goes beyond anything stated in it. But as it was taken for granted that this *mishnah* follows inexorably from the written law, no attempt at proof or citation was made. This method—or absence of method—is true throughout the Mishnah. The value of the law is, in a sense, independent of its pedigree. The rabbis' judgments had an authority independent of the written text. These men knew their Torah. They would have recognized immediately the phrase "he that brings an evil name" as used in Deuteronomy 22:19 of one who casts doubt on a maiden's virginity. They had no need for citations. No system of reference by chapter and verse would be in general use for nearly another thousand years.

The sages did not have a mandate to legislate for the community; their claim to power came not from any Torah text but from the tumultuous history of the time and the nature of their studies. They were masters of *halacha,* the rules accepted as God-ordered. The consequences for the Mishnah are that, instead of seeming to mandate statutory law, it conveys the sense of being an ideal statement of God's law. The Mishnah seems interested less in practical concerns than in determining what ideally should be the practice of the community in regard to Sabbath, marriage, or civil and criminal law. The Mishnah sages did not think primarily in terms of power and authority. Indeed, their assumption of authority was uncomplicated because during these formative years they were "masters" of the legal process and so did not have to compromise with any other group. What they discussed, and consequently the major thrust of the Mishnah, is the ideal of a Torah community, the rules that ought to govern Jewish life.

The Mishnah was not shaped and developed solely as a code of practice for the governance of Jewish life. At least one-sixth of its sixty-three tractates, eleven in all, relate to the operation of the Temple, which, of course, was no longer in existence when these tractates were put together. Yet these texts seem to have been studied with the same intensity and attention to detail that the rabbis employed in discussions of immediate matters. The Mishnah is Jewish in a classic Jewish way. It is interested in today, the business of law, and in tomorrow, the business of hope. It lives in two time zones, the present and End Time, when the Messiah will come. When the Temple is rebuilt, it will be necessary to know what is required of those who will serve at the altar.

There was value in discussing such issues as the operation of the abandoned cult. Had not God promised some day to return the sacred fire to the Temple? The very last sentence in the whole mishnaic compendium is one of its few messianic expressions: "R. Simeon b. Halafta said: The Holy One, blessed be He, found no vessel that could hold Israel's blessing except peace, for it is written, 'The Lord will give strength to His people; the Lord will bless His people with peace'" (M. Uktzin 3:12; Ps. 29:11). This hope would be realized, the rabbis believed, when Israel fully and properly obeyed God's will. To their minds, disaster was almost always deserved. They sided with Job's comforters. Israel had sinned, but God is merciful and an obedient Israel might again merit God's favor. Their ideal Torah way was a practical contribution to the political situation because, by following it and obeying God, Israel would regain God's favor.

THE TWO TORAHS

In the fourth century, the material included in the Mishnah and other contemporary halachic compendia came to be known as *Torah she be'al Peh*, "oral or memorized Torah." The phrase, designed as a complement to *Torah she bi Ketav*, "written Torah," was meant to indicate the existence of a second scripture. The piety that both Torahs had been part of the revelation at Sinai, that a two-sided revelation had taken place in Moses' day, later became a commonplace of rabbinic Judaism. On orders from God, Moses had inscribed the written Torah and memorized an oral teaching he had passed on to Joshua without addition or change. In his turn, Joshua had passed this tradition to his immediate successors, and they to theirs. An unbroken chain of respected teachers had preserved this teaching orally and with fidelity down to rabbinic times. The oral Torah is seen as a complementary Torah, part of the original revelation, fully sharing in its commanding authority.

Despite the later popularity of this myth of a two-sided Torah originating at Sinai, it is difficult to imagine men such as Hillel or Akiba, sages of the first and second centuries, accepting it with any literalness. To be sure, they knew of specific traditions labeled *Torah le-Moshe mi-Sinai,* traditions not included in scripture but claiming a pedigree that could be traced back to Moses at Sinai. Surprisingly few of these traditions—actually only two—are cited in the Mishnah. While the sages argued that this oral law was authoritative, they presented the Mishnah on their own authority, not as revelation. The Mishnah text does not include such phrases as "and the Lord said to Rabban Simeon b. Gamaliel, 'Say to the children of Israel.'" Rather, it says, "Rabban Simeon b. Gamaliel said" or, "The sages said" (M. Git. 6:6).

To be sure, the opening paragraph of the Mishnah tractate known as *Pirke Avot,* "Sayings of the Fathers," explicitly states the piety of the oral law: "Moses received Torah from Sinai and gave it to Joshua" (M. Avot 1:1). Recent research has made it clear that *Pirke Avot,* a compendium gathered over many generations, was a late addition to the Mishnah. The earliest datable reference to the two-sided law comes from a Midrash generally dated to the late third or fourth century c.e., in which the titular head of the *Tannaim,* Rabban Gamaliel, responds to someone named Agenitos the Hegemon, apparently a Roman officer, who asked the Master, "How many Torahs were given to Israel," and is told, "two, one oral, one written" (b. Shab. 31a; b. Yoma 28b; b. Kid. 66a).

In the premishnaic era, Sadducees had denied that the unwritten tradition carried authority; and there must have been men of similar views in the community after 70 c.e. Had the early *Tannaim* thought in terms of a second Torah, they would not have undertaken the extensive and elegant efforts they invested in the halachic Midrash, that complex interpretive effort undertaken to prove that rabbinic teachings were derived from a careful reading of the written text. The earliest claim advanced for the Mishnah was not that it was an actual record of God's instructions to Moses but that its tradition somehow participated in the authority of Sinai. The Mishnah text makes this clear since it contains comments by sages who take opposing views and includes references to outdated or once accepted but now superseded Mishnah statements (M. Ket. 5:3; M. Naz. 6:1; M. Git. 5:6; and so on). What was claimed—though the simple folk, as always, took the myth literally—was that the Mishnah and its commentaries faithfully interpreted the Torah, an interpretation that was a blend of the oral and written law to which Israel had presumedly been bound since Sinai.

The Mishnah lays out the fundamentals of that modulation of the Jewish tradition cherished and practiced by the Palestinian rabbis. The Mishnah and its commentaries are rabbinic Judaism's fundamental documents, which over the centuries were studied in the rabbinic academies and cited in rabbinic responses. The *responsa* literature deals primarily with questions of discipline and practice, and only secondarily with questions of belief and doctrine. The clinching argument in a debate is less likely to be the citation of a Torah text than the citation of a decision made by a sage of the mishnaic period. A pronouncement by an *amora,* a rabbi of the third or fourth through sixth centuries, cannot reverse an earlier tannaitic statement; but in their turn, amoraic opinions in the Gemara or in other texts of the period represent a second level of authority accepted by all subsequent generations. Rabbinic authority rests on the rabbinic Torah and on the rabbis.

There is one Mishnah but two streams of mishnaic elaboration and interpretation, two Gemaras: one developed in the academies of Palestine; and the other in the academies of the East, in the area the Jews anachronistically called Bavel, or Babylon. The Palestinian, or Jerusalem, Talmud occasionally, but infrequently, quotes a Babylonian sage. The Babylonian Talmud does cite Palestinian sages. But the sages east and west recognized the Mishnah's authority; divergences in interpretation which developed between the Palestinian and the Babylonian academies, as codified in their respective

Gemaras, dealt primarily with marginal rather than with central issues. Had this not been so, Palestinian and diaspora Jews would have based their lives on distinctly separate scriptures and serious divisions between the communities would certainly have arisen.

A thousand years after the publication of the Mishnah, Catholic missionaries were puzzled that their proselytizing sermons made so little impact on Jews. An occasional apostate tried to explain to these fishermen for Jewish souls that the Jewish tradition was talmudic rather than biblical; and that to understand Jewish piety, they would have to steep themselves in rabbinic literature. No easy task. The Talmud is massive, only partially edited, written in various Aramaic dialects and mishnaic Hebrew. Moreover, Christians had been taught as a matter of doctrine that Judaism had been spiritually inert since the once-chosen people rejected Jesus and had been rejected by God; that the synagogue was blind and its Talmud nothing but a compendium of superstitions and follies. As early as 553, the emperor Justinian, in his *Novella Constitutio,* signals this approach when he condemns the study of the second scripture: "But the so-called second tradition [Deuterosis] we prohibit entirely. For it is not part of the sacred books, nor is it handed down by divine inspiration through the prophets, but the handiwork of men, speaking only of earthly things, and having nothing of the divine in it" (146, chap. 1:ii, quoted in Baumgarten 1980, p. 37). Most Christians believed there was little motivation to study the Talmud, that it really was fit only to be burned.

Still, the apostates spoke fair. The Jews affirmed a Torah tradition that rested on the Mishnah far more than on the Bible. Over the centuries, many a *yeshivah* student spent his years studying the Talmud, yet rarely handled the scrolls of the Prophets.

THE DISCIPLINE OF TALMUD TORAH

In contrast to the care and ceremony with which Jews treat Torah scrolls, no formalities were attached to the Mishnah either in the synagogue or in the schools. The Mishnah played no major role in synagogue liturgy. Several paragraphs found their way into the prayer book, but the Mishnah itself was never systematically read out. Nor did the Mishnah receive the careful editorial oversight the masoretes gave to the *Tanakh*. No formal scribal conventions developed to govern its manuscript presentation; and, once printing was available, no effort was made to continue producing Mishnah or Talmud manuscripts as the scribes continued to produce Torah scrolls. The Mishnah was a utilitarian work. From the beginning, scholars felt free to add notes in the margins of its text. With the development of the Gemara, the Mishnah text was broken up into blocks, to each of which was appended the amoraic commentary. To be sure, if a copy of the Mishnah were accidentally dropped on the floor, the clumsy reader would pick it up hastily and kiss it, but he would act the same way with a prayer book or any other text that contained the name of God. If one were to judge a scripture solely by whether it is treated as a sacred object, the Mishnah would not qualify.

The Mishnah was a school, rather than synagogue, text. The Mishnah was recited, usually from memory, in an atmosphere that invited debate. One participated in a school of Mishnah and Talmud in order to learn what it meant to be a Jew. The written Torah had its ceremony, public reading in the synagogue; the second scripture never developed a formal public ritual. Instead, it became the fixed content of a key religious discipline, Talmud Torah. Often mistranslated as "Bible study," Talmud Torah was a much broader discipline.

Talmud Torah was a new rabbinic obligation. No rule mandating Talmud Torah appears in the written law. It was a rabbinic enactment to which the rabbis gave great weight: "These are things for which no measure is prescribed: cleansing, first fruits, the festal offering, deeds of loving kindness, and *Talmud Torah* equals all of these" (M. Peah. 1:1). "These are things whose fruits a man enjoys in this world while the capital is laid up for him in the world to come: honoring father and mother, deeds of loving kindness, making peace between a man and his fellow; and *Talmud Torah* is equal to them all" (b. Shab. 127a).

Among the Jews, learning was praised for its importance in character formation. Talmud Torah, the virtue of study, was a discipline quite unlike what any modern means who talks of schooling. We think of the classroom as the place where a student masters a body of useful knowledge. We read silently and seek to grasp the key facts and to discover ways to solve, or at least understand, a problem. Once we have learned a discipline's vocabulary and methods, we are satisfied if we know where to look up the rest. Learning equips us primarily with survival skills; and, despite John Dewey and others of his convictions, we have no illusions that knowing how to build a bridge or write acceptable prose will make us better people.

Talmud Torah taught the Jew how to please God and, in the process, become a better person: "The more Torah, the more life" (M. Avot 2:8). The sages, who read aloud to their students and taught them to read aloud ("Let your ears hear what your mouth speaks" [j. Ber. 2:4]), took as only part of their goal imparting factual knowledge of Jewish law and practice. Since basic knowledge of their law was assumed as it governed life in the community, the goal was, rather, that knowledge of Torah would put more Torah inside a man's head. Talmud Torah was a discipline whose value was the discipline itself. Torah presented God's own words. Reciting God's words was a powerful act of identification with God. Knowing God's words was a powerful tool in one's ethical development. The more Torah sings in your mind, the more able you are to live the covenantal life. Through repeated recitation, Jews hoped to imprint the sound of God's words on their minds, to hear them as God had spoken them at Sinai, to respond with the immediacy with which one responds to a spoken command.

Torah was not literature but words derived from God's own speech. Those who chanted from the *Sefer Torah* participated in a divine act, speaking aloud the words God had spoken at Sinai. When they recited the oral law, they sought to hear not only what He had said—the words—but the tone, inflection, and rhythm tradition associated with His speaking.

Many believed that, by reciting and studying these texts, they were learning to free themselves of earthly concerns and joining their hearts to God. Just as the Greek thinkers had believed that the exercise of pure reason led to the activation of the intellect and to a form of transcendence, moral purity, and perhaps even immortality, so the Jew who spent his days with Torah was busy not only with

God's work, helping God out, but—like the monk who spent his life in meditation and denial—approached God Himself.

The learned were not the only ones who accepted the redemptive value of Talmud Torah. In the close Jewish communities of the Middle Ages, it was not uncommon for ordinary working people to form a fraternal society, a *havurah,* around the twin aims of providing mutual aid and a weekly Sabbath regimen of Bible or Mishnah recitation and study. Indeed, these informal *havurot* focused on the Psalms and the Mishnah far more than on the *Sefer Torah.*

Talmud Torah describes an active intellectual involvement, primarily with the concerns of the oral laws. After the third century, advanced education was called Talmud Torah. The advanced student found a master who taught him Talmud, more law, and much more interpretation. The teacher presented the text and repeated it (b. Hor. 13b). These texts were not usually unencumbered statements of Mishnah law, but blocks of commentary and fragments of classroom discussion which defined the teaching and tried to understand its underlying principles. *Gemara* literally means "study." After students memorized a text, there might be discussion of the concepts of law and theology implicit in it or of the appropriateness of the use of hermeneutic rules in its interpretation. As the sages recognized that not all could manage such erudite material, they decreed that someone who can do no more than read or recite the Shema twice a day, morning and evening, has fulfilled his Talmud Torah obligation; but one sage added, "Don't tell him this lest he feel this is all that is required" (b. Men. 99b).

There are tractates on the Sabbath and the holy days, civil and criminal law, matters of personal status, vows, the rule of the Nazarite—all matters referred to in one way or another in the written Torah; but the Mishnah goes far beyond the Torah text. Deuteronomy contains a key liturgical text: "Hear (*Shema*) O Israel, the Lord our God, the Lord is one" (6:4). The Mishnah was primarily interested not in the theology of the Shema but in its practice. Is the Shema only this one sentence? The Mishnah suggests a lengthier recitation and later makes clear that it is referring to a set of three biblical passages beginning with Deuteronomy 6:4–9 and including Deuteronomy 11:13–21 and Numbers 15:37–41. When is the

Shema to be said? Twice daily at carefully stipulated times. Preceding and concluding benedictions are stipulated, and their wording closely examined (M. Ber. 2:2ff.). Rules determine whether one can interrupt the recitation and for what reasons. There are rules concerning the worshiper's posture during the recitation. Voice level is regulated. There are rules governing what to do in case a mistake is made. Certain exemptions are indicated: a bridegroom on the first night of his marriage is not obligated to recite these paragraphs.

We know that the Shema was recited daily. Its central texts are from the *Sefer Torah,* but the Torah contains no law requiring that these texts, or any other, be recited daily or that such recitation be accompanied with a prescribed set of blessings. In rabbinic discussions of the Shema we come upon this statement: "He whose dead lies before him is exempt from reciting the Shema, from saying the *Tefillah* and from wearing *Tefillin*" (M. Ber. 3:1). The *tefillah* is a series of petitional prayers, usually eighteen, which together with the Shema constitute the core liturgical formulas of the synagogue service. *Tefillin* are phylacteries, small boxes containing parchment scrolls inscribed with several biblical passages that a Jew places on his forehead and right hand during morning prayers. The Mishnah here describes existing practices that are not necessarily grounded in the Torah's text. There is no specific Torah text requiring that the *tefillah* be recited or *tefillin* put on.

THE AUTHORITY OF THE MISHNAH

When in the fourth century the Mishnah achieved scriptural authority, it sanctified for Jews a wide variety of customs and practices that had grown over the centuries, and bestowed on them the cachet of equal standing with the Instructions contained in the written Torah. In so doing, it enlarged significantly the body of regulations Jews accepted as obligatory.

As the rabbis took over from prophets, priests, and scribes as the leaders who would transmit to Israel God's words and will, authority came to rest with the learned and their learning. But rabbinic authority, like prophetic authority, was not automatic. As there had been false prophets, so some rabbis fell into error. We hear of rabbis being excommunicated. Not all Jews accepted the full range of obligations the rabbis laid out; but in most of the Jewish settlements, the Mishnah was slowly accepted as fundamental and authoritative. The Mishnah became and remained the basis of a curriculum that was ever after to dominate and condition the Jewish mind. How this came about has never been satisfactorily explained. Where Christian laymen rarely read canon law, Jewish nonprofessionals read the Mishnah, and the Mishnah and the Gemara became the staples of a program of lifelong education. Part of the reason lies in the nature of the school system the rabbis developed, of which the Mishnah was the centerpiece.

The Talmud contains an imaginary drama: Moses descends to earth to visit the school of R. Akiba, perhaps the most renowned *Tanna* of the first half of the second century. Moses slips into a back row and listens attentively, but with growing perplexity. He does not recognize what is being taught in his name. According to the sage who invented this story, Moses is satisfied when he hears Akiba certify his teachings as part of the oral Torah Moses had received at Sinai. The only way one can unpack this story is to suggest that the rabbis acknowledged that Moses did not recognize the teachings being quoted in his name, and could not recognize the practice of Akiba's day (b. Men. 29b). While such admissions of change are rare, the Jerusalem Talmud does say that in three places the *halacha* uproots scripture. The three specifics seem minor: that one may write a divorce document on any kind of writing surface rather than only in a scroll (Deut. 24:1); that the blood of a dead beast may be covered by any kind of growth, not just dust as Leviticus 17:13 requires; or that the ear of the Hebrew slave who during the Sabbatical year refuses his freedom can be pierced with a needle or a bit of glass and not just the awl as Exodus 21:6 requires. In none of these cases is a basic change made in the Torah law: a bill of divorce must be written, the blood of an animal must be covered, the ear of a slave who refuses his freedom must be pierced—but to tinker with even the details of God's own words is no small matter. The written Torah specifically insists: "You shall not add nor subtract from it." That mishnaic Judaism was a new modality, the rabbis rarely acknowledged.

208

By interpreting the law to include both current practice and venerable tradition, the rabbis created a religious discipline and teaching whose texture was quite different from what many Jews had known before. Authority was to rest with a learned élite, precise rules were to govern all aspects of the religious life, worship was provided with a fixed liturgy, part of every day was to be devoted to Talmud Torah, and hope lay not only in the promise of national renewal but in personal immortality. The management of one's private life, the food and drink one consumed, the garments one wore, the care of one's household, even marriage and parent-child relationships were to be governed by a defined and all-encompassing set of rules. What was right was right because it was stipulated. Duty began in obedience rather than in man's conscience. The rabbis believed in doing the right thing for good motives, but they also believed that the force of habit and community pressure to do what is right can often lead to doing right for its own sake (b. Sotah 22b).

Even household practice comes under the law: separate meat and milk dishes, properly slaughtered meat, concern for the purity of food into which other food may accidentally have fallen, rules governing the cleansing of pots and pans which have been ritually contaminated. Neat and precise rules detail how marriage contracts or bills of divorce are to be written, witnessed, and handled. Relationships with non-Jews were carefully regulated, as were the relations of husband and wife. Codes of civil and criminal law were expanded. It is rabbinic regulation, not the written Torah, that requires the separation of men and women in the synagogue and limits the role of women in the synagogue.

MEMORIZING THE ORAL TORAH

Rabbinic education required a good memory. A prayer learned and recited daily is always on one's mind. *Zakhor,* "remember," was for the Jew a mandate not only to keep alive his people's past but to keep alive the terms of God's commandments.

Determined to keep Mishnah unwritten, the sages inevitably confronted the unequal capacities of individual memory. A good memory is not always attached to a good mind. As the Greeks knew of rhapsodists who could recite Homer fluently but had no understanding of the poem's meaning, so the Jews knew of *Tannaim* similarly limited, "A basket filled with books" (b. Meg. 28b). During these centuries, we hear of men who were used as living tape recorders. Lecturers in advanced seminars could ask such men to recite a block of material the lecturers intended to discuss or simply to refresh the master's memory of the exact wording of a particular citation (j. Ma'aser Sheni 5:1). The Talmud warns that, despite their ability to recite blocks of the Talmud, memory professionals were not to be treated as scholars: "The magician mumbles and does not understand what he says; similarly, the memorizer recites but does not understand" (b. Sotah 22a).

The sages' emphasis on memory, in growing out of a conscious decision, differs from the older traditions of the early biblical period when few were literate and orality was inevitable. The sagas and laws were recited in the vernacular, heard and understood by all. In rabbinic times, basic literacy was fairly common, but Hebrew had ceased to be the people's everyday speech; and even the Hebrew of the Mishnah was spoken only by a minority. To be sure, a folk tradition still persisted in rabbinic times: tales, cures, superstition, customs, conventional wisdom, legends, tales of holy men and their magic, popular medicine and therapies, passed on naturally from generation to generation. There were popular storytellers. Fathers taught their sons; mothers, their daughters. There was no need to systematize this knowledge, which penetrated and influenced every aspect of community life, and it was never collected or codified.

The new oral tradition was, on the other hand, élitist, self-aware, artificial in the precise meaning of the word—in being a creation of human ingenuity. The substance of the new oral tradition was a highly sophisticated tradition of religious and juridic analysis with which ordinary folk had little contact. It belonged to a schooled, literate audience of the academy, not to the world of the storyteller. Students learned these traditions from a master, not at home or in the street.

In an academic world that emphasized oral knowledge, the educational system needed to encourage the development of the memory capacity. Beginning students were repeatedly set the task of reciting

Torah verses they had learned in school (b. Hag. 15a–b; b. Git. 58a) or portions of the liturgy (M. Pes. 10:4; M. Suk. 4:5). In the more advanced classes, a teacher might recite biblical verses dealing with the Sabbath or a holy day, and then a block of rules elaborating on Sabbath or festival law, and assign the class the responsibility of learning it all by heart (M. Shab. 7:2, 10:3–5, 12:1–3). When a youth began to study Mishnah, his teacher would recite a block of law, and the student would repeat it until he had it memorized; months of rote preceded any discussion of meaning. Although the masters taught that Judaism rested equally on three virtues—Torah, study; *avodah,* religious practice; and *Gemilut Hasadim,* acts of covenant loyalty—for the advanced student Torah study was primary. He need not leave his studies to attend worship in the synagogue. Told that his son, an advanced student, was spending his time doing good deeds, a rabbi sent him a stiff note that said in effect, "You could have done those good deeds at home. That's not why you are at school" (Tos. Pes. 3:7; see Goldin 1971, p. 179, n.4).

Homework meant repetition and more repetition. The teacher began a lecture by reciting the text to be discussed; then the student repeated the text. It was suggested that a teacher should repeat a verse or portion at least four times to make sure the student had mastered it (b. Eruv. 54b). Some teachers and students were prepared to repeat a lesson four hundred times. Students were instructed to repeat a new section in the evening, review it the next morning, again at noon, and again in the evening (b. Men. 18a). "One should always recite even if one does not understand what one is saying" (b. A.Z. 19a). It is not unusual to hear of a student repeating his master's interpretation over and over until he can summon up the exact tradition at will.

Obviously, few students memorized this vast atomized literature: "Here is the way it really is; of a thousand who start out to learn how to read scripture, only a hundred go further; of the hundred who study *Mishnah,* only ten go further; of the ten studying *Talmud,* only one becomes an authority" (Lev. R. 2:1; Koh. R. 7:28). It was no easy matter to memorize blocks of law or biblical interpretation; both Midrash and Mishnah reflect the pressure for compression. A teacher should present the material to be memorized in the fewest possible words (b. Pes. 3a). A judge or a teacher who made an elementary error, and ruled against the clear intent of the text, was told in no uncertain terms to go back to school and learn it (b. San. 33b).

Yet prodigious feats of memory were commonplace. R. Meir on one Purim found himself in an out-of-the-way spot in Turkey and had no *megillah* with which he might fulfill the command to read that scroll on the holiday. What did he do? He wrote a *megillah* from memory and then read it aloud (j. Meg. 4:1). As late as gaonic times (beginning in the eighth century), legend has it that a scholar shipwrecked in Spain was able to provide that community with a Talmud by dictating it from memory.

Schools were noisy places. The oral law, like the written law, was chanted as it was being learned. A master needed to hear a recitation in order to correct it. Speaking softly or mouthing the words was frowned on. The literature includes monitory tales of students who chanted softly and forgot everything they knew (b. Eruv. 54a).

Students were judged by their memory aptitude: "There are four types of pupils: swift to hear and swift to lose, his gain is cancelled by his loss; slow to hear and slow to lose, his loss is cancelled by his gain; swift to hear and slow to lose, a happy lot; slow to hear and swift to lose, an evil lot" (M. Avot 5:15). Again, "Four types sit before the sages: the sponge, the funnel, the strainer, and the sieve. The sponge absorbs everything; the funnel takes in at this end and lets out at the other; the strainer lets out the wine and collects the dregs; the sieve extracts the coarsely grained flour and collects the fine flour" (5:18).

Mastery of the rabbinic agenda earned status and respect, but the masters could not be certain of retaining their knowledge. Imagine the fears they must have had about possible memory loss caused by fever or illness or old age. When he became ill, Judah ha-Nasi is said to have forgotten thirteen blocks of material from his Mishnah and to have had to be taught these again by others (b. A.Z. 52b). To avoid any lapse of memory, some sages repeated aloud all they knew as they walked or worked. Others disciplined themselves to repeat the entire oral law every thirty days (b. Pes. 68b).

The teacher sat in front of students on a pillow or chair with his disciples cross-legged on floor mats. At public lectures when several masters and students would meet together, a *meturgaman* or *amora* (speaker) was provided. The sage explained the rule to the *meturgaman*, who shouted out the sage's thoughts. Questions were given to the *meturgaman*, who consulted the sage and then elaborated the sage's answer. The *meturgaman* was often something of a scholar though not a master permitted to vote in the council of scholars which had final authority in judicial matters.

Memory was key and king. It was a high compliment when one sage described another as a cemented cistern which does not lose a drop (M. Avot 2:11). There can be no doubt that methods for developing the art of memory were much discussed. The Talmud is full of acrostics and *simanim*, "signs," put there by editors and teachers to help fix particular formulations in the mind.

One *simanha* focuses on a memorable phrase that suggests an extended legal formula. Another device tied together unrelated statements by providing them identical opening formulas, an ancient practice found in the oracles of the eighth-century B.C.E. prophet Amos ("for three transgressions . . . yea for four"). Numbers were useful: "three things must a man say within his house when darkness is descending on the eve of Sabbath" (b. Shab. 2:7). The fallibility of such devices is suggested by a comment unfavorably comparing the memories of the sages of the Galilee to those of Judea: "The sages of Judea retained their knowledge while those of the Galilee did not because they emphasized *simanhas*" (b. Eruv. 53a). Various biblical texts were cited to "prove" the importance of these techniques: "Put it [*Sima*] in their mouths" (Deut. 31:19); "Erect markers [*Tziunim*], set up signposts" (Jer. 31:21). One technique associated blocks of material with some short, easily recalled statement: Thus, the phrase "great is the sanctuary of Moses" suggested to a certain R. Manesseh three statements about charity which begin successively with "great," "sanctuary," and "Moses." While it is hard to project ourselves back into the mental gymnastics of such a totally different culture, we can recognize how the biblical verses memorized in childhood and frequently heard in the synagogue became the lattice on which the sage hung the associated formulas he wanted to be able to recall. He summoned the Torah text to remind himself of all that had been developed from it.

It was suggested that students form an image of the master who had promulgated a rule even as they memorized the rule, thus fulfilling the requirement that a rule be cited in the name of its propounder (M. Avot 6:6). This was a peculiarly Jewish version of a Greco-Roman memorization technique whose method is outlined in the first-century text *Ad Herennium.* The author, an anonymous teacher of rhetoric, considered two aspects of memory: as a natural endowment, and as an endowment whose efficiency and capacity can be increased by careful training. How is one to train one's memory? Since sight, the author believed, is the strongest and sharpest of the senses, the best way to fix something in one's memory is to associate it with a place and with objects there that can be easily recalled to the screen of the mind. The author suggests that the reader walk through a large, multichambered building and fix in his mind the shape of every room and the placement of objects in each room. Then when he wants to memorize a speech or a text, he should associate the various ideas he proposes to put forward with each of the rooms he walked through and each sentence or phrase with an object in the appropriate room. To recall the speech, he has only to walk through the rooms and among their furnishings in his mind.

The Jewish sages seem to have used a written text as the Romans used a building. Paragraphs, words, and letters became keys to memory. The phrases and letters of a memorized text can stand for a place and its various rooms and objects, "for the places are very much like wax tablets or papyrus, the images like the letters, the arrangement and disposition of the images like the script, and the delivery is like the reading" (Yates 1966, p. 7).

LEARNING AND CHARACTER: THE RABBIS

Today students attend a lecture to learn a specific body of knowledge and are relatively indifferent to a professor's private life and character. That learning and character can be separated is a modern attitude, one the ancient world would not have accepted. Classic theories of education treated learning as essential to the development of character. Learning, the Greeks said, is what distinguishes man from brute, Greek from barbarian. Their theory of education assumed that the purpose of schooling is to initiate the youth into his community's ways of life and to lead him to become a good citizen by helping him to know, understand, and conform to its customs.

Learning was seen as more than a classroom-bound experience. The Roman teacher was a pedagogue, often a freed Greek slave, who was with his charge constantly, teaching him not only to read and write but how to behave in all possible situations. The boy was told that his goal should be to pattern himself on his mentor. He was to shape his mind and body into an esthetically and ethically pleasing persona. His studies were not ends in themselves, as they are for us, but ways to develop aspects of character. Philosophy was the queen of the disciplines because it opened the mind to the orderliness of the universe, an order the student was to duplicate in his person.

It was a rare Jew who had his own pedagogue, but the underlying Jewish approach to learning was not very different. The rabbis used *musar* to mean both "instruction" and "correction" as to manners and morals. Proverbs plainly said, "Train up the child in the way that he should go" (22.6); and the sages often quoted as conventional wisdom a maxim spoken originally to quite another purpose, *Ayn am ha-aretz hasid,* which they took to mean that an ignorant man cannot have a good character (M. Avot 2:6). The goal was to lead a righteous life.

The ancient world assumed that the more learning, the more virtue, and that the philosopher would distinguish himself in all areas of life and be the proper leader for his city. Men came to Plato or Zeno not only to listen to their philosophy but to benefit from their example. Similarly, learning presumedly made the rabbis more Torah-like and, therefore, better equipped to guide and organize community life.

Over time, particularly in the Eastern diaspora, the master came to be seen not only as mentor but as exemplar of the Torah way. The student literally attended the master and learned by copying his manner and daily routines as well as by memorizing his recitations. Learning was not simply a matter of mastering a body of knowledge, but involved emulating the teacher whose every action was believed to exemplify Torah, just as his speech defined it (b. Ber. 62a).

Scholars and disciples were distinctly costumed. The rabbi became a role model for his disciples who saw him as a living Torah, whose every act, the way he dressed, ate, conversed, even the way he cleaned himself, was a reflection of Torah. The rabbis' actions as well as their words refracted Torah. Knowledge, self-confidence, and culture breed awe; and rabbis tended to be treated with the awe due a shaman. Some seem to have deliberately traded on charisma. Others apparently restricted themselves to the pieties of study.

Knowledge allowed the rabbis to share some of God's powers, even to the extent of defining God's will. Since Torah is a divine discipline, their advice and deeds ultimately participated in divinity. A late legend makes this point: A debate rages among the sages of the academy of Usha over the ritual fitness of an oven. A vote is taken. All the sages but one declare it fit. The dissenter is absolutely convinced of his view and tells his colleagues that his view is in fact God's. God will back him up. How? God will cause a large tree in the yard to move. The tree moves, the vote is taken again, and the sage remains a minority of one. God Himself cannot stand against the will of those who have the credentials of Talmud Torah (b. B.M. 59b).

The rabbis of the talmudic period were not members of a clerical profession. Unlike the leaders of the Qumran community, most did not withdraw from their communities. Unlike Hellenistic teachers and rhetors, they did not live off tuition or eschew business or the crafts. Those fortunate enough to inherit wealth or to have been born into the priest class lived off their inheritance or tithes. Others earned their living as best they could. Some held public office, some were artisans. All taught—only a very few in large lecture halls; generally a sage recited and discussed Torah with a few advanced students.

Theoretically, the rabbinate was a meritocracy open to all who qualified; but, as is always the case, the sons of the masters, because of their early training as well as family contacts, were at an advantage. One joined a master only after years of patient memorization and a long and arduous education. Joining a master involved a prolonged apprenticeship and faithful personal service as well as attendance at his lectures.

Israel's Second Scripture: The Talmud

Although Jews were not writing books in this period, rabbinic culture was far from antiliterate. These men bent every effort to have their communities establish the first Western mandatory educational system for boys. One of the important rites of the synagogue was the chanting of portions of the Torah, and it was the task of tutors and primary teachers to prepare every male child for this act. The sages were literate but evidence little literary interest. There were compilations but not compositions. Philo had no successor as author of Torah commentary. Josephus had no successor as historian. The books that emerged were not planned. They represent a deposit of academic notes.

The rabbis of the period were literate but not bibliophiles. They studied Torah. They did not write books. They had little interest in establishing libraries. They finalized the anthology of volumes that would ever after be known as *Tanakh,* the written scripture, but their work was at least in part to set aside all other early works. The literature that survived from the Persian and Hellenistic periods did so because of happy chance—the Dead Sea find—and the interest of the Catholic Church (the Apocalypse-Philo). The rabbis were interested only in those texts that suited their purposes.

While there was no book burning or official censorship, the rabbis deliberately decided to limit the curriculum of their schools to those works they accepted as scripture. Whereas a variety of books had played a major role in the schools of the Hellenistic age like Ben Sirah's, they played a minor role in the rabbinic academies. There were few, if any, reading assignments. The Talmud does not refer to a single *yeshivah* library.

We do not know whether Jews other than the *Tannaim* wrote. If any did, the sages had no interest in their work and allowed it to disappear. Out of sight was out of mind, literally: only the material the *Tannaim* cared about survived.

Yet this was not a bookless world. There does not seem to have been an actual ban on writing down rabbinic law, certainly not one that was enforced, although there were traditions known in the schools of the fourth and fifth centuries that no one was to write down the oral laws—*Ayn Kotevim Halachot b'Sefer* (Schol. to Meg. Ta'anit). There were, of course, biblical scrolls. Some sages kept *pinkasim,* "notebooks," which seem to have been little more than private lists of rules, *halachot,* kept by students or teachers as aids to memory. We hear of scholars who kept shorthand notes (*megillot setarim*) of "scrolls of secrets." In the fourth century, students are described as writing out a text of the Mishnah for classroom use. We are told that some Babylonian students made notes on their classroom walls (b. Hul. 60b). There were also rolls of *aggadah,* though in time the same emphasis on oral transmissions seems to have governed *aggadah* as governed the law. One of the founders of the Eastern rabbinic community, Rav, is said to have consulted *Sifrei d'aggadata,* collections of Torah-related midrashic materials (b. Git. 60a). There is a reference to a *Sefer Aftarta,* a collection of sections of prophetic readings used in the liturgy (b. Git. 60a). But that is the sum of it.

What the masters emphasized was memory, and they took for granted that the oral law should be kept oral. There is no evidence from the third to the seventh century, when written collections of Gemara begin to appear, that the sages made any concentrated effort to prepare a standardized text of any rabbinic work. The knowledge and memory of the master, rather than the text of the manuscript, determined meaning. No liturgical mishnaic rituals, no *Keriat ha-Mishnah,* was developed. The Mishnah and other rabbinic anthologies were creations of the school and belonged in the school. Their importance lay in the fact that Torah came out of these schools. As we shall see, after the third century, rabbinic decisions were for the most part given *de facto* authority by those—the patriarchs and the exilarch—required to organize the Jewish community's domestic life; consequently this academic material became the basis of the new Torah tradition.

CONCLUSION

By the fourth century, the concept of the two Torahs had been broadly accepted. The image is of equal elements; but in actual practice, the sages gave their oral Torah the greater weight. It served as the basis of their educational curriculum and legal decisions. Despite the ceremonial care with which they treated the *Sefer Torah,* they did not hesitate to declare flatly: "In three areas the *halacha* [God's law as they taught it] overrides a specific scriptural instruction" (Urbach 1975, p. 294). Illustrations of this attitude can be multiplied: "The covenant was made at Sinai only on account of the oral Torah" (b. Git. 60b). "Both written and oral laws have been proclaimed and we cannot tell which is the more precious, but since it is written *'Al pi* [literally, "by the mouth of"] these words have I made a covenant with you and with Israel' (Exod. 34:33), we infer that the oral Torah [literally, the Torah by mouth] is the more precious" (j. Peah 2:4). Indeed, the regimen of rabbinic Judaism during its formative centuries was singularly free of any bias toward a narrow scripturalism.

In rabbinic thought, the authority of the sage was at least equal to, if not higher than, that of all the prophets except Moses; and we find such statements as: "since the destruction of The Temple prophecy was taken away from the prophets and given to the sages" (b. B.B.12a). The prophet was forced to show signs. The sage was believed on the authority of his teaching (Urbach 1975, p. 306, n.65). Like the prophet, the sage came to be seen as a holy man. He had the spiritual power and knowledge to heal and to intercede and the authority to say, "One does this" and "One does not do that."

The years when tradition had not yet become scripture were a time of development and change. Scripture suggests, "So it has always been." Not so. No historic, time-informed study can accept the proposition that Judaism is simply the sum of its Torah books, or that Jewish disciplines and values are fully set out in these books. That was not the intention of the prophets or sages or the rabbis for whom the book was a tool, not a totality.

 6

THE MEDIEVAL
SYNTHESIS

If you wish to know God who spoke and the world came
into being study *aggadah*.
—Sifre Deut., Aykev 49

The Torah—the twenty-two books that constitute the Hebrew
Bible—had been deemed sacred by the third century C.E. In subsequent centuries, the Talmud—comprising Mishnah and its commentaries, Gemara—defined the rabbinic interpretation of Torah
and the way of life the rabbis held sacred. Until modern times, the
Talmud would vie with the *Sefer Torah* for scriptural pride of place.

With the Muslim conquests of the seventh century, Jewish communities throughout West Asia had to accommodate to yet another
culture. Muslim expansion into Europe—specifically, into Spain in
the early eighth century—fostered sizable Jewish settlements there
and along the North African littoral that linked the center of the Islamic world with Spain. Initially these communities relied on the
gaonic academies, whose political authority came from the caliph at
Baghdad, but as political power in Islam shifted to the West, a new

and independent Jewish life flourished on the Iberian peninsula—the so-called "Golden Age" of the tenth and eleventh centuries. The Muslim rulers could not long withstand Catholic efforts to reconquer the peninsula, and with Muslim defeat, Jewish life there was effectively over by the end of the twelfth century. In other parts of Europe, Jewish life continued—in Lithuania, Poland, the Rhineland, along the Danube, in Italy—overshadowed everywhere by its homelessness: *galut,* exile, was a fact of life and became a state of mind.

THE TALMUDIC PERIOD

The magisterial *A History of the Jewish People* (Ben-Sasson 1976) typically labels the period between the destruction of the Temple in 70 C.E. and the beginning of the Muslim conquests around 640 C.E. as the era of the Mishnah and the Talmud, and there can be no gainsaying the significance of the period and its achievement for the future development of Judaism. Over these centuries, the Jew knew his everyday Judaism through the Talmud, which governed the conduct of life and became the core curriculum for the Jewish school and for continuing Jewish education.

Also, what was true of the Torah proved to be true of the Talmud: the absence of an authorized written text did not prevent a tradition from acquiring a generally agreed-on shape or a broadly accepted power. Within the span of a century or so after the Mishnah's views were collected, they held sway over large portions of the Jewish community.

While there is general agreement that the patriarch Judah ha-Nasi (late second century) authorized a particular Mishnah collection among several being developed, it is not clear when or under what conditions written copies of this authorized Mishnah began to circulate and even less clear under what conditions his version of the Mishnah developed commentary, Gemara. Gemara shows real interest in establishing a text. Many statements begin: "This is not the Mishnah. . . . This is the way it should read." Gemara on occasion suggests that a particular rabbi taught two texts that contradicted each other, and then ponders which statement truly reflected his view or whether, under certain conditions, both statements could. The development of commentary was not a neat process, as evidenced by the frequent appearance of variant readings in the Gemara and in the Tosefta, an enlarged version of the Mishnah probably dating to the fourth century.

Each Mishnah tractate, a discussion of generally related ideas, was treated as a separate unit. The earliest strata of the Gemara tend to be explanatory and clarifying and to elaborate on Mishnah texts; together, they constitute the Talmud, which consists of layers of briefly stated debates, decisions, case law, and comments on various types of law as they had accumulated in the academies where Talmud was reviewed and studied.

THE AUTHORITY OF THE TALMUD

The Talmud emerged in and from the major *yeshivot*. It was the creation of an intellectual caste, primarily the result and record of the discussions they held in a few central academies in Palestine and in Babylonia. These are long and complicated texts, the Babylonian Talmud almost twice the length of the Palestinian. They were edited in each generation and did not reach closure—that is, achieve their final form—until after the editorial labors of the *savoraim,* sixth- and seventh-century scholars who apparently worked on the various parts piecemeal. Certainly, the editorial efforts of many hands are apparent. The two Talmuds—the Babylonian and the Palestinian—reflect slightly different tendencies. There is more evidence of later editing in the Babylonian than in the Palestinian Talmud. As each generation of sages debated the positions taken by their predecessors and looked for general principles which would explain why earlier sages ruled as they had or had disagreed, they discussed relevant cases and legal procedures and sometimes brought into the discussions tannaitic traditions that had not heretofore been included.

Just as most Judeans during Temple days never saw a Torah scroll, so most Jews during the talmudic period never saw a Talmud scroll. During the third and fourth centuries, there was little need to publish this material. The sages represented a small, though slowly enlarging, group within the community, but until they became part of the official administrative apparatus—as they finally succeeded in doing in Palestine in the third century and in Babylonia a bit later—they had no authority to impose their way. Many Jews were simply not interested in the sages' complicated and often esoteric academic discussions. Even if interested, ordinary folk could not master the details. Many acknowledged the spiritual authority of individual masters, seeing them as holy men who could heal the sick and exorcise evil spirits. Most knew the Talmud only as they heard a preacher or a teacher speak of it or, more significantly, as its teachings affected their daily lives. It was the Talmud that codified what they could and could not eat, when they should worship, how they were to regulate marriage, divorce, and adoption, how criminal and civil court cases were to be managed, and like matters. Many accepted the essential elements of the rabbis' Torah, the Talmud, insofar as it affected daily living. But they were far from accepting the idea that Talmud Torah—the reading of scriptures—required of all Jews a discipline of lifelong study of Mishnah and Gemara texts; that view lay well in the future. First there had to be texts; then there had to be a reason to master these texts. For most Jews, the ability to read a few lines of Torah was hard enough.

Talmud scrolls were not as readily available as Torah scrolls. Copies of the Mishnah did not begin to circulate before the fourth century, and none but the major communities before the eighth or ninth centuries had a copy of even one of the talmudic tractates. Some teachers had notes on one or another of the emerging blocks of talmudic commentary, but these *pinkasim* were reserved for the use of a few favored students and colleagues. *Megillot setarim*—literally, "secret scrolls," but in all probability simply a student's private notes—are known to have existed in early amoraic times (third century). There is every reason to believe that some students made unauthorized records of some portion of the texts they memorized. But the oral law was intended to be oral. Though most masters knew most of the Talmud of their day by heart, they had as a member of their school staff a "living book," a *meturgaman,* who could fill in any of their lapses.

Talmud scrolls were not yet readily available in the diaspora during the seventh to eighth centuries.* The diaspora's lack of and longing for a Talmud is personified in an eighth-century legend whose hero, aspiring to become the head of one of the academies and despairing of his prospects, leaves Baghdad for Spain. When he lands in his new home, he finds there no copy of the Talmud, and proceeds to remedy the situation, as only a master of the oral law could, by writing one out from memory. Not until the eleventh century were copies of the Talmud sufficiently widely distributed that the diaspora communities—and the scholars who lived in them—were no longer completely dependent for copies on the academies or on the remarkable memories of professional memorizers and scholars.

Despite both its manifest centrality in Jewish life, and the fact that it became the people's second scripture, the Talmud was never treated with the same formal care as the Torah. Efforts of editors such as the *savoraim* notwithstanding, the Talmud—or rather, the two Talmuds—were never subjected to the rigorous editorial process that would have produced a single accepted text. Little effort was made to create a clean text. Indeed, there probably never existed a uniformly recognized text. There was no formal order for the presentation of Talmud. Various versions circulated, generally alike in shape and content but full of variant readings and inconsistent selections.

The work of copying out these long and complicated texts did not begin to be seriously undertaken until the emergence of the great centralized academies during the eighth and ninth centuries in Palestine and in the areas east of it called Babylonia, now modern-day Iraq and Iran. The expense and effort involved in writing such extended manuscripts suggests that copies were available only in the centers where patronage was available, in such administrative academies as Sura, Pompedita, and Mahoza, which flourished under the

*Surviving correspondence between diaspora communities and the academic centers includes petitions from the communities asking that the academies send them, through the merchant-messenger who presents their petition, a copy of the Talmud because none was locally available. One ninth-century *responsum*—that is, a letter answering such a petition or an inquiry from a diaspora community—makes special mention that the head of the academy, the *gaon*, had had a copy of the Talmud written at the request of Spanish Jews.

Ommayad and Abbasid caliphates in the eighth and ninth centuries. For the first time, there were the will and the means, in a prosperous Jewish community that had grown up around the powerful Muslim courts, to carry out the expensive task of setting scribes to make copies of this voluminous text.

THE AUTHORITY OF THE RABBIS

The Talmud's authority was established, as I have said, by and through the authority of rabbis, by their reputations and their activities as administrative and judicial officers in the community. What was unique about the talmudic period was that it saw the successful marriage of the religious and secular authorities of the Jewish community. The Roman and the Sassanian emperors, who adopted long-established West Asian patterns of minority self-government, were eager to have someone responsible for the domestic peace in each of the many minority communities that made up their empires. These emperors assigned this role among the Jews—the patriarch, or *nasi,* in Palestine; and the exilarch or *resh galutha,* in the East—to certain men of noble birth and wealth, generally to those who claimed descent from the Davidic dynasty; these men paid for the office, which included certain tax-farming rights through which they generally recouped their investment. To maintain domestic peace, which was among the requirements of their commission, these officials needed a committed administration; they found a ready-made one in the rabbis, who had the necessary skills and interest and general recognition of their authority, as well as their own rabbinic-juridic agenda. The rabbis seized this administrative opening with the stipulation that the secular authorities—if we can call them that, since both the patriarch and the exilarch had religious authority as well—grant them the right to administer the laws of personal status and of justice according to the tenets the rabbis held to be sacred. In this way, rabbinic law became slowly, but surely, the norm in Jewish life. It was an instance of legal practice preceding its formulation in a legal code. The code, the written Talmud, appeared centuries after talmudic law had become widely accepted.

When Islam came to rule in West Asia, the caliphs continued the pattern of minority self-government. The effective spread of rabbinic authority can be traced to the military conquests of Islam and the centralization of caliphate authority over the areas where Jews lived. Rabbinic law became the almost universal norm in the communities of the diaspora under the strong central authority of the academies, which were empowered as agents of law and justice by the Abbasid caliphate (*c.*750–1258). After 750, the caliph devolved power on the leaders of the tolerated non-Muslim minorities (*dhimmi*) to govern themselves, and the academies enthusiastically took on the responsibility of being the exilarch's agents, two of them—Sura and Pompedita—moving to Baghdad to carry out their new charge more effectively. In order to organize the proper governance of the *dhimmi,* the caliphate empowered over each community one of its own to keep the peace and to collect taxes. In the Jewish community, the exilarch had his offices at the caliph's court in Baghdad and turned to the Baghdadi academies to provide him with a cadre of legal officers and knowledgeable administrators. The heads of these academies—the *gaonim,* literally, "eminences"—were significant authorities between the seventh and twelfth centuries.

The rabbis' functions as officials help to explain the theoretical bent of much of the Gemara, which, as the years passed, moves increasingly away from descriptions of proper practice toward a search for the general principles behind discrete and separate practices. The Mishnah had said most of what needed to be said about practice. The rabbis of the third through sixth centuries, the *amoraim,* tried to understand the spirit behind the mishnaic ideal of practice, the nature of God's will, and to work out how they and their colleagues could use the courts to bring community practice up to that ideal; thus, the Gemara's use of details of specific cases and citations of precedent.

THE CONTINUING AUTHORITY OF TORAH

The emphasis on the Mishnah and Gemara as the key documents of this period leaves the unfortunate impression that the Palestinian

226

and Babylonian Talmuds are in many ways proof of the intellectual élite's indifference to scripture. Not so. Israel now had a scripture. While the sages of the mishnaic and talmudic period ruled on their own authority, they and those for whom they ruled believed that all the rabbis spoke and wrote grew out of and depended upon the written Torah as interpreted by their predecessors. The Mishnah and its commentary, the Gemara, represent the thoughts and convictions of the rabbis. Much of the material is presented on rabbinic authority and much of it reshapes or transcends the scripture. It is also true that every talmudic tractate is replete with scriptural texts.

The written law was often cited, and all talmudic citations, significant or insignificant, show a close reading of the Torah text. The Gemara of Berakhot, the opening tractate in the Babylonian Talmud, contains quotations from every volume of the written scripture except four of the minor prophets, Ezra, and Chronicles. At the beginning of Berakhot, where the issue arises of establishing the proper time for the public recitation of the Shema, the Mishnah sets out to establish the evening hour before the morning hour. Why? Because of the sequence explicit in a Torah text: "and thou shalt recite them . . . when you lie down and when you rise up" (Deut. 6:7). And if one text were not enough, another sage offers a text from Genesis: "And there was evening and there was morning, one day" (1:5). Thus, if the rabbis made the oral law in a sense their law, took it as the final word, they did not diminish in any way the authority or the symbolic value of the written Torah text.

The rabbis took it as their responsibility to encourage as well as to instruct Jews, often ending a tractate with an encouraging or consoling *midrash*. At the end of Berakhot a certain R. Eleazar draws on Isaiah and Psalms: "The disciples of the wise increase peace in the world, as it is said: 'And all your children shall be taught of the Lord, and great shall be the peace of your children'" (Isa. 54:13). Read not "your children" (*banayik*), advises R. Eleazar, but "your builders" (*bonayik*). There then follow lines from the Psalms: "Great peace have they that love your law and there is no stumbling for them" (119:165). "Peace be within your walls, prosperity within your palaces" (122:7). "For my brethren and companion's sake I will say, peace be within you" (122:8). "For the sake of the House of the Lord our God, I will seek thy good" (122:9). "The Lord will give strength unto His people, the Lord will bless his people with peace" (29:11).

One of the unique features of early rabbinic Judaism was, as I have noted, its lack of interest in any books other than those it accepted as scripture. By the third century C.E., the pattern of Jewish education was largely fixed, the *Sefer Torah* has become and remained the basic text for elementary education, now required for all Jewish males five years of age and older. Everyone—every male, at least—knew some scripture. The elementary school system, which had been spreading across the whole Jewish landscape during the previous several centuries, assured by its concentration on the Law and, to some degree, the Prophets, that the language of the Bible would be an essential part of the community's everyday idiom. Most Jews never went beyond elementary schooling. One sage estimated that for every one hundred boys who started their education at the age of five, only ten proceeded to study the Mishnah at about the age of ten, and far fewer, perhaps only one, went on to study with a Talmud master. While abler students learned to read portions of the Prophets and Writings as well as the *targum,* it appears that most dropped the systematic study of the written scripture at about the age of ten; for those who went on, education centered on the Talmud. Students at the secondary level learned a proper version of the Mishnah; and perhaps the schoolmasters taught a few of the brightest, upper-level students some Talmud, but more probably those who were ready for such intellectual efforts were passed on to the academic centers, where advanced students were increasingly going to study.

But we must not minimize what the old-fashioned, rote education accomplished for most Jews. The young man had heard the language of the Bible—Hebrew. He understood many biblical phrases and knew many biblical stories. He had been brought into a universe of discourse which gave cohesion, coherence, unity, and direction to Jewish life. If he could not read from scripture during public worship, he knew the Torah blessings and appreciated why the Torah was read and could nod his head sagaciously when a preacher made a telling textual point. The Torah was his.

228

Every community had at least one synagogue, and every synagogue had at least one *Sefer Torah,* probably many more. Everyone heard it read on the Sabbath and market days and on fast days and festivals. Most synagogues probably also owned scrolls of the Prophets and Writings. During the early rabbinic period, it became common practice to add to Torah readings a thematically related portion (*haftarah*) from the latter sections of scripture. So the Jew was conditioned to the Bible. It was the Bible to which he returned during worship week in and week out. In school he had memorized many biblical phrases; and he sprinkled them through his daily speech, whether he spoke Greek, Aramaic, Latin, or Arabic.

For all Jews, the learned and the half-literate, the Bible was the basic text. *Keriat ha-Torah,* the reading of Torah, was a basic redemptive rite. Mishnah and Talmud, as elements in an educational curriculum, were treated with utmost seriousness; they were the technical education, if you will, of the Jewish community, the way a Jew mastered the rabbinic way of thinking and living. Talmud education was treated with great gravity; but it was the assumptions and teachings of the basic text, the Bible, which gave the Jew his tie with God and with his people. To ninety-five out of one hundred Jews, the Talmud was unexplored territory. Only advanced learning, reserved to an élite, was talmudic.

Clearly, the emergence of rabbinic Judaism should not blind us to the steadily growing importance of *Mikra* during these first seven centuries after the destruction of the Second Temple. The sages who worked on Talmud were steeped in biblical study, quoting from the Bible repeatedly and extensively in their discussions of *halacha,* the law, and *aggadah,* the stories. They approached all biblical texts as equally sacred and important, since all were part of God's message. Their conception of biblical unity prepared Jews to accept the exegesis they heard in sermons which bound together ideas and sentences without what we would consider any self-evident logical or temporal connection; the conventional exegesis sometimes linked unrelated biblical verses or sentences on the basis of an identical word or similar-sounding words. The sages insisted that "a sentence never loses its plain meaning [*peshat*]" (b. Shab. 63a), but read the Bible so that each sentence had both its plain meaning and an almost infinite number of possible meanings. Jews were conditioned by such readings to a different perception of context than ours. Torah, as they knew it, consisted of God's speech, was of God's devising, a miracle. Though they might not have phrased it this way, they believed that God's words were not confined by the familiar canons of common sense and context or by the laws of logic. These categories were applicable to human compositions, not to God's. God's speech had its own laws. Everything they ever heard about the Torah emphasized its divinity, its depths, and its mysteries.

The sages saw the written and oral laws as in spirit one and the same. Much of their effort was directed at making explicit the underlying unity they assumed. Having satisfied themselves through their investigations of the law, *midrash halacha,* that the oral law was implicit in the written, the sages developed a new dimension of meaning for the term *Torah.* Torah was not only the written text but all that could "legitimately"—that is, within the bounds of their exegetic point of view—be deduced from it. Scripture became the sum and substance of what the rabbis knew it to be. Thus, we hear sages speak of using Torah to establish Torah: *Mei Torah?* What is Torah? *Midrash Torah.* Torah is what has been searched out and found through rabbinic exegesis to be Torah.

SERMONS AND MIDRASH

Only in these talmudic centuries, when the Torah was accepted fully as scripture, did Torah develop a full-blown midrash. The midrashic comments, originally discrete statements, were ultimately drawn together by sages and editors into presentations, sermons, or sermon outlines, which followed, more or less sequentially, the texts of the books of the Bible or were related to the themes of a reading reserved for some special occasion.

The rabbis were concerned, particularly in talmudic times when their authority did not yet reach throughout the diaspora, that the community understand and accept that the whole scripture was in fact this larger entity. Popular sermons served as one effective way to make the point. Often on the Sabbath and festivals, a homily or sermon would be given. Although sermons sometimes, as in the examples to be cited here, introduced the scriptural portion, they were generally offered after the scriptural reading. The preacher generally sat during his delivery. Noted speakers used a *meturgaman* (literally, "translator") as a human megaphone. The speaker spoke his thoughts to the *meturgaman,* who cried them out to the congregation, a convention apparently devised to increase the respect in which the speaker was held. Sermons were not free-wheeling affairs but followed strict conventions that tested a speaker's originality and pluck. Typically, the speaker would take a sentence or theme from the Prophets or Writings—at first glance, thematically unrelated to that day's *Sefer Torah* portion—and by stringing together a number of texts, pass from text to text, from idea to idea, until he came, *mirabile dictu,* to the text that began the week's Torah portion.

One example can stand for many. A preacher began with a line from Ecclesiastes: "The words to the wise are as goads, and as nails well planted are those that are composed in collections; they are given from one shepherd" (12:11). Why, he asked rhetorically, are the words of the Torah likened to a goad? His answer: Just as the goad directs the heifer along the furrows in order to bring forth life from the earth, so the words of the Torah direct those who study them away from the paths of death to the paths of life. Then he noted a problem with the analogy: A goad is movable. Are the words of the Torah movable, transient? Obviously not. Therefore, the text says "nails." He noted another problem: A nail does not grow. Do the words of the Torah not grow? Therefore, the text adds "Well planted": just as the plant grows and increases, so the words of the Torah grow and increase. He continued with the analysis of the text's implication: When those who occupy themselves with the Torah disagree—some pronouncing unclean and others pronouncing clean, some prohibiting and others permitting—a man seeing this division of opinion might say, "How shall I learn Torah from men of such divergent views?" Therefore, the text says, "They are given from one shepherd." One God gave them; they were spoken by the mouth of the Lord of all creation, Blessed be He, for it is written, "And God spoke all these words" (Exod. 20:1)—which brings us to the opening line of that week's Torah portion, which presents the Ten Commandments.

Assuming the unity of the scripture as they did, the sages went about the business of interpretation using the unsystematic and atomistic approach that is Midrash; they had no need of a sequential and systematic one. Any text they reached for was related to every other. The Torah became text, context, and pretext. Midrash examined it all down to the most minute detail. Even the shape of a letter or the unusual spelling of a word might reveal God's teaching. Through Midrash, preachers and sages developed the myriad ideas they found in scripture and in experience, and bound disparate texts into what was to them a single, unified whole—God's words.

Midrash in its classic form is biblical interpretation as practiced during the formative period of rabbinic Judaism. The great collections were begun in the third century and developed until about the seventh, although collections continued to be built up for another five hundred years afterward. Midrash collections from the talmudic period fall into two general categories, one dealing with legal matters and the other sermonic or homiletic. The first one, *midrash halacha,* tends to investigate biblical texts; the other, *midrash aggadah,* tends to investigate sermons of the time, most of which were based on biblical texts.

Sermons seem to have had a threefold purpose: education, encouragement, and entertainment. The sermon was an effective way to teach Jews about scripture, about the unity of its texts, about the requirements of the rabbinic Torah, and about the teachings of the faith, about such themes as God, the nature of Torah, divine providence, immortality, and human nature. That the scripture was constantly raided to develop this wide variety of themes is evidence of its importance in community thought and of the detailed familiarity that even unlearned Jews had with its narratives and wordings.

Paradoxically, this assumption of unity allowed the sermonizer a great deal of freedom. Since he began with God's word, the source guaranteed the value of his observation. If he took a position that contradicted that taken by another sage, he did not have to worry that his point of view in all respects be dogmatically correct. His hearers could assume either that he was mistaken—as, being human, he could, of course, be—or that two sages had derived different insights from the same phrase or text. Jewish life never imposed aggadic uniformity. "Both this view and another are the words of the living God" (b. Eruv. 13b).

Sermon subjects were chosen from themes as wide as life's experiences. Some tied together what we might describe as loose textual ends. Some united popular folk traditions with more official traditions. Some simply made observations on aging, on men and women, or the meaning of life. Some reflected on contemporary political conditions. Unfortunately, no full text of a sermon from the talmudic period survives. What we have are the bare bones, an outline or a précis of the points made and the texts used. One element is certain: these talks frequently ended with an encouraging reaffirmation of the messianic hope, a confident restatement of God's care for His people or a prayer for redemption. The rabbis were well aware that the people's longing for redemption was evidence of difficult times, even for a community steeped in faith. "In the past when money was plentiful one longed to hear a word of the *halacha* but now that money is scarce one longs to hear a word of *aggadah*" (Yalk. Exod. 271).

Speakers in all ages have found that a light touch will draw a far larger audience than a dry and austere message: you can instruct people only if they will listen. Since the sermon was a significant feature of Jewish life in talmudic times, the preacher had to learn the art of entertaining. Women and children as well as men came to the sermon, the illiterate as well as the literate. The sermon's popularity testifies to the skills of those who spoke and to the audience's thirst for an encouraging word and for the pleasure of being cajoled by one who knew how. Even listeners who really did not know the sources were eager to be entertained and enticed. There was a rabbinic saying that what is done for a less than high-minded reason often comes to be done for the best of reasons. Those who came to be entertained often left inspired.

Even in the absence of complete examples, the sermon more than any other feature of talmudic times illustrates the degree to which the Jewish community's speech was impregnated with the language of scripture. The outlines of sermons that survive in collections of *midrashim* are usually arranged as if they provide a running commentary on a biblical book. Biblical phrases were on every tongue, and these phrases kept Hebrew alive. As aggadic *midrash* truly began to flourish in the talmudic age, several midrashic collections began to take shape, particularly *Genesis Rabbah, Leviticus Rabbah,* and *Pesikta de Rav Kahana.* The opening chapter of *Leviticus Rabbah,* usually assigned to the fifth century, is another example of the midrashic method. The sage picks a text—in this case from the Psalms. Though there is no apparent link between it and the other materials he chooses, he moves nimbly through the scriptures until he arrives at a connection between the psalm and the opening of the Book of Leviticus: "and the Lord called unto Moses."

"Bless the Lord, ye messengers [*malachim*] of His, you mighty in strength who fulfill His word, hearkening unto the voice of His word" (Ps. 103:20). The midrashist asks, of whom does the text speak? He answers, on the basis of etymology, that *malachim* designates both human messengers and angels. He reasons that human messengers are intended here; otherwise, the sentence would be more inclusive: "all you his messengers." He then equates messengers and prophets, on the basis of a second text that refers to a prophet: "Then spoke Haggai, the Lord's messenger." In a short but interesting digression, someone asks, "Who are the mighty in strength who fulfill His word," and promptly answers, "Those who observe the sabbatical year." Why these particularly? Because unlike all others who observe a commandment for a day or a week, the one who observes the sabbatical year must see his field remain untilled for a year and still pay his taxes. When he does this in an uncomplaining manner, he fulfills God's command. Is there anyone who with greater might or strength fulfills a greater obligation than this? Turning to the task of relating the psalm text to Leviticus 1:1, the midrashist quotes a rabbi who said that a task too difficult for one man can easily be done by two. The midrashist observes that the reverse is impossible; that a burden too great for sixty myriads, the sixty thousand Israelites at Sinai, cannot be done by one man. Yet that is precisely what Moses did. The Israelites at Sinai were afraid to hear the voice of God "lest they die" (Deut. 5:22). Moses heard it and lived. So "the Lord called unto Moses" (Lev. 1:1) and no one else.

The word *midrash* comes from the root *darash,* "to investigate," "to search out and expound." The beginnings of Midrash go back to the imaginative embroidery of old narratives and traditions by Israel's early storytellers and rhapsodists. Many suggested etymologies of proper names in scripture are a primitive form of Midrash. An instance is of two place names that have generally the same sound and meaning: "Abraham called the name of that place *Adonai-Jireh,* as it is said to this day: 'In the Mount where the Lord is seen [*Be-Har Adonai-Ye'raeh*]'" (Gen. 22:14). Biblical editors used Midrash to adjust texts to correspond to the people's expectations of a story line, a hero's behavior, or the unity of the biblical tradition. David did not give Solomon plans for the Temple he should build to honor God (2 Sam. 7:13; 1 Kings 2), but the priest-editors of Chronicles made up for this unfortunate lapse: "and David gave to Solomon the son the pattern of the Porch" (1 Chron. 28:11) and "the detailed working out of the plan" (28:19). The priestly editor of Ezra reported that his hero "set his mind to investigate [*li'derosh*] the Law of the Lord in order to teach effectively its statutes and ordinances" (Ezra 7:10)—as precise an explanation of Midrash as one could hope for.

The midrashist approaches the text with the psalmist's prayer, "Hide not your commandments from me" (119:19); and when he achieves his ends, he repeats the psalmist's contented sigh, "The opening of your words gives light" (119:130). In many ways, it is best to look on Midrash not as a logical search for what can be deduced from a text, but the other way round—as an imaginative search for what the midrashist believed to be Torah. We suppose that the rabbis had little sense that they were imposing their ideas on the text. Since the text was a unique literature, God's own words, and therefore of infinite depth and breadth, it already had all ideas in it. The midrashist believed he was simply uncovering the full meaning of a text, although he inevitably moved well away from the plain sense of a text. One of Amos's most damning condemnations is addressed to a king who "oppresses the poor and oppresses the needy" (4:1) and, after citing many sins, concludes with a frightening message of doom: "Be prepared to meet your God, O Israel" (4:12). A thousand years later, the Midrash tradition, lacking any more apposite and obvious text in scripture for a lesson in proper synagogue attire, turned this threat into a command that those who came to worship God should be properly dressed: "Prepare yourself properly to meet your God, O Israel" (b. Ber. 23a).

Midrash is a response to an age-old problem common to all scriptural religions. Affirming the scripture as sacred, as a reflection of God's omniscience, leads to the affirmation that it contains all that needs to be known and can be known. On the other hand, the religion must always develop new ideas to meet new problems—that is, ideas not readily perceptible from its scripture's text. In a scripture-based tradition, the new must be derived from the old and must seem old.

Interpretation develops far more naturally and exuberantly when a scripture is in the original language assumed to be God's own, than when, as in Christianity, the scripture is a translation. When the holy book is a translation—the New Testament is in Greek, not Aramaic, which was Jesus' tongue—interpretation and commentary can deal with ideas, themes, and typologies but not with ideas that derive from the text's words, phrases, syntax, and spelling. When these are reported in God's own speech, they must be assumed to have meaning. For the Muslim, God spoke Arabic and the Koran is His speech. For the Jew, God spoke Hebrew and the Torah is in His native tongue. In Islam and Judaism, interpretation can be contextual and go beyond the world of concepts and doctrine to a world of language where every detail and nuance can be assumed to have meaning. Jews developed both *peshat*, the plain-sense meaning of sentence and paragraph, and midrash, the meaning of the way a word was spelled or a letter shaped, or of a particular vocalization, the absence or presence of an unexpected letter, the numerical value of the letters or of a word, even of the way blank spaces occur in the text.

Obviously, to go so far beyond the contextual meaning of phrases and sentences is to open the text to an infinite range of possible meanings. Midrash is an assemblage of discrete and varied statements, some of which stand in direct contradiction to others. Yet flat-out contradiction was impossible in *halacha*—the law as God meant it to be—for in matters of law contradictions are unthinkable. The text was assumed to be truth awaiting discovery.

236

The common practice of the rabbis, therefore, created a unity of *midrash halacha*. They agreed, for example, on how to develop an *eruv*, the rabbinic fiction that enlarges the area in which activity on the Sabbath is permitted, or to manage the dietary rules. The legal consensus was largely completed by the end of the tannaitic period, about the first half of the third century. Later halachic discussion in the Gemara tends to deal less with practical issues, as I have noted, and more with understanding the basis and philosophy of the laws.

Gemara treats *halacha,* the law and legal ideas, with great circumspection. The bulk of a student's effort was invested in legal studies. These were the staff of life, the bread that held the Jewish body and soul together. The interpretive, aggadic traditions provided the wine and the joy of life. They occupied a minor place in the school curriculum and were treated with less circumspection.

While *aggadah* was seen as a useful study, suggesting the various ways in which man approaches God, comes to understand the meaning of the spiritual, and to appreciate His hopes and the messianic vision of His people, it was not *halacha,* not the basic structure and substance of Jewish life. In the height of the gaonic period (ninth to tenth centuries), the general principle was that one does not depend upon *aggadah.* What, then, was the value of aggadic study of the text? "If you wish to know God who spoke and the world came into being study *aggadah,* the more you will recognize Him and cleave to His ways" (Sifre Deut., Aykev 49).

For *aggadah*—tales, incidents, stories without the force of law— uniformity was never required and great flexibility was allowed. Sages' disagreement on a point of etiquette or ethics simply revealed their fallibility as humans. *Aggadah* is not authoritative. A sage might be excommunicated for teaching against the halachic consensus, but would not be if he questioned an aggadic *midrash*—even on such elements of faith as free will or a particular scenario of End Time and even in a way that violated the prevailing rabbinic consensus. Such variety could be tolerated because of the conventional assumption that this whole wondrous body of scripture was, in all its parts, from God. God is one; ultimately, God's truth is singular; in the end the truth will out.

How to make the new seem old and familiar is one of the arts of

Midrash. The rabbis looked on Midrash as an inspired rather than a critical discipline. They devised critical rules of interpretation, but ultimately the truth of Midrash depended less on the canons of logic and analysis governing its use, than on imagination, inspired study, and the acceptance of an interpretation by one's peers. Midrash comments, but not to provide an extended interpretation of a given chapter or section; its commentary is an individual statement, phrase, or word, analyzed for its unique meaning. James Kugel, a student of biblical language and literature, is useful here: "*Midrash* might best be translated as 'research,' a translation that incorporates the word's root meaning of 'search out, inquire' and perhaps as well suggests that the results of that research are almost by definition *recherché*, that is, not obvious, out-of-the-way, sometimes far-fetched" (Kugel 1983, p. 144). The rabbis accepted as self-evident the thesis "that every reading has a mother," which is to say that every biblical sentence has a history that ties into all that was revealed at Sinai, and in sum makes each word pregnant with potential meaning—God's (Sifra Lev. 12:5).

Because rabbinic Judaism approached the sacred text armed with the assumption that everything in the text related to all its parts, the midrashist had no qualms about taking a phrase or a word out of what we would call its context, or of giving the text a reading that common sense does not permit. He was not limited to the idea that a straightforward sequential reading might suggest: every word, every anomaly, spelling, or syntax, every turn of phrase was suggestive. Because the midrashist knew he was dealing with a sacred, not an ordinary, text, he could believe that even the trivial—an unusual spelling or place name—could be turned into a meaningful term, that the use of one enigmatic expression rather than another had meaning. Midrash deconstructs scripture to explore its depths and details, but with far different methods and purposes from those of modern literary critics who assume a series of apparently unrelated meanings in the various parts of a work. Midrash assumes that behind the world of detail and meanings lies an absolute and eternal truth, an unyielding and unbending Torah text.

Despite its sometimes fanciful approach, Midrash is uncongenial to word play or interpretive games employed only for their own sake. The sages were believers. They held a coherent faith: God does not speak to contradictory purposes. They were observant. They were dealing with a text they accepted as divine and whose teachings they accepted as binding. God had placed much wisdom in the text: one source, one truth. Their challenge was to draw that wisdom out, to explore its depths.

MIDRASH AND THE TWO TORAHS

Over time, as I have said, the talmudic, halachic, and aggadic agenda acquired the name that emphasized its authority: *Torah she be'al Peh,* the oral, memorized Torah. The Talmud ascribes the terms to Hillel and Shammai, the first-century Pharisees (b. Shab. 31a); but it is more likely that the phrase did not become conventional until the third or fourth century. In its final form, the myth held that God had revealed through Moses all of *Sefer Torah*—the Torah—and *Torah she be'al Peh,* a complementary oral revelation that had passed down to the present generations without significant change and without ever escaping from the control of reliable transmitters. The two Torahs had been interpreted by generations of responsible leaders who through Midrash had woven them together into the single entity they, in fact, were.

As a technique for weaving a twofold Torah into one, Midrash had one structural disadvantage: it was without self-evident limits. Since the sages' techniques of interpretation were artificial, in the sense that they artfully transcended logic, there was no obvious limit to what could be claimed as Torah. Elegant interpretation can make black white and permit the forbidden. The rabbis limited the authority to do Midrash only to qualified sages by setting aside *midrashim* of which they disapproved, by reining in the imagination of the young, by limiting discussion to those few who were educated and already deeply committed, and by confining to these circles the development of collected blocks of *midrashim.* This concern for control, for protecting the rabbinic authority over the developing tradition, was also an original motive for drawing together and editing midrashic collections. In so doing, the rabbis imposed standards.

Since writing was not particularly encouraged, Midrash, like so much else, was mostly memorized; that which a sage did not deem worthy of being enshrined in memory generally disappeared.

Most of the Midrash that has come down to us is presented atomistically, as terse, single-sentence comment. Many such comments undoubtedly floated about the schools and were ultimately lost. Others, for various reasons, became part of a block of tradition a teacher had his students memorize. Some traditions melded because they shared a stylistic element. Others were hung onto the opening sentence of a Torah section or some other biblical portion. Since Midrash was still at this time a central part of the rabbis' oral culture, in most cases its organizing principle was simply to make memorizing easier and surer.

Midrash rests on paradox: on the one hand, it is based on the premise that all ideas are rooted in scripture, and encourages belief in the coherence of the whole tradition; on the other, it reflects not a single point of view but rather diversity of insights and doctrines. This great effort of synthesis is full of contradiction and is not frightened by this fact. A single formulaic statement can be given various readings. Without context, it is often difficult to know exactly what the midrashist intended. Often the only connection between *midrashim* is that they circulated in a particular school or were of interest to a particular compiler.

Midrash testifies, above all, to the continuing deep interest in the written scripture. It is simply not true that with the Talmud, the focus of Jewish interest switched from the written to the oral law. That assumption is based on little else but the late medieval practice by European Jews of setting talmudic studies above all else. True, in the *yeshivot* of Slobodka or Volozin, the *Tanakh* was not systematically studied; and in every Lithuanian and Polish town, the most prestigious continuing-education circles studied talmudic tradition rather than the Bible. But, even then, when the Bible was not studied systematically, knowledge of its teachings was assumed and fairly correctly so: it remained the curriculum of elementary education, the text of weekly synagogue ritual, the subject of occasional sermons; and its language remained basic to the people's speech.

In talmudic times, and persisting later in the Muslim world, knowledge of the written Torah played a major role in all that constituted Jewish studies. Indeed, in the Islamic environment, there were those eager to study the written Torah and willing to simplify the oral tradition to do so. In any Arabic community, Talmud remained the code of Jewish life without imposing on the community, in the name of Talmud Torah, the monumental task of mastering its intricacies or commentaries. During the early centuries of Muslim dominance, many Jews were unable or unwilling to devote the time and effort such mastery required; they were heirs of tradition that required only the more active religious rituals. In the Islamic world in the ninth through twelfth centuries, the custom developed of preparing précis of talmudic law, codes of practice, arranged topically but without methodology. Moses Maimonides' *Mishneh Torah* was simply the most famous of the codes prepared so that far-flung communities and their judges could operate without the presence of a fully qualified talmudist. Higher rabbinic education was presumedly to be left to the great academies of Babylonia and Palestine. This simplified codification was an attempt to reform rabbinic Judaism without challenging any of its major affirmations. The codifiers were good scholars, but knew that talmudic erudition was beyond the average Jew. Whenever Jewish life has been able to gain a significant degree of access to the larger business and professional world, as was true for Jews in many parts of the Arab world during the eighth and ninth centuries, Jews have tried to move away from a learning that is parochial and all-absorbing so as to have time to participate in the larger world.

HEBREW POETRY

During talmudic times, an extensive literature of Hebrew poetry developed, based on themes and idioms taken primarily from the *Tanakh* and designed primarily to fill out the still spare worship service. These poems generally dealt with biblical themes and deliberately used biblical Hebrew and biblical idioms. They kept alive the language of the Bible as well as biblical and folk stories about biblical heroes. This form of literature, the *piyyut*—apparently a Hebrew form of the Greek *poietes,* "poet"—began to appear in the third century C.E., particularly in Palestine, and was destined to have a creative run of over a thousand years.

The importance of Palestine rather than the diaspora as the center of scripture-based interest needs to be understood and emphasized. Babylon, in the Sassanian empire (third to seventh centuries), had rabbinic academies, became the political center of Jewish life, and produced the better of the two Talmuds, the Babylonian written in Aramaic. But pride of rank in exegesis and *aggadah* goes to the Palestinian sages. Almost all the Midrash collections come from Palestine. The *piyyut* emerges in Palestine and flourishes almost exclusively there right down through the early centuries of the Muslim period. In the eighth and ninth centuries, Karaite masoretic studies (see pages 249–50) flourished in the Galilee, stimulated rabbinic interest in such studies, and brought that thousand-year-old discipline to a triumphal conclusion. I suspect that the fact of Palestine as a center of *aggadah* had something to do with the naturalness of Hebrew in that environment. Hebrew, after all, was the language of the Jewish story.

Then, too, the Palestinian schools had a head start of a century or two on those of the diaspora. Palestinian cultural eminence may have acquired some of its force from the preference of the Palestinian synagogues for a three- or three-and-a-half-year cycle of Torah readings—a practice maintained throughout most of the first millennium—whose shorter portions inspired greater intensity in study and discussion. Finally, the history of the two communities is instructive. The Palestinian history is one of uninterrupted creativity. The East was an ancient center, but we hear of little that is creative after Ezra in the fourth century B.C.E. and before the rabbinic revival of learning there in the third century C.E.

The Book of Psalms is a recognized classic of liturgical poetry, a feature as old as the Hebrew tradition. While the Psalms stand on their own, the *piyyut* differ in depending heavily on the Bible, the *targum,* and midrashic explanations. Poems were composed for each of the Sabbaths of a three-year cycle; as insertions or substitutions for portions of the *amidah,* the traditional heart of the service; as additions to the blessings that precede the saying of the Shema; and for a variety of other liturgical purposes, including, some believe, as a substitute for the *amidah* during periods of persecution when the Byzantine authorities ordered that it not be publicly recited.

We know little—sometimes not even their names—about the personalities of the early *payyetanim,* the authors of the liturgical poems. They were generally the men who chanted the service. At a later period, these poet-singers were also called *chazzanim,* those whom we would today call "cantors." During the talmudic centuries, the synagogue service developed a set form, though its contents were not completely fixed. Particularly the Sabbath and festival services needed much more structure. At first, the *payyetanim* sought to provide compositions that could supplement or supplant the still undeveloped and unstandardized portions of the service. Writing for their own congregations, *payyetanim* provided verses that added substance and freshness to the service and allowed the *payetan* to display his skills. Some poems were like the sermons of the day, recapitulations of the weekly Torah portion. Some selected a festival theme, like that of the awesome priestly confession on Yom Kippur, and enlarged on it for the holy day's additional service (*musaf*). Poems included both *aggadah* and legal materials. Some allude to disputation with other faiths, such as the growing friction with the newly Christianized Roman empire, and later to extortions by Byzantine emperors and Islamic rulers. Some are full of mystical thoughts. Almost all, like the popular sermons, conclude with some expression of Israel's messianic hope. Some communities, like Tiberias, ultimately produced manuscript anthologies of poems by local writers. Whatever their content or quality, these poems—and their number runs into the thousands—reflect the importance within the community of an effective system of Torah education. Some were written for ordinary folk. Most were full of literary allusions and obviously intended for congregations of the intellectual élite. It is clear that the general audience was expected to understand basic biblical citations, and that the élite were expected to be able to decode a surprising number of recondite references.

Fortunately, we know the names of a few of the important poets of this late talmudic period: Yose b. Yose (fourth to fifth centuries), Yannai, and Eleazar b. Kallir (sixth century) are the best known. Their poems are mostly on biblical themes, each a testament to the depth of biblical knowledge in the community. These men and their predecessors and successors were, of course, heirs to a long tradition of poetry, and their work reflects stylistic patterns of both biblical and midrashic traditions: for example, parallelism, alphabetic acrostics, and a fourfold division of verse in which each division has two accented terms. Early Hebrew poetry, like the Psalms, tends to avoid rhyme. It is too easy to rhyme a language in which case endings are common.

A typical early *piyyut* written by an unknown author is a complement to the prayer for rain introduced into the service from fall to spring.

> *I shall sing praises now that the time of the singing of the birds has come, and I shall answer in song: go in peace, rain.*
> *I shall look at the deeds of my God, so pleasant in their season, and sweetly say: come in peace, dew.*
> *The rains are over and gone, the winter is past; everything is created with beauty: go in peace, rain.*
> *The mandrakes give forth their perfume in the lovers' garden; sorrows are past: come in peace, dew.*
> *The earth is crowned with new grain and wine, and every creature cries, go in peace, rain.*
> ("Go in peace, Come in peace" in Carmi 1981, p. 203)

The imagery clearly taken from the Song of Songs and the Psalms is evident throughout. Indeed, we cannot imagine most of these songs without reference to biblical antecedents.

Much of the poetry, particularly that which relates directly to the weekly portions of the Torah cycle, has a more apparent and immediate connection to the *Sefer Torah,* as does the following poem by Yannai, at the beginning of the classical period of the *piyyut* (mid-sixth to late eighth century), which refers to Moses' vision of God at the Burning Bush. The author combines, as do most of these poets, biblical themes with those that derived from the Midrash and were clearly as well known—here, for instance, the *midrash* that Moses at the Burning Bush had been transformed into an angel, and that the experience of looking at the Bush allowed him to become an adept in fiery visions:

244

> Into the wilderness the Messenger drove his flock; into
> the wilderness he would lead his people like a flock.
> Without feet he ran, rushing his herd to the place where
> he would see his vision of God.
> Green crops sprang up before him, then were swallowed in
> his wake.
> In a single day he travelled a long distance, for He who
> loves straightness straightened the path before him.
> When he reached the Mountain of God, he was eased of his
> hardship and relieved of his toil.
> At first an angel appeared before him to change his form
> into that of an angel.
> Then the Lord taught him to look at fire, to be expert in
> fiery visions.
> His heart was strengthened by looking at the flame, so
> that he might be able to withstand all manner of fire.
> The Pure One revealed His splendour in the midst of
> Egypt's defilement; the High One proclaimed His glory from the
> lowly bush—
> For His people's distress is His distress, and their
> salvation is His own.

("Moses the Messenger" in Carmi 1981, pp. 219–20)

TRANSLATION AND COMMENTARY

Bible translations continued to be made throughout the talmudic centuries into Aramaic, Greek, Syriac, and other tongues; and the existence of several strands of *targum* show that there was a continuing and flourishing interest in biblical concerns and studies in Palestine and later in the East. The semi-official *targum* of the *Sefer Torah* was developed in Palestine although it was edited in the East, in Babylonia in the sixth century C.E., there to become the official *targum* of the synagogue—*Targum Onkelos*. The *Onkelos* tradition avoided all anthropomorphism and mandated the proper rabbinic interpretation of the law.*

---

*It is likely that *Onkelos* is a corruption of the name of Aquila, a second-century translator of the Bible into Greek. Aquila was a convert; Onkelos is so described (b. Git. 56b). Biographical similarities about the two men are reported in the Talmud. It seems plausible that the facts and legends surrounding the life of Aquila were attached to an important *targum* tradition about whose author little was known. *Targum Onkelos*, like almost all other works of the age, was a composite achievement, and therefore neither the personality nor identity of its purported author is truly important.

In addition to the *Targum Onkelos* to the Pentateuch, there was a similar *targum* to the Prophets; it also was begun in Palestine and developed there for several centuries before it, too, was transported and finally completed in Babylonia around the same time as *Onkelos,* during the sixth century. A number of *targumim* of the Holy Writings were done at the same period.

The *targum* was treated with the same formality that governed the public reading of the Torah in the synagogue. It had been created, after all, as an adjunct to that reading, to guarantee that the reading was properly understood by Jews who no longer knew the classic Hebrew. According to talmudic prescription, the *targum* has to be read, never recited by heart, after each verse of the portion of the week and after every third verse of the *haftarah*. A minor could read from the *targum* in the synagogue, but not from the Torah; and in the Cairo *Genizah,* the synagogue storeroom, a few twelfth-century letters praise youngsters for this achievement. Sometimes a *targum* added midrashic tales to the biblical text it was translating or paraphrasing. Portions of scripture—like the story of Reuben (Gen. 35:22), the second account of the Golden Calf (Exod. 32:21–35), and the Priestly Benediction (Num. 6:24–26)—were forbidden to be translated. The Priestly Benediction was deemed too holy to be translated; while the suspicion that the Golden Calf might have had divine powers, since it emerged fully molded out of the gold tossed into the fire, led to the prohibition against reciting that portion.

THE GAONIC PERIOD

The rise of Islam brought many changes to Jewish life. Islam, like Judaism, and unlike Christianity and Zoroastrianism, believed that the truth was in a revelation, written out in God's own language. Duty and practice lie at the heart of that revelation. Like Judaism, and unlike Christianity, Islam insists on a pristine monotheism. Unlike Persian, Greek, or Latin, Arabic is a Semitic tongue, whose grammar approximates Hebrew. Arabic grammarians made the study of the Koran an act of devotion and developed significant grammatical ideas which proved useful to Jews in their understanding of scripture: for example, Arab linguists discovered the trilateral root of Semitic words. Jews quickly picked up Arabic as everyday speech and did not hesitate to write major religious works in Arabic, although usually using a Hebrew script. Both Islam and Judaism spawned cadres of independent scholars and jurists who set out to organize their community's judicial system. The eighth-to-ninth century development of the science of Arabic jurisprudence, Shariyah, corresponds with the heyday of the authority of the great eastern academies of Sura and Pompedita, which quickly moved to the center of caliphate power, Baghdad. For the first time in nine centuries, Jewish life had a political focus. The authority of the academies and their responses to queries from the widely scattered Jewish communities defined practice and established the texts and the curriculum of rabbinic Judaism.

In the gaonic period, the early centuries of Muslim rule, the Talmud was one element in the curriculum of adult education but not yet the whole of it. The growing effort at this time to simplify Talmud into codes of laws which could be readily and easily consulted had as one consequence the diminution of the rabbi's role. He was no longer the third living Torah. More books existed. Schools, and even private homes, had their own libraries. Information was more readily available. People had become familiar with the rabbinic way. Authority was more centralized in the powerful academies in Baghdad, where scholar-jurists studied the law and ruled on legal matters. Jews still looked on certain men as holy men and miracle workers, though these were not necessarily the great rabbis. The idea that one man's life illustrates Torah began to disappear. Informed by the authority of the exilarch, expressed through the bureaus and the courts, the sages made rabbinic law effective over issues ranging from family status to criminal law, all with the goal of obedience that would earn the end of exile. It was rabbinic belief that the obligations required by their law, the oral Torah, were normative: an individual who obeyed that law merited life in the world to come, and an obedient community hastened the day when God would end their exile, restore the Temple, and bring the Messiah.

THE CHALLENGE TO THE ORAL LAW

During the first centuries of the Muslim period, there were several violent messianic uprisings against authority, by such men as Abu Isa of Isfahan and his disciple, Yudghan. Limited largely to rural areas, these rebellions testify not only to the intensity of messianic hopes but equally to the fact that rabbinic law had not yet been fully accepted. The little we know about the domestic rules of the breakaway groups suggests that they did not slavishly follow rabbinic law.

In most communities, rabbinic law became official practice, observed by everyone, although it was interpreted and controlled only by the intellectual élite of the rabbinic *yeshivot,* the academies, whose heads—the *gaonim*—wielded strong and centralized authority. Accepting the piety that the Talmud had remained an oral teaching until political circumstance made its inscription urgent, the academies depicted their predecessors in the sixth century as recognizing the urgency and responding to it—Rabina leading the compilation process of the Jerusalem Talmud, Rav Ashi for the Babylonian.

How much time and attention, but not how much authority, to give to the written and oral law, respectively, was an issue faced by all who affirmed the rabbinic teaching about the authority of the two-sided scripture. Not all Jews did. All Jews affirmed the written Torah, but not all accepted the rabbinic piety of the two Torahs: that is, not all accepted the self-proclaimed authority of the rabbis to organize Jewish life according to their understanding of the oral law. In every generation, there were Jews who observed the Sabbath and holy days, worshiped in a synagogue, recited the Shema, adored the *Tanakh,* believed in repentance, resurrection, the Messiah, and an ultimate return to Zion, but did not feel compelled to accept the authority of the rabbis or many of their rulings. Until rabbinic authority had behind it sufficient political clout to insist on conformity—that is, until the late eighth century—these groups apparently simply continued to be Torah-true in their ways, living quietly on their own. With the rise of Islam and the centralization of imperial power in the caliphate and of effective power over the Jewish community in the exilarch and the rabbinic academies, these groups were forced out into the open.

The *b'nei mikra,* or Karaites (*Karah* comes from the same root as *Mikra,* "scripture"), were Jews who challenged the authority of the oral law and consequently of the Talmud. The history of the Karaite challenge is complex. It was catalyzed in the eighth century by, as challenges often are, a disgruntled figure from within the establishment. Anan belonged to the exilarch's own family. Legend has it that he had been passed over for that office. The facts are hard to ascertain, but he certainly focused a lot of local discontent and directly challenged rabbinic authority. He is sometimes reported as saying, "Forsake the words of the Mishnah and the Talmud and I will make you a Talmud of your own."

Anan's teachings were not antinomian. His Talmud increased the range and rigor of Jewish obligations, but rabbinic obligations not specifically prescribed in the written law—Hanukkah, the second day of holidays, and use of a calendar based on astronomical calculation—were discarded. Anan took literally the idea that no light should be lit on the Sabbath, and that everyone should stay at home (Exod. 16:15). Karaite communities enlarged the list of relatives with whom marriage was prohibited; and in many communities, all meat was forbidden except deer and fowl.

Anan, like Luther, had a complex, difficult, and authoritarian personality. The challenge he raised was to the oral law, which he defined as not Sinaitic but rabbinic, as no more than the interpretation of certain sages. He compiled in Aramaic, using rabbinically favored hermeneutics and exegesis, his own Book of Precepts as a direct challenge to the Gemara. Anan and his followers found halachic authority in all the books of the *Tanakh,* not just the five scrolls of the *Sefer Torah.* In his eyes, there was no long-standing, correct, God-defined interpretation, no oral law; there were only the rabbis' own fanciful interpretations. Like the Protestant reformers much later, Anan insisted on his right to confront the text directly. Some of Anan's disciples would go further and insist on the right of everyone to interpret scripture. Beginning with Karaite sages such as Benjamin Nahavendi (ninth century) and Daniel al Kumisi (early tenth century), Karaite schools replaced Aramaic with Hebrew as the vehicle of teaching and made the study of biblical exegesis a major academic discipline. As one would expect, the

Karaites lavished great care on the written text. Indeed, many of the most important masoretes were Karaites; and the standard masoretic text, the Ben Asher Codex, was the work of members of their community.

The early history of Karaism is not so much that of a cohesive movement as of a series of localized protests against rabbinic authority, often triggered by messianic expectations and complaints about rabbinic rapacity. The rabbis seemed to be settling comfortably into *galut,* "exile." They had power and prestige and were free of taxation. Karaite practice combined a strong element of asceticism and of Zionism's impatience with the *galut.* The fire of the messianic hope still burned bright in many breasts. Karaite liturgy sought to reproduce the worship of the Temple. In the ninth and tenth centuries, Karaites established pilgrimage to Jerusalem as an act of obligation; and many stayed on there as *avelei Zion,* mourning for Zion and praying for its re-establishment, as a protest that emphasized the right of interpretation unconstrained by a defined and authoritative tradition. Karaism in its early phase was more a diverse movement than a single-minded protest and included various schools of interpretation. How could it be otherwise when leaders, wishing to spur their followers to individual study, insisted on a principle they put into the mouths of several leaders: "Search thoroughly in the Torah and do not rely on my opinion"?

In order to have Muslim authorities treat them as a separate, self-governing community, the Karaites had to persuade the administrators that they had their own laws and courts and no need of the rabbinate or exilarchate. The Karaites accomplished this aim and, over time, developed their own post-Torah tradition, the so-called *hevel ha-yerusha,* "yoke of inheritance."

Separation gave the Jewish communities a chance to see what they had in common as well as what they did not share. They were both Israel. Gradually a *modus vivendi* developed, and the bitter quarrels of the early centuries lost much of their importance. The Karaites shared Israel's fate and even began to permit intermarriage. The later Karaites accept rabbinic rules except in a few specific areas where their traditions differed. Karaism had raised the issue of what is scripture and, in part, had answered it. The authority of the

Tanakh had been underscored: it was beyond challenge. But the authority of the Talmud, the rabbis' second Torah, had been challenged as it would again be challenged in modern times. Karaism's challenge had also made it clear that a naked scripture was not enough: a disciplined faith requires a body of authorized tradition and interpretation. Karaism could not survive with only the Bible: scripture requires interpretation and elaboration because community requires definition and agreement. Protestant Christianity would relearn the lesson centuries later at no inconsequential cost. Karaism remained a force for many centuries, and tiny remnants of the community survived into this century. Neither Karaism nor the single-scripture issues it raised would ever completely disappear.

THE ACADEMIES AND THEIR WORK

A grammatical tradition began to develop around the text in gaonic times, and a small number of manuscripts survive. Some were vocalized; and some, like one produced for Hai Gaon (eleventh century), included useful linguistic and grammatical comments. Though the Mishnah circulated in an unvocalized form and the Gemara generally followed suit, readings were standardized by the learning songs that accompanied their study in schools.

The Talmud became the scripture of the secondary schools in the eighth and ninth centuries. Students expended prodigious effort in memorizing blocks of text. The Baghdad academies of advanced study also employed memory professionals to make sure that only the accepted text was discussed and taught. Formality governed discussion in the academies. Completion of a tractate of "readings" was celebrated as a festive occasion. The Kaddish prayer, which praises and thanks God for the privilege of study, may have had its origins as a blessing on such occasions.

By its very bulk and its many halachic interests, the Talmud seems, as we have seen, to be not only an attempt to rearrange and to elaborate Jewish law into positive codes but to create a new world of discourse, including *aggadah,* history, discussion of exegetical principles, legal methodology, and unresolved legal issues. There could be no mistaking the importance of this world of discourse. It was the oral law, given at Sinai, nurtured by generations of leaders and sages, understood as God's will for the organization of Israel's communal life.

Yet the Islamic-Jewish world's developing concern for precision and order was a bit put off by the Talmud's dense complexity. Attempts were made to present issues with some sense of order. The learning charts of the academies of the East emphasized correct pronunciation and meaning. Discussions were conducted with a care and ceremony that would be conspicuously lacking in later European *yeshivot.* A *gaon* aided by both a provost (*av*) and a scribe presided over academic meetings. Seating in the academy was arranged hierarchically: each row had a head, and discussion was carried on by a strict rule of seniority. Twice each year, public lectures (*kallot*) were organized. The *gaon* chose a particular treatise as his subject for a *kallah,* and various officials would add their remarks to his. Visiting scholars who were present were expected to carry home decisions and formulations from the *kallah.* The academies were sustained by gifts accompanying requests for legal answers and decisions and by income from lands donated to them. Academic scribes prepared letters for various communities, which reported on the *kallah* and answered specific questions on chosen texts and others asked by the communities. These questions and answers constitute the *responsa* literature, the most characteristic contribution of gaonic times, which was added to the body of Jewish law in a role similar to that of case law in the English and American legal systems.

One of the principal advantages of this correspondence was that it closed debate, particularly where the academy had made a specific ruling on an issue the Talmud had left open. Effective authority therefore lay in the institution rather than in the text. The great academies were the center of Talmud study. Occasionally circumstances or appointment would prompt an advanced student or a scholar from the academy to leave for other parts; it was unlikely that he would teach in a community without proper authorization from one of the academies. Once settled, he might set up a school for a few favored scholars, almost never more than a half-dozen or so. Some may have preached in the synagogue, but I suspect their impact was greater in and through the courts and the schools. The rabbis looked to the teacher, not the text, to propagate their ideas. The teacher could explain and clarify, put teachings in context, and bring new ideas to bear on the issues.

In an environment where the major faith was based on a written scripture, Jewish thinkers began to take a closer and more systematic look at the written Torah. Of the translations into Arabic, the most important was the *Tafsir* of the *gaon* Saadya b. Joseph (882–942). With many additions by other hands, it became the quasi-official Bible of the Jews who lived in Arab lands.

The work of the masoretes was brought to effective conclusion. For the first time, there was systematic interest in *peshat,* the grammatically accurate understanding of the text within the context of its original history, literary style, and language. Biblical scrolls were systematically annotated, in both Arabic and Hebrew. Growing interest in the text of the written Torah prompted further development of collections of sermonic *midrashim*—running commentaries on the Five Books of Moses and the five scrolls called *megillot* (Ruth, Esther, Song of Songs, Lamentations, and Ecclesiastes). Hebrew and Arabic poetry flourished, much of it created in biblical style. Records found in the Cairo *Genizah* indicate that, during the entire medieval period, groups met in the evenings and on Sabbath afternoons to study *Tanakh.*

NEW ACADEMIC APPROACHES

Though rabbinic practices were widely accepted as normative, some men questioned the spiritual benefit of spending all one's energies sorting out the subtleties of rabbinic reasoning. The many-sided interests of Islamic civilization encouraged Jews to study philosophy, mathematics, and medicine, as well as Torah. *Shelemut ha-Nefesh,* "spiritual perfection," communion with the spirit of God, was not believed to reside, as many European sages would later argue, in a single-minded immersion in the give-and-take of talmudic discussion. For Jews influenced by Islamic attitudes, it lay, rather, in a thoughtful immersion in the whole of Torah literature.

Many took a practical approach toward the Talmud as a source of law and wanted to make it possible for the communities to have access to the law. They argued that much of the halachic debate was tiresome and much of the *aggadah* uninspiring. They had no argument with the functional parts of the Talmud. Alfasi (eleventh century) prepared a synthesis of the Talmud, brilliantly elucidated the practical *halacha,* and deliberately eliminated most *aggadah.* A scholar like Maimonides knew but had little patience with the *masa-u-matan,* the endlessly unresolved legal debates of the Talmud, and so brought to a consummate conclusion in his *Mishneh Torah* several generations of efforts to systematize the talmudic approach—the way, not coincidentally, that Muslim scholastics had presented the Shariyah. Maimonides felt not only that the *Mishneh Torah* showed that in every respect the oral and written law were woven of one thread, but that the *Mishneh Torah* also had the practical benefit—because of its comprehensiveness, clarity, and imaginative organization—of obviating the need to spend endless hours mired in the exhausting, and not necessarily rewarding, effort of talmudic discussion. Of course, not everyone was happy with this approach. To many scholars, the Talmud was a liberating discipline, the key to all wisdom.

While one finds among the Jews of the Islamic world a certain impatience with talmudic study as an end in itself, they evinced a strong appreciation of the dramatic myths and evocative language of the written Torah. *Peshat* became a favorite literary approach for everything from philosophy to love poetry. The intellectual centers of the Islamic world were attracted by philosophic speculation, and many Jews preferred to approach doctrinal comments or apologetic or mystical speculation through the simple and affecting texts of the written scripture rather than through the complex mass of *aggadot.*

Under Karaite and rabbinic influence, and aided by the linguistic science and literary interests of the dominant Muslim culture, biblical exegesis thrived. By the tenth century, there was an official Hebrew text, the masoretic text, which became the basis for all subsequent biblical studies. A burgeoning new discipline, biblical commentary, in both Hebrew and Arabic differed sharply from the older Midrash because it eschewed noncontextual exegesis, preferring to search through texts for meaning by using the most advanced tools of scientific grammar available. From the tenth through the fourteenth centuries, primarily in the Arab world but also in Western Europe, there were literally dozens of commentaries on individual books or on the whole *Tanakh*. The most important of these were texts by Abraham ibn Ezra (1092–1167), Solomon b. Isaac of Troyes (Rashi) (1040–1105), Moshe b. Nachman (Nachmanides or Ramban) (1195–?1270), and others who developed all possible aspects of the biblical text. With the rise of printing in the late fifteenth century, certain of the more popular of these were chosen to be printed alongside the biblical text and the *targum,* in what came to be seen as an official scripture.

Ibn Ezra declares the intention of all such commentaries:

I shall be concerned with analyzing each word grammatically and only then proceed to the interpretation of the meaning. . . . I shall not dwell on the reasons and explanations by way of *derash* [homiletical interpretation] which the men of the tradition gave in their day, for these do not belong at all to the subject . . . and are useful only for young children in elementary schools. I shall also not make use of the emendations of the later scribes but take into consideration only the *targum,* for its rendering is correct and made all the obscure passages clear and comprehensible.

(*Introduction to Commentary on Pentateuch*)

One brief example can stand for all such analytic efforts, the story of Jacob defrauding Esau of the birthright: "And Esau despised his birthright" (Gen. 25:34). Ibn Ezra tends to be apologetic, arguing that Esau thought so little of the birthright because their father, Isaac, was then a poor man who had nothing to give; and his "proof" is that Isaac favored Esau because he had brought soup to supplement Isaac's rather spartan diet. Nachmanides, agreeing with Ibn Ezra's methodology, scoffs at the errors of his ideas and explains that Esau's role as a hunter put him in mortal danger—he held no hope of outliving his father. Rashi, the least grammatically sound of the three, gives the simple answer: that as a rough man, Esau despised all that had to do with God's service.

THE SEARCH FOR MEANING

Where in the talmudic period the sermon or lecture had pulled texts from here or there to teach the unity of the written Torah, beginning with the Saadya Gaon in the tenth century, the more philosophically minded rabbis fixed on the search for the meaning of the whole. Intellectuals began to occupy themselves in constructing "philosophies of Judaism." Talmudically trained and observant, they nonetheless tended to make greater use of the texts and images of the written Torah than their predecessors had. They found in the laws and narratives of the Torah, in the statements of the Prophets, and in the literature of the Writings, that God had revealed what could be known about Himself, Divine Providence, free will, human nature, election, atonement, resurrection, and the Messiah. To those who became fascinated by matters philosophical and apologetic, the written Torah regained pride of place.

Apparently in practice the Talmud was seen as the scripture for positive law and the Torah as scripture for faith and philosophy. Why philosophy? The answer would seem to lie in a new and more relaxed attitude toward scripture and in a broader definition of learning. Islam made many converts, particularly among worldly and ambitious Jews and non-Jews; these converts had a new faith but essentially no faith. An interest in the sociology of religions, which reached back to Plotinus and Zeno, was enlarged to include inquiry into the differences between Islam and Judaism.

A faith that claimed to base belief in God on reason was popular. Saadya Gaon not only translated major parts of the *Tanakh* into Arabic but produced a major philosophical work, *The Book of Beliefs and Opinions,* the opening gun in Israel's attempt to adjust scripture and reason. In it, he quotes from the *Tanakh* over thirteen hundred times and from rabbinic works, including the Mishnah and the Talmud, fewer than eighty. Maimonides' classic *Guide of the Perplexed* quotes from Genesis as often as from the Mishnah and both Talmuds.

Why this heavy use of biblical ideas and language? Part of the answer lies in the distinctive natures of the biblical and the talmudic texts. The Talmud is laconic, sometimes gnomic. It does not offer the reader fully developed sentences or a fully fleshed-out text.

Much of the biblical text is spare, but it is fully developed; its language is uncomplicated and potentially allegorical, claiming our interest. An intellectual élite who knew Bible and Talmud, and were heirs to a particular biblical tradition, developed a new interest in Jewish philosophy; and their biblical commentary was based on the brilliant advances of Arab and Jewish grammarians and linguists.

Saadya's *Beliefs and Opinions* defines not only reason and revelation but tradition. Tradition, as Saadya defines it, embraces revelation embodied in scripture, the established interpretation of scripture, and religious custom. He is saying that, to be properly understood, scripture must be interpreted in terms of tradition. Philosophers agree that knowledge can come through observation, experience, reason, logical inferences, and through tradition. Reason, Saadya says, may never be used to contradict the tradition, but reason may require the text to be interpreted allegorically. Saadya's concept of tradition went back to Torah and reflects extreme reverence for the past. It is scripture updated but by logical inference rather than by contemporary arguments. The concept that scripture must be interpreted in terms of tradition lies behind most—indeed, all—medieval Jewish philosophy.

THE KABBALAH

As far back as the seventh century B.C.E., and possibly before, biblical phrases were already being used as talismanic amulets. The magical use of the name(s) of God is a constant of the tradition, continuing throughout gaonic times and beyond. In the twelfth and thirteenth centuries C.E., magic and mysticism melded into Kabbalah, a vast literature that had its beginnings in late talmudic times and can be traced for well over a thousand years, dealing primarily with theosophy, the nature of God.

According to the Kabbalists, there were several scriptures. There was the familiar scripture of commandments and narratives—important, full of obligation, operative, but not the original Torah. Behind the phrases of the familiar scripture lay a secret or mystical scripture that consisted entirely of the names of God. This mystical scripture was part of the hidden, yet real-life, energies of God which the Kabbalists defined in terms of ten *sefirot* (singular, *sefirah*), or "emanations." Generally, they equated the secret scripture with the second *sefirah, binah,* "understanding." Presumably, an adept might glimpse the secret of the names and so move toward a fuller knowledge of God and consequently have greater power on earth.

Kabbalists did not deny the authority of the familiar scripture. Though they were part of the self-validating Jewish world, their active interest lay not in "you shall" and "you shall not" but in the nature of the Godhead and man's relationship to it. And so they spent hours and days in mystical communion. Phrases and letters of the scripture were studied to pierce through to the secret of the names. Theosophy rather than theology was their métier. The mystical Torah was really a manifestation of God's most private life. God manifested Himself in a primal state as a thinking God, and each stage in God's exposure to the "real" world was part of the process of God's thought manifesting itself. The Hebrew letters are the building blocks of the world beyond—the planets and constellations and the universe as we see and know it. But, according to the rabbis, the Torah that God had looked into to guide Him through the difficult time of Creation is not the same Torah as the one in the synagogue ark; it is a different Torah, yet these two Torahs are not absolutely distinct. Both are composed of the names of God: but in our synagogue Torah, the names have been scrambled; while in the celestial Torah, God's names are readily apparent. Over its thousand-year history, Kabbalah developed many variations on the notion of an existing Torah through which men can sometimes glimpse the Torah of God's names. It is a thesis that encouraged esoteric commentary and theosophic speculation but did not challenge the authority of the known Torah in everyday matters.

THE CHRISTIAN WORLD

For Jews, Christian Europe was quite a different environment from that of the Islamic world. Unlike the mosque, the medieval Church did its best to keep its Bible out of the hands of laymen. The ties between canon law and scriptural text were not self-evident. Laymen were to trust the priest rather than the text. In the early Middle Ages, folios of the Bible were actually chained to the desks of monastery libraries.

The Church felt that since Jews and Christians shared the Old Testament, it should be easy to convince Jews of the Christian belief that the Bible promises and prophesies the second coming of the Christ. The Church saw the Talmud both as blasphemous and an obstacle to Jewish conversion. Already in the Justinian Code (sixth century c.e.), there was a Christian attack on the Talmud as a second law. This second law offered one explanation to Christians of Jewish obstinacy: Christians believed the Talmud had reinterpreted the Bible to deny the christological prophecies that Christians believed the Hebrew scripture contained. Christians explained their lack of success in persuading Jews to convert by the fact that the Jews had over the centuries deliberately altered the Torah.*

During the Middle Ages, the imperial Church had no patience with Jewish obstinacy. Apostates explained to churchmen that their sermons fell on deaf ears because the Jews had a second scripture, the Talmud, which had effectively replaced the first, and that it contained, beside all manner of superstitious belief, blasphemies of the worst kind about Jesus, Mary, and Christians generally. Busy rooting out Christian heresies, the Church still found the energy to turn its attention to the Talmud and found much of it pernicious. In Italy, Dominican censors blue-penciled offending sections. The French church and Dominicans were more zealous, consigning to the flames cartloads of Talmuds and other Hebrew works in 1215, the first of many book burnings in medieval Europe.

Rabbis were forced to defend the Talmud before courts of priests and Christian nobles, men whose minds were already made up. Such attacks made the Talmud even more precious to the Jew. It must be powerful, indeed, if the Church had to unleash the Inquisition

---

*Indeed, one of the reasons the Jesuits who came to China in the sixteenth century were eager to visit the Jewish community of Kaifeng was their hope that they would find there Torah scrolls in pristine form. Because tradition reported that Jews had come to China before Jesus' day and been cut off from their co-religionists since then, Christians assumed that the Torah of China was original and would include the references to the Christ they believed the rabbis of the West had excised.

against it. It was a mark of its value that the Talmud was included in the first published list of books prohibited by the Sacred Office.

Culturally, medieval Europe was a much narrower world than that of Islam, particularly during the tenth to the twelfth or thirteenth centuries. European Jewish elementary schools had only one text, the Torah. Jews learned to read from the Bible and then to read the Bible with Rashi's rather straightforward commentary (eleventh century). The idea of a Judeo-Christian tradition was nonexistent. Not only were the Jewish and Christian religious communities socially, culturally, and politically separate; but they did not, in fact, share a common scripture.

In European Jewish communities, advanced education was almost entirely talmudic. Talmud study was an end in itself. Lifelong education centered on mastering the intricacies of the Talmud, which often meant manufacturing questions for no better reason than to show erudition. The Talmud became the center of a vast superstructure of commentaries—as is visibly demonstrated by a page from a printed Talmud. Since the first folios were printed in 1520, the printed Talmud has followed a generally similar form: in the center of the page is a block of Mishnah and/or Gemara; it is surrounded on all sides by large columns of commentary in smaller type, usually by Rashi and his students, the Tosefists, and in another column, cross-references to other parts of the Talmud, various medieval codes, and brief additional notes by various rabbis.

Caught between the narrow preconceptions of the medieval Christian and Jewish worlds in the sixteenth century were individuals from marrano families who, raised and educated as Catholics in Spain, had managed to escape, probably as much out of fear of the Inquisition as out of deep loyalty to Judaism. Once free, they sought to rejoin the Jewish community. Society was corporate; there was no other place or community for them to be part of. In Venice, Amsterdam, and Leghorn, they presented themselves, at times full of enthusiasm, only to find that their limited knowledge of Jewish practice and their education at Catholic schools, where they learned something of the Old Testament but nothing of the oral tradition, did not prepare them to understand the Judaism of the communities they had now rejoined. Christianity defined Jews as the once-chosen people, the people of the Old Testament. The Church condemned the Talmud as anti-Christian, a mass of superstition. Marranos knew little of the rich rabbinic tradition and were not prepared to appreciate its texts or methods. They found it hard to understand why the Bible should not be understood as they had heard it interpreted in Catholic Spain, where it would have been worth their lives to follow the dietary laws or worship on the Sabbath. Never having seen a Talmud, they found it hard to speak or think of it as scripture.

Perhaps the most dramatic of these stories is that of Uriel da Costa (1585–1646), a Portuguese marrano whose revealing autobiography has all the hallmarks of a Greek tragedy. Here is the story of a man who seeks faith but cannot find peace. Born in Oporto, Portugal, da Costa was troubled by the Catholic teachings his father avidly espoused, and began to work out what he believed to be a more philosophic and rational faith, one he identified with the Judaism of his ancestors. He did so in the only way he could, from a careful reading of the Old Testament. Satisfied that he had found his truth, he escaped with his family to Amsterdam and eagerly joined the Jewish community, only to find that their Judaism was not what he had expected. Unhappy and puzzled, he lashed out from the depths of his Catholic conditioning and Jewish need against the "Pharisees of Amsterdam" who were totally absorbed with what he considered trivia. He was finally excommunicated for publishing a bitter pamphlet expressing his views. Da Costa left Amsterdam, but there was then no neutral ground; he was, in effect, a man without a country—not a Christian, yet excommunicated by the Jews. He returned, recanted, and asked to be readmitted to the Jewish community. He was readmitted. His pain, however, was not over. Da Costa had begun to espouse advanced deistic ideas and to doubt the authority of all religions. He renounced Judaism and tried to prevent other marranos from rejoining the synagogue. There was a second excommunication. Again, he was out in the cold and, again, he needed to belong. He petitioned for readmission. The community elders agreed but required that he make a public confession and submit to thirty-nine lashes. He did so, but his spirit was broken; and shortly after this purgatory, he committed suicide.

While other returnees had trouble with the oral Torah, da Costa was one of the first Jews to question the divine authority of the written Torah. In this sense, he was far ahead of his time and stands out in the history of changing attitudes toward scripture.

CONCLUSION

The oral Torah was not the only oral tradition Jews kept out of books as long as they could. The basic form of the synagogue worship service was established and accepted for well over half a millennium before written copies were readily available (tenth century). Authors of philosophy and Kabbalah, which began to appear in the eighth century, often indicated that the heart of the matter, the secrets, had only been hinted at, and that knowledge of these could be gained only from a knowledgeable teacher and private tutorial instruction.

Even though the Arab cultural environment encouraged the writing of books and the maintenance of significant libraries by those who could afford them, Jewish learning consisted largely of memorization. Maimonides in his code, the *Mishneh Torah* (1180), insisted that a student will forget what he has not reviewed and recited aloud: the heart of the Jewish educational enterprise remained "letting your ears hear what your mouth has spoken"; "If one recites aloud while studying, what he learns will remain with him. He who reads silently soon forgets" (M.T. *Talmud Torah* 3:12). Muslim learning was of the same order; that is, it began with the memorization of portions or all of the Koran. As books became ever more widely available, they played an ever-increasing role in Jewish life, but the old spirit was not dead. Major protest movements—Karaism, Hasidism, Reform—emerged when groups felt that undue weight was being given to the authoritarian, book-dominated side of tradition. Jews were not anti-book or anti-learning. Quite the contrary: they valued education and literacy. But their goal was an active knowledge of all that was considered Torah, rather than a veneration of books.

In the medieval world, the Torah came to occupy a special place in Jewish life as did the Talmud, the prayer book, certain codes, and biblical commentaries like the Kabbalists' Zohar. However much Jews respected Torah literacy and loved Torah books, the sages were generally not prepared to make the living faith dependent on the written word. Texts were not only fallible, susceptible to scribal and printed error, but fixed, limiting. A written sentence gives no indication of time, inflection, or emphasis. The word of teachers took precedence over a written text. The sages did not write books: they taught. Their classrooms were not like ours, filled with students busily writing down all that is said. The sages spoke. The class listened. The first order of business was to memorize the material one was hearing; discussion came later.

God did not write to Israel: He spoke. The answer to "Why must I?" was not "So it is written" but "So it is taught." The difference seems slight, but the reference to authorized speech is significant. Paul, with his usual tendency to excess, claimed that the letter kills. The Jewish sages believed that the letter kills only when it is left naked of commentary, a discipline they used easily and successfully. To comment is to interpret, to suggest ever new levels of meaning. Rabbinic understanding regarded the memorization of the Law and its commentaries as both intellectual necessity and ethical discipline: you are what you know.

THE AUTHORITY
OF SCRIPTURE IN
THE MODERN
WORLD

[The man of today] must read the scriptures as though
they were something entirely unfamiliar, as though they
had not been set before him ready-made, at school and
after in the light of "religious" and "scientific" certain-
ties, as though he has not been confronted all his life with
sham concepts and sham statements which cited the Bible
as their authority. He must face the book with a new attitude as something new.

—Martin Buber

The power of the idea that the faith was announced at Sinai lies in its
simplicity and in the simple confidence with which it is asserted.
This idea, which was universally affirmed by medieval Jews, sets the

faith apart at its source and seems to provide it with a sure, clear, and permanent identity. But it is an unacceptable claim for our historical and linguistically conscious generation, which no longer accepts the thesis of an original, complete, once and for all times, revelation. Simply put: If I cannot believe that God dictated the Torah in its present form to Moses, yet am told that it is the fact of that revelation which gives Judaism's teachings their authority, then the text's authority is no longer compelling. In emphasizing the event as crucial, rather than its content or the functional value of the teaching, Judaism puts itself at risk. If there was no Sinai, then what is there to depend on? Only a faith that seems to be based on elegant but improbable legends—and who wants to make ultimate commitments to a set of teachings that are clearly not what they have long been claimed to be?

Rabbinic Judaism had presented its teachings as timeless. Modernity introduced the dimension of time into all religious discussion. Joseph Albo, who lived during difficult times in early fifteenth-century Spain, was a philosophically-minded sage who developed in his *Sefer ha-Ikkarim* (*Book of First Principles*) a neat model of the Torah tradition. He likened the Torah to a sprig planted by the events at Sinai. Like all young trees, its basic shape, though underdeveloped, is already in place. The trunk represents the existence and unity of God: the branches, providence, covenant, election, immortality; the smaller branches, the *mitzvot*, the commandments. Over the years, study and interpretation nourished the tree, which has grown taller and sturdier in all its parts; but its shape has remained as it was when planted. To be sure, there have been changes. Each year the tree leafs out and blossoms appear. These are the customs appropriate to each generation which, like the leaves, fall to the ground to be replaced the next season; but nothing essential changes.

History challenged this model. Over the last two hundred years, countless careful studies have shown that a fully mature monotheism took centuries to develop, that the doctrine of physical resurrection did not emerge until the time of the Book of Daniel (second century B.C.E.), that the concept of two Torahs first appeared in the second and third centuries C.E., and so on. Pious Jews, loving the Torah and its familiar themes and sagas, reacted to the challenges historical evidence flung at them, and began to search in the tradition for themes that seemed to reach back in time to the beginning. Many well-trained minds undertook this task of apologia, but ultimately the search found what the seekers were prepared to find. The modern orthodox found the twofold law. The moderate reformers discerned a national spirit acting and reacting on the tradition. The more radical reformers emphasized an ethic that spoke to and about moral principles rather than traditional practices. Given the religion's three-thousand-year history on all the continents of the world save the polar caps, it is not surprising that evidence could be found for diverse and divergent portraits of Judaism.

THE COMING OF MODERNITY

To the premodern Jew, scripture had been fully formed from the beginning, and later authorities only filled in the details. With modernity came a new awareness of the inevitable changes that take place in all times. With that awareness came the recognition that the religions of the world are like all other human institutions, subject to development and change.

This new understanding of history met with stubborn resistance, eager embrace, and nearly every response between. Some were willing to trust their own thoughts, to look for confirmation of their faith to the mind and to experience rather than to a scripture—a willingness that is the hallmark of modernity. Others clung to established patterns of thinking and believing, while still others searched for and devised ways to wed change and tradition. The efforts and attitudes of some of our predecessors struggling with modernity's challenge to scripture may be instructive to us.

NON-ORTHODOX BELIEVERS

Perhaps modernity's most persistent quarrel with the old claims that the two Torahs constitute a seamless scripture is with their prescriptive nature. Torah not only sets out rules and disciplines as God's will but assumes that the community will enforce these obligations. Yet one sign of the modern spirit, at least in the West, is the loss of control by religious authority and a suspicion of all authority. Unless derived from a voluntary social contract, authority is seen as arbitrary and suspected of being entirely self-serving. It is generally, though not universally, held that political and religious loyalties should be freely chosen, church and state should be separate, and the pattern of one's life freely established.

Unhappiness with the coercive elements of religious traditions has its premodern roots in the rationalist assumptions about religion developed during the Enlightenment in the philosophies of men such as John Locke, in the spread of education beyond the clergy, and in the growing dissatisfaction among the newly powerful urban merchant class with the churches' support of traditional class-based privileges. This concern with the heavy hand of religious authority provided the theme for what was perhaps the first modern tract dealing with the Torah: *Jerusalem: On Religious Power and Judaism*, which was published in 1783 in Berlin by one of the first Jews admitted into non-Jewish academic circles, the gifted philosopher Moses Mendelssohn (1729–86). He once won first place—over, among others, Immanuel Kant—in an essay contest sponsored by the Prussian Academy.

An observant Jew, Mendelssohn set out to separate personal belief and practice from institutional authority. He argued that religious institutions ought to be concerned only with enhancing man's relations with God and making clear how that relationship created the values by which one's private life should be shaped. As the Torah was the focus of these values, Mendelssohn prepared a German translation of the Torah in Hebrew letters so that it might be understood by the body of ghettoized Jews who, he believed, would profit from learning refined German.

The state has every right, Mendelssohn argued, to regulate the activities of individuals to enlarge the common good. Religious institutions, on the other hand, can only teach, encourage, and persuade. When Palestine was a Jewish state, in Roman times, the Torah was its operative law; when the Torah is no longer an operative law, it may not be imposed, but it remains a religious obligation to be followed out of personal conviction. In Mendelssohn's day, the Berlin Jewish community could regulate or control the lives of its members only by social pressure and, in extreme cases, by excommunication. He strongly opposed the practice of excommunication and argued that neither the state nor the religious authorities may intrude in matters of conscience.

Mendelssohn was a paradox. Strictly observant, willing and able to hold to and carry out the prescribed rituals without any of the usual religious assumptions that normally engender such loyalty, he failed to see the inherent contradiction in his position or to foresee its disruptive consequences: Mendelssohn's grandchildren would no longer be Jews. But he had raised perhaps the major problem of modern faith: What to do with the medieval assumption of the overriding authority of scripture?

In the medieval world, corporate entities had been the accepted pattern of community organization. Wherever they lived, Jews belonged to a separate corporate body and were treated as a community apart. They governed their communal life, always accommodating to the particular, rarely benevolent, requirements of the local ruler.

By the first half of the nineteenth century, the corporate character of life had begun to break down. Jews in Western Europe and the United States could, for the first time, become citizens of a state. By the middle of the century, some were admitted to the universities of Central and Western Europe. For the first time in European history, some Jews could come out of the isolation that had been the norm in the Middle Ages for all, and that for Jews lasted down to the nineteenth century. New ideas, new political constructs, and new institutions were casting doubt on ways of life that had been taken for granted. The new values of the larger world challenged the values of the traditional Jewish world. Some Jews began to feel constrained by the authority the religious community exercised over major elements of their personal lives. Many resented anyone telling them they could not shorten the prayer service or add a sermon in German, their vernacular, or teach girls together with boys in their schools.

In Eastern Europe, where Jewish self-government and corporate responsibility persisted for another century, the issue of religious freedom and Torah authority remained smoldering. Eastern European Jewish communities were more resistant to new ideas and change, in part responding to the resistance of their societies, which were generally less educated than those of Central and Western Europe.

Modernity was not a condition that described all segments of Jewish life. The modern spirit came to Frankfurt and Philadelphia in the early decades of the nineteenth century, to Warsaw and Lublin more than half a century later. It never penetrated the hamlets and villages of the shtetl. When it came, it often came suddenly. The Jews of Europe did not have the time to enjoy a Renaissance, a Reformation, or an Age of Reason. Many who bought steamer tickets in Hamburg and disembarked eight weeks later in New York were thrust into a modern world they had no preparation for.

Mendelssohn's *Jerusalem* raised, albeit indirectly, a question that has faced Jewish life ever since. As long as the *Sefer Torah* was accepted as scripture, God-inspired, the unity of all its parts could be assumed. Modernity destroyed this comforting consensus. From the world outside Torah, modern Jews brought to Torah ideas they found satisfying.

Mendelssohn was one of the first to articulate the growing belief among Western Jews that scripture had ceased to be the sole source of revealed doctrine and became largely a confirmation of what the age of reason taught. Mendelssohn himself was a son of the age of the Enlightenment, the *Aufklärung*, the belief then popular among many intellectuals that revelation could not disclose any ideological truths that were not also discernible through reason and experience. Theologians of the age translated this idea to mean that there are three elemental religious truths: the existence and oneness of God, Divine Providence, and the immortality of the soul. To be sure, one finds these cardinal beliefs enunciated in scripture, but one can also find there much else—the resurrection of the dead, various messianic themes, the special creation of human beings—that is not self-evident. Mendelssohn acknowledged that the three central beliefs were unmistakably self-evident, arising naturally in the human mind. These truths are universal truths, as valid in Christianity as in Judaism. They do not depend on scripture. Therefore, Judaism does not wholly depend on scripture.

Mendelssohn's philosophical system, based on ideas of the Enlightenment, shaped his religious beliefs and led to his insistence on the three cardinal doctrines. Judaism is, according to Mendelssohn, a combination of these three essential doctrines and a revealed code of practice. To him, it was manifestly clear that "you are not commanded to believe, for faith accepts no commands; it accepts only what comes to it by reasoned conviction" ([1783] 1969, p. 71). Yet he went on to argue that scripture does, in fact, command a special discipline, the familiar and eternally valid code, to which the Jew should give assent because it is God's generous gift, designed to confer distinction on and give a sacred purpose to Jewish life. Ceremonial law is obligatory; doctrine is not.

As we have seen, generations of Jews before Mendelssohn had also shaped their religious beliefs according to the ideas of their times—but in the belief that they were simply interpreting the text; they were not conscious of bringing a set of preconceptions to scripture. By contrast, however much we moderns appreciate elements within scripture, we consciously bring to it outside material. We no longer make the connection our ancestors would have assumed: that somehow out of scripture's depth the truth that we seek will emerge. We may read appreciatively, but we also read critically. The scripture is not our world; rather, we bring our world to scripture.

Modernity developed quickly in nineteenth-century Europe. From a few favored Jews and exceptional individuals like Mendelssohn, it grew into a way of life and thought popular with many Jewish businessmen and intellectuals. Again and again, Jews challenged the old assumptions of a fixed and all-encompassing truth expressed by scripture. Some laymen were eager to introduce German sermons and texts into the liturgy and to introduce into worship a modern aesthetic. Some took advantage of citizenship and converted to Christianity. Others worked out their own ways of adjusting tradition to their beliefs. There were those, who—like Elijah, *gaon* of Vilna, the leading rabbinic light of the eighteenth century—held to traditional religious ways and practices while encouraging a broad secular education.

In the nineteenth century, the best-known advocate of this last approach was a German rabbi, Samson Raphael Hirsch (1808–88). He took a mishnaic statement attributed to Rabbi Gamaliel—"an excellent thing is study of Torah combined with worldly occupation for toil in them both puts sin out of mind" (M. Avot 2:2)—and interpreted "worldly occupation" to signify not simply "employment" but the high culture of the day. Hirsch's motto, *Torah im derech eretz*—Torah, together with a contemporary standard of manners and culture—encouraged a scrupulous observance of the *halacha* and legitimized a curriculum that included modern learning and science as well as the written and the oral law. Those who followed Hirsch's way read the creation stories literally and midrashically as a source of some truths but not necessarily of science; yet they did so in a reverent manner, accepting the general authority of the Torah. While not unaware of studies that were finding the biblical accounts of Sinai inconsistent and inconclusive—evidence was piling up that many tribes of the confederation were never in Egypt and that the Mosaic law reflected both earlier and later conditions than those of the Sinai years—they judged this irrelevant to Torah study; yet they did not insist that all the details of the Exodus and the Sinai revelation be taken literally.

Hirsch insisted that the task of the modern Jew is not to question the mystery of revelation but to search out and, as best one can, understand its meaning and live up to its obligation. His followers were not simple literalists who would join a search for Noah's Ark on Mount Ararat, but they affirmed on faith that the whole Torah is revealed, full of wisdom, and authoritative; and that, combined with the disciplines taught by the oral law, it provides the basis from which the values of modern life are to be judged. They believed that Jews have in the Torah a standard against which any and every contemporary philosophy or value system should be judged. They were adamant on the revelatory nature of the Torah and took seriously the tripartite division of the written scripture: The Law, the Prophets, and the Writings.

Toward the oral law they tended to take a similar position. They readily acknowledged that the Mishnah and the Talmud are not identical with the *Torah she be'al Peh* but insisted that the understanding derived from pious study and living by generations of sages (tradition) is inspired and authoritative. They took delight in much of the *aggadah* of the Talmud and Midrash but did not look on these as literally true. Many engaged in careful study of the history of talmudic composition but with the assumption that the rules set down there are authoritative and the teachings consequential.

In neo-orthodox congregations where the authority of the two Torahs was affirmed, affirmation was more a matter of faith than of liturgical proof. The Torah is revelation, a unique document, a miracle that God in His kindness gave to Israel through His prophet, Moses. It is the source of Israel's faith and contains liberating truths that the generations have sought to make real in their lives. Unlike some modern orthodox Jews who see the secular university as a threat, Hirsch's spiritual heirs rejoiced in the knowledge explosion. While standing on the foundation of Torah, Hirsch's disciples accepted as useful modern knowledge of all kinds: insofar as knowledge is true, they say, it cannot be a threat because the seal of God is truth. They challenged the logic of modern knowledge only where it touches the nature of Torah: the Torah is *Torat Emet*, true in every way.

A former classmate of Samson Raphael Hirsch at the University of Bonn, Abraham Geiger (1810–74), provided the best-known statement of the liberal position. Geiger was especially influential because of his reputation as an exceptional scholar whose learning encompassed virtually all Jewish thought and history. In a series of theological essays, he described Judaism as a religious culture always in the process of becoming. There had been revelation at Sinai and, subsequently, to the prophets, out of which had emerged the insight that there is one Creator, God, who is known primarily by knowledge of His moral will. Priests, Wisdom teachers, and sages developed these ideas, criticized some, elaborated some, and developed others. The *Tannaim* did not simply interpret what they received, but accepted new ideas according to their needs. Revelation was not a once and only phenomenon, limited to a single event that presumably defined the tradition for all time. Geiger taught that revelation takes place at many times and in many ways—his concept of "progressive revelation"—and is vouchsafed not only to prophets but to poets, artists, and scientists. New truths are constantly being discovered, and any theological tradition that claims to be committed to truth must adapt itself to this fact. By definition, then, no scripture can contain all truth.

Geiger did not see Judaism's development as ever upward. Sinai had set Israel on the way. Inspiration, piety, concern, commitment, and an openness to new ideas kept it on the way. Once the Talmud was in place and the philosophical-minded like Maimonides had made their contribution, Judaism had, unfortunately, closed itself off from the sources of life and truth. As a leader of reform in his day, Geiger was moved to preach on the imperative of reawakening the tradition's slumbering vitality. He believed that some of the disciplines of observance, which such men as Mendelssohn had praised, discouraged the best spirits of his age, whose interests and aesthetics required new forms of expression. He emphasized instead the centrality of the moral law and, following Isaiah 42:6, urged his followers to be "a light unto the nations."

Just over a century after Mendelssohn, the noted Hebrew and Zionist master Ahad Ha-Am (Asher Ginzberg, 1856–1927) published a fiery essay in which he protested against the insistence of traditionalists that justice and morality are fully and satisfactorily defined by a scripture developed long ago by sages facing quite different circumstances. He worried that the people of the Book had surrendered their souls to the book, to the arbitrary and sometimes anachronistic authority of the written word:

> The book ceases to be what it should be, a source of ever-new inspiration and moral strength; on the contrary, its function in life is to weaken and finally to crush all spontaneity of action and emotion, till men become wholly dependent on the written word and incapable of responding to any stimulus in nature or in human life without its permission and approval.
>
> (Ginzberg 1894, p. 59)

Ahad Ha-Am argued that life, not ancient legal formulas, must govern a community's concept of morality and justice. He illustrated his argument with a story he had found in a poem by the Hebrew writer A. D. Gordon: A Talmud student goes abroad to make a living. He leaves his young wife behind. Years pass. He does not send for her, and she meets a man she would like to marry. She writes asking for a divorce; the husband agrees and has a scribe prepare the appropriate document. But when it arrives, the local rabbi discovers a single, trivial scribal error and declares the document invalid. A corrected copy is requested but never arrives. The husband has by now been lost at sea. There are no survivors of the shipwreck; and since rabbinic law requires at least one witness to certify a death, the woman becomes an *agunah*, a deserted wife, forbidden by Jewish law to remarry out of fear that her husband might some day turn up alive.

Ahad Ha-Am wanted to end Judaism's reliance on texts and rescue it from the lifeless, frozen orthodoxy he believed it had become. To restore Judaism, more than words were required. It was necessary for Jews to move from minority status in a non-Jewish world into their own world—Zion. He was convinced that in Zion, in Palestine, in the Promised Land, their own land, Jews could create a social and cultural life that would inspire others. More important, the new life would enable Jews to re-create themselves as a people. His is one of the first voices to call for a Jewish people bound together by other than purely religious ties.

ORTHODOX BELIEVERS

There are still groups who readily and without reservation accept the Torah's authority. For them the infallibility of the tradition is a matter of faith and historical fact. For them the Torah's description of the thousands who were at Sinai, who saw God's presence descend on the mountain and heard His voice and later Moses' proclaim the teachings, is the best possible evidence that these events happened just as the Bible describes them. In their eyes, the text is sacred and the source, together with the oral law, of all significant truth. Such believers accept obedience to God's instruction as the key to redemption, both for the individual and the nation: "This Book of the Law shall not depart out of your mouth, but you shall meditate therein day and night that you may observe to do according to all that is written therein; for then you shall make your way prosperous and you shall have good success" (Josh. 1:8).

Members of such groups within the Jewish community generally send their children to parochial schools whose teachings reinforce their religious assumptions and equip the child with knowledge of the rich tapestry of ideas and tales the sages and folklore have drawn from or into the texts. Those texts are, they believe, far more extensive than the *Sefer Torah*: together with what we call the Bible, they include the Talmud, the *midrashim*, the codes, the philosophers, the Kabbalah, and the Responsa, the literature of questions and rabbinic answers. To all these texts, save the *Sefer Torah*, critical analysis can be applied; but they insist that the *Sefer Torah* is God's word and therefore unique, exempt from such examination. They do not question the Torah's authority over their lives. Indeed, they say they are saddened by the indifference of most Jews to the pattern of life-long study and commitment they call the Torah way.

There is a world of difference between neo-orthodox Jews, such as Hirsch's followers, who are today exemplified by the faculties of Bar Ilan and Yeshiva universities, and the groups who continue as if the knowledge explosion of the last several centuries had not taken place. For these, Torah study is the only knowledge that counts for anything. The world outside has little of value to teach. They continue the pattern of culture of European Jewry before it was challenged and reshaped by modernism. They live to a surprising degree in and for books—more specifically, in and for Torah. In that European Jewish world, men spent their lives studying the Talmud and its commentaries. Other, simpler folk spent hours each day reciting Torah texts as an act of devotion. Book study was held to be a consummately worthy way to spend one's life—but study only of the books of the Torah, which were held to contain all wisdom and even the presence of God.

THE PEOPLE OF THE BOOK TODAY

In the early days of printing, many Hebrew books contained a title page called *sha'ar*; the usual introductory information was printed within the outline of a gate bearing a motto that suggested that all who passed through it, and studied what lay beyond, performed a pious act: "This is the *sha'ar* [gate] of the Lord, the righteous shall enter therein" (Ps. 118:20). Talmud Torah, Torah study, was seen as a virtuous way to spend one's life and accepted as a technique of moral and spiritual improvement, as a key to the mysteries, and as a way to approach God.

It is this premodern European culture that gave rise to the conventional judgment that Jewish culture is book-centered, even book-dominated. Telling the extensive and fascinating story of the authors, editors, scribes, and printers who developed and made available the literature of the Jewish people, *The Hebrew Book* (edited by Raphael Posner and Israel Ta-Shema, one of a series of single-theme volumes developed from the materials prepared for the 1974 *Encyclopaedia Judaica*) rehearses this conventional judgment: "Not for nothing has the Jewish people been known as the 'people of the book.' The most important object in Judaism is—albeit in scroll form—a book, the Torah. And the cultural history of the Jewish people is a story told, not in pictures, buildings, or statues, but in books" (introduction, n.p.). This is a clumsy version of Jean-Paul Sartre's mordant observation that "Jews live in books, not in landscape," and its elegant elaboration in "Our Homeland, The Text," the title of an essay by George Steiner, a European critic-playwright who makes sporadic forays into matters of Jewish interest (1985). The judgment, however conventional and popular, is a strange one for a people who, as we have seen, made prodigious efforts to prevent just the fate of being smothered by texts.

There is today no synagogue without an ark and no pattern of synagogue worship without *Keriat ha-Torah*, the ritual of reading from the *Sefer Torah*. Orthodox congregations follow the traditional cycle of Sabbath and holy day readings, while non-orthodox groups may read only a section of the weekly portion each Sabbath. All congregations read at least a few verses. *Keriat ha-Torah* was, and remains, the central Jewish ritual act honoring the tradition. Unhappily, one of the hallmarks of modern life is its swift pace; few come regularly to the synagogue, and those who come no longer linger in God's courts. There is so much else of interest for Jews to do. Yet few Jews would deny the value of *Keriat ha-Torah*. Its old forms are maintained. The number called up to read from the Torah, or more customarily simply to offer the blessings, has remained fairly constant over the centuries: seven on the Sabbath, three on the weekdays. In every congregation, the reading is preceded and followed by familiar blessings that thank God for the gift of Torah, which is seen as the sign of Israel's election and, as such, the source of Israel's immortality as a people:

> Praised be you, O Lord, our God, King of the universe, Who has chosen us from among all peoples and given us his Torah. Praised be you, O Lord, giver of the Torah.
> Praised be you, O Lord, our God, King of the universe, Who has given us a Torah full of truth and in so doing planted within us eternal life. Praised be you, O Lord, giver of the Torah.

Nineteenth-century liberal congregations fought for the right to meet, teach, and organize the life-cycle events in their own ways. Such a synagogue was receptive to the music, art, and culture of the day and used them in worship. Its congregants recognized ideas from other cultures and other ways of life and were willing to adapt these to Jewish practice. This eclectic approach assumed that what the rabbi and congregants felt to be valid had validity—and what they did not, did not.

In Europe, there was a mixed pattern of congregational autonomy, varying from region to region. In some regions and cities, local Jewish councils limited the ability of liberal Jews to experiment, to drop old rituals and create new ones. In other regions, liberals gained control of their local councils and ensured that their way was acceptable to the Jewish community and to the local non-Jewish authorities, to whom all changes in worship and unresolved frictions within the Jewish community had to be submitted.

In the United States, where there was no tradition of Jewish corporate life, from the beginning there was full congregational autonomy. Each congregation organized itself on its own authority; and during most of the nineteenth century, there was no official national body that could impose its will. All efforts to treat the American Jewish communities as a single organism, and to put communal restraints on changing attitudes, were unsuccessful.

Perhaps the central issue on which attitudes were changing was the authority of scripture—changes that applied equally to the first and the second scriptures. In Europe, the issue could not be avoided, for if it led to strife within the Jewish community, the local government stepped in. In the United States, it was not an issue that disturbed the outward unity of the Jewish community. There was little unity to begin with. Scriptural translations and commentaries were many and varied, and communal standards no longer encouraged obedience to the Torah's full authority.

The issue did not disappear in the United States. There were always fervent orthodox believers; and with the creation in the mid-twentieth century of the State of Israel, the issue became a matter of increasing concern and national division: What degree of authority shall an organized, yet pluralistic Jewish community give to the bodies who claim to govern in the name of Torah?

The reach—or limits—of scriptural authority has been defined in several contradictory ways in modern times. Some Jews accept scripture. Some see only claims they can no longer affirm, and categorically deny any divinity to scripture: if the texts are inspired at all, it is the inspiration that comes to artists and poets. Some see the scriptures as interesting but archaic. Others see their seminal role in Western civilization and the continuing power of some of their ideas; in their eyes, the Bible is a classic but no longer a commanding voice. Or if it is a commanding voice, the orders it gives are so nobly and broadly ethical as to be capable of affirming what one wishes to affirm. Some claim that Judaism's long reliance on texts stands in the way of the sense of immediacy in religious experience; the call to obedience to the text overwhelms the emotions and feelings that play so great a part in the religious life.

Those who accept scripture—to be exact, *both* scriptures—sense God in the word. Some accepting believers become belligerent about their faith, perhaps because the rising tide of fundamentalism in the outside world reinforces their faith in "Bible." Other believers may have doubts but allow the evidence of centuries of a rich Torah-based culture to silence their doubts. They treat the Torah as inspired, unique, a miracle. They believe that the rabbinic ethos, their understanding of Torah, remains authoritative. They insist that they—and they alone—do not bring foreign fires to the altar; and that they, and they alone, are open to the specialness of God's will.

For other Jews, the scriptures have become simply a series of documents that reveal various concerns and interests of Judeans and Israelites over the course of the first millennium B.C.E. From this secular vantage, many of the Bible's constraints do not commend themselves today and cannot be accepted on faith or on any other basis.

To many more Jews, the scriptures have become a seminal document, the source but not necessarily the substance of their traditions. Accepting the idea that Torah law is inspired and therefore, necessarily, good, they nonetheless do not accept the position of those who wish to impose it. They see Judaism as a living, changing religious culture which began at Sinai and was afterward constantly in the process of development. In the nineteenth century, this view of the Torah as the catalyst but not the all-inclusive teaching was generally combined with that century's confidence in progress.

The liberal traditions in the West, as they were developing a hundred years ago, put forward arguments based on then-current ideas about human progress. Confident that science and technology were improving human life, that what was early was necessarily primitive and what was contemporary was "advanced," liberal Judaism trusted that there had been and would be many revelations, not just one. Vivian Simmons, a mid-twentieth-century English liberal rabbi, has expressed these thoughts in popular form in *The Path of Life*:

Liberal Judaism cannot accept the old teaching of the verbal inspiration of Torah. Nevertheless, Jewish tradition, the best of Jewish tradition, a great deal of it, is still sacred to us. The scroll of the law is still the outstanding symbol of Judaism. In the Synagogue it plays a prominent part. Though it contains only the Five Books of Moses, it stands for the great Jewish principle that man is bound by law. But to Liberal Jews it is not only Jewish law. That is binding upon us only insofar as it harmonizes with the best thought and the circumstances of our own age. For us religious truth and command mean: all those spiritual and moral obligations, whether expressed in the Law of Moses or in *any other form*, ancient or modern, which we acknowledge as commands for us to obey, though naturally we look primarily to Jewish law and tradition. The scroll of the Law is the symbol of our human duty—to God, to our neighbours, to ourselves. It stands for the supreme principle of Revelation: the belief that God reveals Himself and His will to man, not in one age, but in every age, not in one form, but in many.

(1961, p. 48)

Simmons describes the use of the scripture in a liberal synagogue:

We still read out of the Scroll of the Law at the services of the Synagogue. But we do not read all of it, as is done in Orthodox synagogues. We read those parts that have for us a present-day meaning, and are either the source or an illustration of the moral and spiritual teachings which guide our lives.

(Pp. 46–47)

His explanation that the traditional customs and rules "are not divine in origin, and are therefore subject to change and replacement" (p. 48) makes clear that the scriptures have become sources from which critical spirits choose what is satisfying to them; and, further, that the scroll's "prominence in the Synagogue does not imply a pledge to accept all its teachings or to obey all of its commands." Arguing that the central command is "justice, justice shalt thou follow," Simmons says that the Mosaic code is justice "in an early form," and "our interpretation of what justice means and demands has gone far beyond the Mosaic Law in its application to the life of today. It is by means of these progressive conceptions of justice that the Jew and his neighbours advance towards the ideal of human society" (pp. 48–49).

What all non-orthodox views of scriptural authority have in common is acceptance of the value of the scripture as a seminal and suggestive document, even though it has been drained of the divinity that gave it its original authority and power. The Bible's value is as a chronicle of the extraordinarily significant development of the idea of ethical living and of the attempts of a nation to build a way of life on the basis of new ideas and structures. The non-orthodox belief that neither the first nor the second scripture actually presented God's words has in no way eroded the conviction that the two scriptures made critical contributions to Jewish civilization. Modern ideas about history and historiography influenced liberal Jews to recognize that revelation must always be transmitted through human minds and is, therefore, inevitably conditioned by human circumstance. Sinai reveals as much about Moses as about God— perhaps more.

When scripture, while remaining scripture, began to be read as literature—as material that could be classified as myth, saga, narrative, law, and psalm—parallels could be and were found in other West Asian cultures, and studies were made of the distinctiveness of the Torah: how, for example, its law codes differed from Hammurabi's. The question that faced everyone was whether the Bible was, in fact, just another national literature, albeit one that had played and continued to play an unusually important role in the development of Western civilization.

Despairing of being able to use history to prove the Bible's distinctiveness, some began to speak of transcending history. The search for the essence of Judaism became a search for Judaism's existential meaning: What does the tradition as I know it mean to me? Modern Jews like Franz Rosenzweig (1886–1929) and Martin Buber (1878–1965) argued that religious truths are not found by applying some philosophical or sociological judgment to what people have said and written. There are, in fact, no objective and universal truths. What there are are moments of intimacy and personal moments of revelation when one confronts another's concerns or ideas and finds that they speak to one's innermost needs and awaken new ideas and feelings. The Bible, and presumedly also the Talmud, are to be seen not as a copy of some divine dictation but as records of humans, like ourselves, opening themselves to ultimate reality. The Bible is the record of a dialogue between God and Israel, and this unique quality gives it its power and moral and spiritual authority. The ultimate seriousness of the original experience has not been completely lost in the reporting.

Martin Buber wrote of the Hebrew Bible as a compilation of the records from that centuries-long dialogue between a speaking God and human beings who were ready to listen. The value of scripture for the modern is that, if we would devote time and sensitive attention to the texts, we could listen in to that original conversation. We, too, can stand at Sinai or with Joshua at Bethel.

One of the challenges faced by moderns who seek to present the aliveness of the Bible to a generation of silent, critical readers, is to get them to hear its voice. We find Martin Buber encouraging reading aloud, reading over and over, letting the words and cadences wash over the reader, letting the Bible speak rather than simply reading it. The German translation that Buber and Rosenzweig undertook, as well as their encouragement of reading aloud, meeting the text, sought to breathe life, immediacy, into Bible-reader relationships:

> The man of today has no access to a sure and solid faith, nor can it be made accessible to him. If he examines himself seriously, he knows this and may not delude himself further. But he is not denied the possibility of holding himself open to faith. If he is really serious, he too can open up to this book and let its rays strike him where they will. He can give himself up and submit to the test without preconceived notions and without reservations. He can absorb the Bible with all his strength, and wait to see what will happen to him, whether he will not discover within himself a new and unbiased approach to this or that element in the book. But to this end, he must read the scriptures as though they were something entirely unfamiliar, as though they had not been set before him ready-made, at school and after in the light of "religious" and "scientific" certainties; as though he has not been confronted all his life with sham concepts and sham statements which cited the Bible as their authority. He must face the book with a new attitude as something new. He must yield to it, withhold nothing of his being, and let whatever will occur between himself and it. He does not know which of its sayings and images will overwhelm him and mold him, from where the spirit will ferment and enter into him, to incorporate itself anew in his body. But he holds himself open. He does not believe anything a priori; he does not disbelieve anything a priori. He reads aloud the words written in the book in front of him; he hears the word he utters and it reaches him. Nothing is prejudged. The current of time flows on, and the contemporary character of this man becomes itself a receiving vessel.
>
> (1936, p. 181)

One further mode—a purely academic one—of dealing with the scripture in the mid-twentieth century is perhaps best illustrated by the new Jewish Publication Society translation of the Torah, first published in 1962 and revised in 1967. One of its goals is to be as accurate and exact as possible, identifying textual errors and untranslatable words: "Meaning of Hebrew uncertain" appears throughout. The new translation admits openly that a variety of English translations are possible for given Hebrew sentences, and even that there are sentences in the Hebrew that cannot be translated. Raising the question, albeit indirectly, of whether the Torah represents the word of God, this approach ascribes fallibility to scripture itself. Academically sound, the translation denies any literal acceptance of Torah.

This is perhaps the final step in a gradual acceptance of the idea that the scripture is not God's words. Israel's scripture has become for many a human document, a classic work inspired in the sense that successful art is inspired, but no longer an unquestioned source of authority or an all-knowing, unquestioned guide to deed and doctrine. In that sense, for many Jews there is no longer a scripture. The power of the book and the value of many of its ideas are acknowledged, but it is no longer altogether holy.

For many, the model of their religious tradition is no longer Albo's tree, but a river, a great river like the Mississippi. It begins in small fresh-water lakes in Canada and Minnesota and flows several thousand miles across the North American continent to the Gulf. The current flows in one direction. Its past is present but not necessarily visible. At St. Louis, the river is quite different from the way it is at its source or at its mouth. Over its course much changes. Rains fall. Tributaries flow in. The sun evaporates water from the surface. Cities draw out water for their reservoirs, and farmers for irrigation. At times, pollution enters the river. From high in a plane, one can see the whole river. Science can today color a water molecule and follow its passage. Some may make it to the Gulf. Others won't. There is continuity and significant change.

Scriptures do not fit easily into such a model. A scripture is fixed. The text is frozen. Some say that Judaism has come full circle, and that we are back at the time when there was Torah, tradition, but not yet a *Sefer Torah*. For many, scripture has again become simply a part of tradition, its value beyond debate but its authority not beyond question. The age of scripture as authority is for many over and done.

In the creative ebb and flow of Jewish life, the rise and fall of scripture has played a key role. But there was a distinctive faith tradition long before a written scripture appeared, and the tradition can adjust to its dethronement. What it may not be able to adjust to is the radically different world views that exist now within major segments of the community and determine their attitudes toward authority and faith.

In the late twentieth century, there are still Jews who would sacrifice life to text. Much of the political struggle in Israel with the extreme right-wing, the so-called Black Hats, is over this issue of Torah authority. In 1948, the government of the new State of Israel, for political reasons and following the old British mandate law that each religious community govern according to its own traditions, gave to traditional religious authorities control over the laws of personal status: marriage, divorce, issues of inheritance, adoption, and the like. From that day, the battle has been joined between those whose idea of a Jewish state is one governed by the two scriptures and those who would take a modern stance and follow the model of the United States Constitution by creating secular laws and separating state and synagogue. Since Ahad Ha-Am's day, the issues of conflict between those who go by the Book, and those who insist that the Torah often blurs real justice and equity, have multiplied: autopsies, women as religious leaders, the authenticity of nonrabbinic interpretations of Judaism, the rights of non-orthodox Jews to have their marriages and conversions accepted. Ahad Ha-Am feared Torah fundamentalism, and the acts of those orthodox Jews who desecrate graves of reform rabbis in Israel show that he had reason for his fears. He worried that "'a people of the book,' unlike a normal people, is a slave to the book. It has surrendered its whole soul to the written word" (Ginzberg 1894, p. 59).

Since 1948, Israel has been the focus of a heated struggle between those who insist that a Jewish state must be governed by God's law, Torah, and those who insist that in matters of belief each should do what is right in his or her own eyes. What happens in Israel has repercussions throughout the diaspora. In American communities before 1948, it was a matter of live and let be. Today there are pressures to obey the Torah as law. American Jews of Conservative or Reform groups may not be able to settle in Israel unless their marriages, divorces, and adoption procedures follow certain *halachot*. The fiery battles over Torah authority that worked themselves out in Europe and America in the nineteenth and early twentieth centuries are flaring again in Israel today and are major causes of division. Since the world thinks of the Jews, and the Jewish people think of themselves, as a single body, the issues that divide them are not purely philosophical.

Modern non-orthodox Jews are conditioned by the societies they live in. Though ours may be a "post-Christian" society, traditional Christian norms still shape its thoughts and attitudes. Christianity emphasizes the experience of the mass and the presence of the spirit. It is, therefore, to the service, rather than to the scripture, that many modern Jews are conditioned to look for the sacred. Many such Jews have come to think that the only valid religious experience is one that is immediate and intensely personal. Seeing what we are prepared to see, interpreting sensation and experience in terms appropriate to our time and place, we hope for intensity in a conversion experience and for the sense of peace within a sanctuary. One can, of course, use the texts as a worshiper uses a cathedral, as an environment in which God's immanence is felt as present. The great religious traditions have, after all, incorporated into their scriptural texts the records of what individuals have felt in the presence of the sacred, so that the texts and their recorded traditions can be used as supportive models of custom and practice. But few moderns are prepared or willing to explore those possibilities. Not the scripture, but the service, seems the place where sacredness may dwell.

Thus, Jews who search for a scripture will probably seek it in the prayer books. The language of the worship service is generally non-specific, broadly human, yet phrased in traditional idioms, often those of the Bible. Its themes are noble, capable of the most varied interpretations. Past statements and present needs are fused and offer a way to touch scripture: the cycle of Torah reading, a selection from some traditional passage, a talk that can bring in relevant and acceptable bits of the rabbinic tradition.

The time is appropriate to clear up as far as one can the conventional idea about Jews and their books. Since book learning was increasingly prized in the modern world Jews began to move into, talk of Jewish traditions of book learning emphasized the intellectual nature of the Jewish ethos. Jews secularized their unique tradition of sacred learning as they entered civic life in the larger world. At a time of industrial transformation, when trained minds were in great demand, Jews found that their age-old habits of education could become the basis of economic success in the West. All the accomplishments of their traditional world—literacy, cultivation, erudition, achievement—were admired in their new one.

But book learning is one thing; the Jewish tradition of Talmud Torah, quite another. Torah recitation is not speed reading; it is not keeping abreast of the research in one's field, dabbling in world literature or political analysis, or an acquaintance with contemporary writers. It is a process of immersing oneself in a special culture. What the rabbinic world called *lernen*, too easily translated simply as "learning," was and is a discipline intended to transform scripture into life.

When Jews in the twentieth century began to apply to themselves the label "the people of the book," they meant it as both a literary compliment and a passport into the larger arena. Sharing, as they did, with the Christian world love of "the book" allowed them to emphasize a bond they hoped the other people of the book would also feel. In their minds "the book" was the basis of a new entity, which they called the Judeo-Christian tradition.

It is my argument in this book that the Jewish spirit did not set out to develop a scripture; that during most of the biblical period a written scripture played no significant role; that the rabbis made prodigious efforts to mitigate the limitations imposed by the existence of a scripture; that the concept of an oral memorized law in part reflects these efforts; and that until the European centuries, Judaism more or less effectively escaped the limitations of scripture.

Judaism is not and never has been just the teachings of a set of authorized books. The text is not our homeland; life is. Commentary reads in as readily as it reads out. Our books were meant to become part of us, the living voice of God and tradition. Except under rare circumstances in Jewish history, the texts did not define life. Far more than has generally been recognized, life defined the texts.

⇢⇢⇢ BIBLIOGRAPHY ⇠⇠⇠

ORIGINAL SOURCES

A.R.N. (Avot d'Rabbi Nathan)
b. (Babylonian Talmud)
  A.Z. (Avoda Zarah)
  B.B. (Bava Batra)
  Ber. (Berakhot)
  B.M. (Bava Mezia)
  Eruv. (Eruvin)
  Git. (Gittin)
  Hag. (Hagigah)
  Hor. (Horayot)
  Hul. (Hullin)
  Ket. (Ketubot)
  Meg. (Megillah)
  Men. (Menahot)
  Pes. (Pesahim)
  San. (Sanhedrin)
  Shab. (Shabbat)
  Sotah
  Tem. (Temurah)
  Yoma
Ber. Rab. (Bereshit Rabbah)
Cursor M. (*Cursor Mundi* [*The Cursor of the World*], a Northumbrian poem of the 14th century in four versions), Richard Morris, ed. London: Early English Text Society, 1874–1893.
Dead Sea Scrolls
  Commentary on Habakkuk (1QpHab)
  Damascus Document (= *The Damascus Rule*, CD, 6QD)

Genesis Apocryphon (1QapGen)
Hymns (*Hodayot*, Thanksgiving Hymns, 1QH)
Manual of Discipline (= *The Community Rule, 1QS*)
Temple Scroll (11QT)
j. (Palestinian [Jerusalem] Talmud)
  Ber. (Berakhot)
  Hag. (Hagigah)
  Horayot (Hor.)
  Ma'aser Sheni
  Meg. (Megillah)
  Peah
  Ta'anit
Jubilees (*Pseudepigrapha of the Old Testament,* trans. R. H. Charles [Oxford, 1913])
Koh. R. (*Kohelet Rabbah*) (Midrash Ecclesiastes)
Lev. R. (*Leviticus Rabbah*) (Midrash Leviticus)
M. (Mishnah)
  Avot (= *Pirke Avot*)
  Ber. (Berakhot)
  Git. (Gittin)
  Hag. (Hagigah)
  Ket. (Ketubot)
  Kid. (Kiddushin)
  Naz. (Nazir)
  Peah
  Pes. (Pesahim)
  San. (Sanhedrin)
  Shab. (Shabbat)
  Shevi'it
  Sotah
  Suk. (Sukkah)
  Uktzin
  Yoma
Schol. to Meg. Ta'anit (Scholia to Megillat Ta'anit)
Sifra (Midrash Sifra on Leviticus)
Sifre (Midrash Sifre on Deuteronomy)
Soferim
Tanhuma
Tosefta (Tos.)
  Pes. (Pesahim)
  San. (Sanhedrin)
  Sotah
Wisdom of Ben Sirah
Yalkot Shimoni

BIBLIOGRAPHY

TEXTS CITED

Ad Herennium. Rhetorica Ad Herennium. Ad C. Herennium. De Ratíone Dicendi; with an English translation by Harry Caplan. Loeb Classical Library. Cambridge, Mass.: Harvard University Press, 1954.

ALBO, JOSEPH. 1929. *Sefer ha-Ikkarim (Book of First Principles).* Philadelphia: Jewish Publication Society.

Aristeas' Epistle. 1951. *Aristeas to Philocrates: Letter of Aristeas.* Edited and translated by Moses Hadas. New York: Harper.

AUGUSTINE. *On Christian Doctrine.* Translated and with an introduction by D. W. Robertson. Indianapolis: Bobbs-Merrill, 1958.

BAUMGARTEN, ALBERT I. 1980. "Justinian and the Jews." In Leo Landman, ed., *The Rabbi Joseph H. Lookstein Memorial Volume.* New York: Ktav.

BEN-SASSON, H. H. 1976. *A History of the Jewish People.* Cambridge, Mass.: Harvard University Press.

BUBER, MARTIN; AND ROSENZWEIG, FRANZ. 1936. *Die Schrift und ihre Verdeutschung.* Berlin.

CARMI, T. 1981. *The Penguin Book of Hebrew Verse.* New York: Penguin.

DELMEDIGO, JOSEPH SOLOMON. 1631. *Koah Ha Shem.*

Documents of Vatican II. 1966. New York: Herder & Herder/Association Press.

FISHBANE, MICHAEL. 1986 [1985]. *Biblical Interpretations in Ancient Israel.* Oxford: Clarendon Press.

FRAZER, J. G. 1898. *Pausanias's Description of Greece.* London: Macmillan.

GINZBERG, ASHER. 1894. "The People of the Book." In Leon Simon, *Ahad Ha-Am.* Oxford: Philosophica Judaica, East and West Library, 1946.

GOLDIN, JUDAH. 1971. "Several Sidelights on a Torah Education." *Ex Orbe Religionum* 1.

GOODENOUGH, ERWIN R. 1964. *Jewish Symbols in the Greco-Roman Period.* Volume 11. Symbolism in the Dura Synagogue. Bollingen Series 37. New York: Pantheon Books.

GOODY, J., ed. 1968. *Literacy in Traditional Societies.* Cambridge, England: Cambridge University Press.

HALLO, WILLIAM W. 1980. In C. D. Evans, W. W. Hallo, and J. B. White, eds., *Scripture in Context.* Pittsburgh: Pickwick.

HALLO, WILLIAM W. 1988. "Sumerian Literature—Background to the Bible." *Bible Review* 4 (3 [June]).

HUGO, VICTOR. 1871. *Notre Dame de Paris.* Paris: Librairie Hachette et Cie.

IBN EZRA, ABRAHAM. *Introduction to Commentary on Pentateuch*. Translated in Louis Jacobs, *Jewish Biblical Exegesis*. New York: Behrman House. 1973.

JOSEPHUS. *Antiquities of the Jews*. 1926–65. *Josephus*. London: Heinemann; New York: Putnam. Vol. 4–9.

JOSEPHUS. *Contra Apion*. 1926–65. *Josephus*. London: Heinemann; New York: Putnam. Vol. 1.

JOSEPHUS. *The Jewish War*. 1926–65. *Josephus*. London: Heinemann; New York: Putnam. Vol. 3–4.

KUGEL, J. 1983. "Two Introductions to Midrash." *Prooftexts* 3.

LORD, A. B. 1960. *The Singer of Tales*. Cambridge, Mass.: Harvard University Press.

MAIMONIDES, MOSES. *The Guide of the Perplexed*. Translated with an introduction and notes by Shlomo Pines. Chicago: University of Chicago Press, 1963.

MAIMONIDES, MOSES. *Maimonides' Commentary on the Mishnah Tractate Sanhedrin*. Translated with an introduction and notes by Fred Rosner. New York: Sepher-Hermon Press, Inc. 1981.

MAIMONIDES, MOSES. *Mishneh Torah. The Book of Knowledge*. Book 1. Translated with notes by Moses Hyamson. Boys Town Jerusalem Publishers. 1962.

MENDELSSOHN, MOSES. 1783. *Jerusalem: On Religious Power and Judaism*. Translated by Alfred Jospe. New York: Schocken, 1969.

ONG, WALTER. 1982. *Orality and Literacy*. London and New York: Methuen.

PAUSANIAS. *Pausanias Description of Greece*. Translated by W. H. S. Jones, in six volumes. Loeb Classical Library. London: William Heinemann; New York: G. P. Putnam's Sons. 1926.

PHILO. *De Specialibus Legibus*. Translated by F. H. Colson. Cambridge, Mass.: Harvard University Press, 1960.

PHILO. *The Contemplative Life*. Translated by F. H. Colson. Cambridge, Mass.: Harvard University Press, 1960.

PHILO. *Vita Moysis*. Translated by F. H. Colson. Cambridge, Mass.: Harvard University Press, 1960.

PLATO. *Phaedrus*. Translated by B. Jowett. New York: Tudor Publishing.

POSNER, RAPHAEL; and TA-SHEMA, ISRAEL. 1974. *The Hebrew Book*. Vol. 8 in *Encyclopaedia Judaica*.

PRITCHARD, JAMES B. 1950. *Ancient Near Eastern Texts*. Princeton: Princeton University Press.

PSEUDO-PHILO. *Biblical Antiquities*. In James Charlesworth, ed., *The Old Testament Pseudepigrapha*. Vol. 1. New York: Doubleday. 1983.

RICHARDSON, E. C. 1914. *Biblical Libraries*. Princeton: Princeton University Press.

ROBINSON, JOHN. 1963. *Honest to God*. Louisville, Ky.: Westminster John Knox Press.

SAADYA BEN JOSEPH, GAON. 1948. *The Book of Beliefs and Opinions,* New Haven: Yale University Press.

SANDERS, J. A. 1967. *The Dead Sea Psalms Scroll*. Ithaca, N.Y.: Cornell University Press.

SIMMONS, VIVIAN. 1961. *The Path of Life*. London: Valentine-Mitchell.

290

BIBLIOGRAPHY

SMITH, M. 1979. *Palestinian Parties and Politics That Shape the Old Testament*. New York: Columbia University Press.

STEINER, GEORGE. 1985. "Our Homeland, The Text." *Salmagundi* 66 (Winter/ Spring).

URBACH, E. E. 1975. *The Sages—Their Concepts and Beliefs*. Jerusalem: Magnes Press, Hebrew University.

VERMES, GEZA. *The Dead Sea Scrolls in English*. Third edition. New York: Penguin. 1987.

YADIN, YIGAEL. *The Temple Scroll I - III*. Jerusalem: Israel Exploration Society. 1983.

YATES, FRANCES A. 1966. *The Art of Memory*. London: Routledge & Kegan Paul.

INDEX

Aaron, 75, 92, 98, 99
Abbasid caliphate, 225, 226
Abihu, 99
Abortion, 8, 13
Abraham: destruction of idols by, 93; and Hagar, 3; midrashic versions of early life of, 182–83; and purchase of Machpelah, 47; visit to Egypt of, 164
Abu Isa, 248
Academies, 224–25, 251–53
Accuracy, 8–9
Acrostics, 183, 213
Ad Herennium, 214
Adonai, 146
Adultery, 4
Agenitos the Hegemon, 201
Aggadah, 181–83; poetry and, 242; questioning of, 237; scrolls of, 218
Agunah, 274
Ahad Ha-Am, 273–74, 284
Ahl-ul-kitab, 25n
Akiba, R., 157, 163, 193, 208
Albo, Joseph, 265, 283
Alexandria, 129, 130, 143, 155
Alfasi, 254
Alphabet: beginnings of, 19–20; of early Hebrew scribes, 55; Greek, 130; as numbers, 134–35, 163
Al-sahib, 40
Amidah, 242–43
Amoraim, 202, 204, 213, 226
Amos, 64, 235–36
Amulets, 29, 70
Anachronisms, 34
Anan, 249

Angel of the Presence, 182
Ani, 145
Anochi, 145
Apocalypse, 139, 170
Apologetes, 142–43, 169
Arabic, 35–36, 246–47
Aramaic, 109–12, 146–47
Aristeas, 117n, 143–44, 147, 155
Ark: for holding scrolls, 23, 162; Noah's, 54, 72
Ashi, R., 162–63, 248
Ashurbanipal, 58
Ashurit, 110, 144–45
Aufklärung, 269
Augustine, 33
"Authoritative" texts, 130
Authority, 4; and covenant at Sinai, 74–75; in Israel, 284–85; in modern world, 266–67, 278–79; of rabbis, 186–92, 219, 225–26, 248; of Talmud, 207–9, 222–25, 248–51; of Torah in talmudic period, 226–30
Av, 252
Avelei Zion, 250
Avodah, 188, 211
Ayn Kotevim Halachot b'Sefer, 218
Azariah, Prayer of, 134

Babylonian Exile, *see* Exile
Balaam, 64, 68, 114
Baraitot, 194
Baruch, 65–66, 92
Bat Kol, 179
Beit ha-Keneset, 105, 155

297

INDEX